PREP

PREP
FOR BETTER READING

Third Edition

W. Royce Adams
Santa Barbara City College

HOLT, RINEHART AND WINSTON, INC.
New York Chicago San Francisco Philadelphia Montreal
Toronto London Sydney Tokyo

Senior Acquisitions Editor: Charlyce Jones Owen
Developmental Editor: Kate Morgan
Senior Project Editor: Lester A. Sheinis
Senior Production Manager: Pat Sarcuni
Design Supervisor: Robert Kopelman
Text Designer: William Gray
Cover Photographer: Richard Haynes

Library of Congress Cataloging-in-Publication Data

Adams, W. Royce.
  PREP : for better reading.

  Includes index.
  1. Reading (Higher education)   2. College readers.
3. Vocabulary.   I. Title.   II. Title: P.R.E.P.
LB1050.42.A33   1988   428.4′07′11   87-8562

ISBN 0-03-013324-6

Copyright © 1988, 1984, 1980 by Holt, Rinehart and Winston, Inc.

All rights reserved. No part of this publication may be reproduced or transmitted in any form or by any means, electronic or mechanical, including photocopy, recording, or any information storage and retrieval system, without permission in writing from the publisher.

Although for mechanical reasons some pages of this publication are perforated, only those pages imprinted with an HRW copyright notice are intended for removal.

Requests for permission to make copies of any part of the work should be mailed to: Permissions, Holt, Rinehart and Winston, Inc., 111 Fifth Avenue, New York, NY 10003.

Printed in the United States of America
Published simultaneously in Canada

8 9 0 1   016   9 8 7 6 5 4 3 2 1

Holt, Rinehart and Winston, Inc.
The Dryden Press
Saunders College Publishing

Preface to the Third Edition

Changes in this third edition of *PREP: For Better Reading* are basically in the reading selections and the Unit Check Tests. Of the twenty-one reading selections in this edition, thirteen are new. Only those selections unanimously agreed on by reviewers were retained from the last edition. Of the eighteen major readings in each of the nine units, eleven are new, as are two of the three essays in the Unit Check Tests. Most readings are textbook-type selections similar to what students will confront in their other college courses. Changes in the Unit Check Tests include a four-part check rather than three.

For those of you new to this text, *PREP* still contains three units consisting of three chapters each. At the end of each unit is a Unit Check Test based on the content of each unit's three chapters. Each chapter has a list of its objectives at the beginning. Chapters are divided into four parts: P, R, E, and P. "P: Prereading Drills" presents a selected vocabulary list plus word usage and visual discrimination drills based on words from the reading selection in the chapter.

"R: Reading Drill" presents a reading selection using a modified Directed Reading Thinking Activity (DRTA) method. A tear-out comprehension check follows each selection for submission to the instructor. Using the Fry Readability Formula, reading selections range from approximately fifth to tenth grade level. Infrequently there is an excursion into higher levels when passages from college textbooks are used.

"E: Exercises in Vocabulary" presents word-attack skills of all types and word-knowledge skills in a variety of drills ranging from phonics to Greek and Latin word parts. Again, a vocabulary check tear-out sheet is provided for the instructor's use.

"P: Perfecting Reading Skills" provides practice in everything from comprehending short phrases and idiomatic expressions to interpreting maps, tables, and graphs. All chapters end with another reading selection and comprehension check. Although comprehension questions are not labeled as such, skills covered include recognizing main ideas, sequence of events, cause-effect relationships, author's bias, drawing inferences, following directions, and organizing information. Charts for recording test results appear in the back of the text. Answers to all drills as well as their rationale appear in the Instructor's Manual.

The Instructor's Manual provides the rationale for the design and the use of certain types of drills in the text. It offers some suggested readings from books and journals for instructors who wish to improve their own knowledge of teaching reading skills at the college level, as well as giving some suggestions for using the text. The manual may be obtained through a local Holt representative or by writing to the English Editor, College Department, Holt, Rinehart and Winston, 111 Fifth Avenue, New York, NY 10003.

PREP can be used in a classroom situation or in an individualized reading program. There is much self-directed student activity involvement. Although each chapter builds on the other in difficulty, particularly in vocabulary concepts, a careful examination by the instructor will show it is not necessary always to assign each chapter in numerical order, nor will all students need to do all the drills in the book. In addition to this book, instructors may wish to examine other Holt texts in reading, among them *Developing Reading Versatility* and *Reading Beyond Words*, in order to select the texts most appropriate for their classes.

Appreciation is given to Kate Morgan, Lester A. Sheinis, Pat Sarcuni, and Robert Kopelman at Holt for their vital help in revising this edition. Appreciation is also given to the following reviewers: Robyn S. Browder, Tidewater Community College; Betty Marshall, Grambling State University; Elizabeth Montague, Utah Technical College at Salt Lake; Kathryn E. Moore, St. Louis College at Meremac; Margaret Jane Payerle, Cleveland State University; Edwin C. Reeves, Glassboro State College; and Meralee Silverman, Westchester Community College.

WRA

Contents

Preface v
PREP Talk: What It Takes to Catch Up   1

UNIT 1   3

Chapter 1   5

Objectives   6

P: Prereading Drills   7

    Words to Know   7
    Warm-up Drills   7

R: Reading Drill   11

    Reading and Thinking About What You Read   11
    "Succeeding on Campus"
    by Adam Ribb   11
    Comprehension Check   14

E:	Exercises in Vocabulary	17
	Drills	17
	1: Part A, The Alphabet	17
	1: Part B, Expanding Words	17
	2: Consonant Blends	18
	3: Vowel Sounds Review	18
	4: Double Vowels Review	20
	5: Homonyms, or Words That Sound Alike	21
	6: Definition Review	21
	Vocabulary Check	22
P:	Perfecting Reading Skills	25
	Comprehending Phrases	25
	Comprehending Sentences	26
	Comprehending Main Ideas: Paragraphs	29
	Comprehending Main Ideas: Essays	34
	"How to Use a Library"	
	by James A. Michener	35

Chapter 2 — 41

	Objectives	42
P:	Prereading Drills	43
	Words to Know	43
	Warm-up Drills	43
R:	Reading Drill	47
	Reading and Thinking About What You Read	47
	"We Are What We Think We Are"	
	by John Hubris	47
	Comprehension Check	50

E:	Exercises in Vocabulary	53
	Drills	53
	1: Expanding Words	53
	2: Expanding Words	54
	3: Vowel Review	54
	4: The Schwa (ə)	56
	5: Homonyms, or Words That Sound Alike	57
	6: Definition Review	57
	Vocabulary Check	58
P:	Perfecting Reading Skills	62
	Comprehending Idiomatic Phrases	62
	Comprehending Sentences	63
	Comprehending Main Ideas: Paragraphs	65
	Comprehending Main Ideas: A Chapter from a Psychology Textbook	67
	"The Search for Self-actualization" *by Dennis Coon*	68

Chapter 3 — 74

	Objectives	75
P:	Prereading Drills	76
	Words to Know	76
	Warm-up Drills	76
R:	Reading Drill	80
	Reading and Thinking About What You Read	80
	"How to Study-Read" *by Michele Learned*	80
	Comprehension Check	82

E:	Exercises in Vocabulary	87
	Drills	87
	1: Dictionary Entry Words	87
	2: Dictionary Abbreviations	88
	3: Pronunciation Keys	89
	4: Word Meanings in Context	90
	5: Using the Dictionary	92
	6: Definition Review	94
	Vocabulary Check	95
P:	Perfecting Reading Skills	98
	Comprehending Sentences: Idioms	98
	Comprehending Paragraphs: Main Ideas and Interpretation	99
	Comprehending Main Ideas: A Textbook Passage	103
	"Mnemonics—Memory Magic" *by Dennis Coon*	104

Unit 1 Check Test (Chapters 1–3)   110

1: Word Knowledge   110
2: Word Usage   111
3: Comprehending Paragraphs   113
4: Essay Reading Comprehension   115
"The Uses of Error"
by Isaac Asimov   115

UNIT 2   119

Chapter 4   121

Objectives   122

P: Prereading Drills   123

	Words to Know	123
	Warm-up Drills	123
R:	Reading Drill	126
	Reading and Thinking About What You Read	126
	"Reading the Social Sciences"	
	by Scott Forbes	126
	Comprehension Check	130
E:	Exercises in Vocabulary	133
	Drills	133
	1: Root Words	133
	2: Prefixes	133
	3: Suffixes	134
	4: Syllables and Vowels	135
	5: Context Clues and Dictionary Definitions	136
	6: Definition Review	140
	Vocabulary Check	140
P:	Perfecting Reading Skills	143
	Comprehending Sentences: More Idioms	143
	Comprehending Paragraphs: Main Ideas and Interpretation	144
	Comprehending History Textbook Passages: Marking and Underlining	148
	"The Kennedy Administration"	
	by George E. Frakes and W. Royce Adams	151

Chapter 5

157

	Objectives	158
P:	Prereading Drills	159

	Words to Know	159
	Warm-up Drills	159
R:	Reading Drill	164

Reading and Thinking About What You Read 164
"Computers and Work"
by Arthur Luehrmann and Herbert Peckham 165
Comprehension Check 168

E:	Exercises in Vocabulary	171

Drills 171
1: Prefixes 171
2: More Prefixes 171
3: Suffixes 172
4: Compound Words 174
5: Homonym Review 175
6: Words in Context 176
7: Definition Review 177
Vocabulary Check 178

P:	Perfecting Reading Skills	181

Comprehending Sentences Using Idioms 181
Comprehending Paragraphs: Main Ideas 183
**Comprehending Health Textbook Passages:
Applying Study-Reading Techniques** 186
"Do Large Doses of Vitamin E Retard the Aging Process?"
by Eva May Hamilton and Eleanor Noss Whitney 186

Chapter 6 192

Objectives 193

P:	Prereading Drills	194
	Words to Know	194
	Warm-up Drills	195
R:	Reading Drill	199
	Reading and Thinking About What You Read	199
	"On Teaching the First Grade"	
	by Carl Sagan	199
	Comprehension Check	201
E:	Exercises in Vocabulary	204
	Drills	204
	1: *Words Often Confused*	204
	2: *Prefix Review*	205
	3: *More Prefixes*	206
	4: *Suffix Review*	206
	5: *More Suffixes*	207
	6: *Compound Words*	207
	7: *Words in Context*	208
	8: *Definition Review*	209
	Vocabulary Check	210
P:	Perfecting Reading Skills	213
	Comprehending Sentences	213
	Comprehending Paragraphs	214
	Comprehending Science Textbook Passages: Applying Study-Reading Techniques	219
	"Origin of the Earth"	
	by Arthur Beiser and Konrad B. Kranskopf	220

Unit 2 Check Test (Chapters 4–6)		224
1: *Word Knowledge*		224
2: *Word Usage*		225
3: *Comprehending Paragraphs*		226

    4: *Essay Reading*   **227**
"Big Business: Selling Cancer"
by Walter Raleigh   **228**

UNIT 3   233

Chapter 7   235

Objectives   **236**

P: Prereading Drills   **237**

    Words to Know   **237**
    Warm-up Drills   **238**

R: Reading Drill   **242**

    Reading and Thinking About What You Read   **242**
    "The Development of Writing"
    by Susan and Stephen Tchudi   **242**
    Comprehension Check   **246**

E: Exercises in Vocabulary   **249**

    Drills   **249**
      1: Synonyms   **249**
      2: Antonyms   **250**
      3: Using the Correct Word   **251**
      4: Word Formation   **253**
      5: Definition Review   **254**
    Vocabulary Check   **254**

P:	**Perfecting Reading Skills**	**257**
	Comprehending Paragraphs	257
	Comprehending, Interpreting, and Evaluating	261
	"How to Spell"	
	by John Irving	262

Chapter 8   268

	Objectives	269
P:	**Prereading Drills**	**270**
	Words to Know	270
	Warm-up Drills	270
R:	**Reading Drill**	**275**
	Reading and Thinking About What You Read	275
	"Newspaper Reading, How to"	
	by Nancy Cage	276
	Comprehension Check	279
E:	**Exercises in Vocabulary**	**282**
	Drills	282
	1: Greek Word Parts	282
	2: Latin Word Parts	284
	3: Root Words	284
	4: Definition Review	286
	Vocabulary Check	286
P:	**Perfecting Reading Skills**	**289**
	Comprehending Newspaper Headlines	289

Comprehending Paragraphs: Main Ideas and Support	290
Comprehending Essays: Skimming and Scanning	294
"Making TV Commercials" by Roy Wilson	295
Comprehending Bias and Inference	298
"News Is Meant to Inform, Not to Make an Impression" by Andy Rooney	298

Chapter 9 — 302

	Objectives	303
P:	Prereading Drills	304
	Words to Know	304
	Warm-up Drills	305
R:	Reading Drill	309
	Reading and Thinking About What You Read	309
	"Increasing Aesthetic Comprehension" by W. Royce Adams	310
	Comprehension Check	313
E:	Exercises in Vocabulary	316
	Drills	316
	1: Word Categories	316
	2: Greek Word Parts	317
	3: Latin Word Parts	320
	4: Root Words	321
	5: Words in Context	322
	Vocabulary Check	324

P: Perfecting Reading Skills — 326

    Comprehending Reference Materials — 326
    Comprehending Maps, Tables, and Graphs — 334
    Comprehending What You Read — 340
    "The Killer Ideas"
    by Kurt Vonnegut, Jr. — 340

Unit 3 Check Test (Chapters 7–9) — 346

1: Word Knowledge — 346
2: Word Usage — 347
3: Comprehending Paragraphs — 348
4: Essay Reading — 350
"The Right Answer"
by Roger von Oech — 351

Appendixes
    Appendix I   *Roots and Affixes Reference Lists* — 358
    Appendix II   *Student Record Charts* — 363

    Index — 366

PREP Talk: What It Takes to Catch Up

Let's be straight. Chances are you are a college freshman. But chances are you don't have a terrific high school grade record. You're probably not too sure why you're in college except that you've been told it's good for you and you'll get a better job if you go to college. You probably are not used to reading or studying much. Perhaps you haven't been in school for a while and you're a little nervous. Maybe you even have a bad self-image. Maybe you've already taken reading courses and don't feel that they have done you much good. And maybe you don't feel too hot about taking a reading course when you're in college because you know you should have the skills this course teaches.

Well, forget all that. It's all past. Now you have a chance to catch up. Working in this book can bring your reading scores and skills closer to college level. The drills you need are here. What's needed now is for *you* to be here—really here wanting to learn. Get off your case, and give yourself a chance to learn what you missed somewhere, whatever the reasons. Now you have a chance to do what you didn't or couldn't do before. Don't waste any more time. Give this book and this course all you've got. It's probably more important than any other class you're taking right now.

As you work through this book, don't be afraid to ask questions. No question is dumb if you don't know the answer. Don't worry about mistakes you may make. Learn from them.

Take this book, this course, and yourself seriously. You *can* learn to read better.

UNIT 1

Chapter 1

Objectives

P: **PREREADING DRILLS**
   Words to Know
   Warm-up Drills
R: **READING DRILL**
   Reading and Thinking About What You Read
   "Succeeding on Campus" by Adam Ribb
   Comprehension Check
E: **EXERCISES IN VOCABULARY**
   Drills
       1: Part A, The Alphabet
       1: Part B, Expanding Words
       2: Consonant Blends
       3: Vowel Sounds Review
       4: Double Vowels Review
       5: Homonyms, or Words That Sound Alike
       6: Definition Review
   Vocabulary Check
P: **PERFECTING READING SKILLS**
   Comprehending Phrases
   Comprehending Sentences
   Comprehending Main Ideas: Paragraphs
   Comprehending Main Ideas: Essays
   "How to Use a Library" by James A. Michener

Objectives

When you are finished working in this chapter, you will

1. Recognize and be able to use at least 90 percent of the vocabulary words presented in the Words to Know section.
2. Have started to develop your ability to recognize words faster.
3. Know what vowels and their basic sounds are.
4. Know what consonants are and what consonant blends and digraphs are.
5. Know what homonyms are and be able to name at least ten homonyms.
6. Have developed your comprehension of the main ideas in phrases, sentences, and paragraphs by noting how key words and phrases are used in sentences.
7. Have experienced answering comprehension questions that help develop your ability to recall main ideas, interpret, and apply what you have read.

P: PREREADING DRILLS

WORDS TO KNOW

Directions: Here are some words that appear in the drills and essay you will be reading in this chapter. Read them aloud, and learn the definitions of the ones you don't know.

1. *distraction*—something that draws or pulls you away from what you are doing.
College has many distractions that can make study difficult.
2. *tendency*—a pattern, trend, or leaning toward acting a certain way.
There is a tendency to skip classes, especially in classes where the instructor doesn't take the roll.
3. *concepts*—ideas, beliefs, feelings, impressions.
Often textbooks are filled with many new words and concepts.
4. *reputation*—the way people think of someone; the beliefs held about someone or something.
Instructors on campus develop reputations.
5. *inspirational*—stimulating an interest; causing excitement.
Ask for the names of instructors who are more likely to be inspirational in their teaching.
6. *plot*—to draw out graphically; to make a chart.
Plot out your schedule on a chart of some type.
7. *contacts*—people you know; connections.
Learn to balance your social contacts so that your study time doesn't suffer.
8. *assuming*—supposing; taking for granted; believing it to be so.
Instructors provide you with reading assignments, assuming that you know how to handle the reading.
9. *preference*—choice; selection; decision; what you prefer.
His preference was to take fewer classes the first semester.
10. *feast*—a large, elaborate meal with many choices.
College is a great feast from which you should choose.

WARM-UP DRILLS

DRILL 1

Directions: Some words are often misread because they are read too quickly. Read each sentence on this page, and look carefully at the two words under it. Then write the correct word in the blank.

1. Here is some commonsense _____ that may help you.
   advise   advice

2. Try to arrange time to study when you are fresh, not _____.
   tried   tired

3. The schedule had an interesting _____ to it.
   partner   pattern

4. He was never _____ how to study.
   thought   taught

5. Steve was never able to _____ his degree.
   compete   complete

6. Learn to balance your social _____ so that you have time to study.
   contacts   contracts

7. Taking good lecture notes is a _____ of its own.
   still   skill

8. Don't wait until you get so _____ or far behind that it's impossible to catch up.
   confessed   confused

DRILL 2

Directions: Move your eyes rapidly across each line. Mark the word by the number each time it appears on the same line. For example:

   1. laugh   tough   laugh   tough   laugh   tough
   2. right   night   night   right   right   night

Don't look back on any line. If you make a mistake, don't stop to change your answer. Keep moving on. Try to finish in less than forty seconds. Begin timing.

1. college   collage college college collage cottage
2. while   white   white   while   whilt   while   white
3. adjust   adjust   adjurn   adjust   adjurn   adjurn   adjust
4. order   odor   order   otter   odor   order   order   odo
5. bunching   bunches bunching bunched bunch   bunching
6. note   note   not   note   not   nose   note   noted   note
7. assuming   assuring assume   assumed assuming assumed
8. master   master   mast   muster   master   mustard master

P: Prereading Drills 9

9. alert   alive allergy alert alive already alert
10. counsel   council counsel council counsel county
11. qualify   quality quality qualify quantity qualify
12. broaden   broad board broaden broken broaden broken
13. discuss   discussed discussing discuss discuss
14. course   coarse course coarse course courage
15. support   support supply suggest support supported

TIME: _____

Now check each line to see if you marked the correct word every time it appears. Make sure you can pronounce all the words. Learn definitions of words you don't know. The words by the numbers all appear in the essay you are going to read in this chapter.

TOTAL LINES CORRECT: _____

DRILL 3

Directions: Follow the same directions as for Drill 2. Remember to work quickly. Don't look back on a line. Don't change any mistakes you may make. Try to finish in less than forty seconds. Begin timing.

1. faintly   faint faints faintly frankly faintly
2. poverty   proverty probably poverty proven poverty
3. granted   grants grant granted grandly grant
4. whack   whacked whopped whacky whack whack
5. frustrates   frustration frustrate frustrates fluster
6. fussed   fussy fuss fussily fussed flossed
7. audition   audio audition audience auditorium audition
8. professional   professor profession profess professional
9. acceptance   acceptance accepted acceptance accent
10. personally   personal professional personally personally
11. expand   expanded expanding expansion expand
12. renew   remove renewal renew renewal renews
13. flurry   furry furry flurry furry flurry
14. praise   praise prize praise pride praise
15. shinnied   shinny shin shinnied shinnied shiney

TIME: _____

Copyright © 1988 Holt, Rinehart and Winston, Inc.

Check each line to see if you marked the correct word every time it appears. Make sure you can pronounce each word. Learn definitions of the words you don't know.

TOTAL LINES CORRECT: _____

R: READING DRILL

READING AND THINKING ABOUT WHAT YOU READ

Directions: Before you read most things, it's good to skim or look over what you are going to read. It helps to get your mind on the reading. In turn, it helps your comprehension. Take a minute to skim over the following article. First, read the title. Next, read only the first paragraph. Last, let your eyes skim over the article just to see what you see. Don't try to read the article now. You will later. After you've skimmed over the article, come back here, and answer the questions that follow.

1. What do you think the article will be about? (Don't just answer by stating the title.) _____

_____

_____

2. What do you think you might learn from reading this article? _____

_____

_____

3. What do you think the title means? _____

_____

_____

Now read the article.

SUCCEEDING ON CAMPUS

ADAM RIBB

Most students who enter college expect to leave with a degree. Less than half actually do; the others drop out. Although there are many reasons for this,

Reprinted by permission of the author.

one of the biggest has to do with the inability to adjust to the demands of college life. Here is some commonsense advice that may help you reach your college goals.

Time Management

Most college counselors recommend that you take fifteen units or fewer of classes your first semester. That's because you are expected to put in at least two hours of study for each hour in class. If, for instance, you are in classes fifteen hours per week and you study two hours outside of class for each of those fifteen hours in class, that's a total of thirty hours of study. Between class time and study time, that makes a forty-five-hour week—a full-time job. If you must work part-time in order to stay in school, then you should not try to take a full load. It would be better to cut down your class load to fit the time you can devote to study.

Get someone to help you plan a weekly schedule that you will stick to. Plot it out on a chart of some type that shows when you get up in the morning and everything you must do until you go to bed. Try to arrange your classes so that you have time to study both before and after classes. Bunching up all your classes together in order to get them over with leaves no time to go over notes after class or to prepare before another class begins. Try to arrange time to study when you are fresh, not tired.

College has many new distractions. You'll meet people whose values and priorities are different from yours. The class lectures and textbooks will offer ideas and suggestions for other readings that you should pursue. Often the real learning does not take place in the classroom at all but in discussions with others, in outside readings, and during those lonely study hours. Learn to balance your social contacts so that your study time doesn't suffer.

There is also a tendency to skip classes, especially in large lecture settings or in classes where the instructor doesn't take attendance. But skip at your own risk. Asking someone to fill you in on what you missed is dangerous unless that person keeps excellent notes.

Study Methods

Many college professors take it for granted that you already know how to study for their classes. They go about their business of providing you with information in lectures or reading assignments, assuming that you know how to handle it all. That may not be the case. Studying in college demands more reading and thinking, and less memorization, than in high school. If need be, take a study skills class that will show you how to approach the reading of textbooks, how to take good notes, and how to manage your time. If you don't have time to take such a class (which could be the most important class you could take), then go to the library or learning resource center, and ask for books on studying. There is a wealth of information on the subject.

Some professors use lectures to discuss information not found in the textbooks. This means you are left on your own to understand the reading assignments and are expected to keep good notes on the lectures. Often textbooks to introductory courses are difficult to read, full of many new words and concepts that you must master in order to understand the information for examinations. Such books require a whole new approach to reading, and taking good lecture notes is a skill of its own that can not only be useful for study later but can also help you stay alert and involved during class.

Getting Help

Each college differs, but almost all of them have support systems. In addition to learning resource centers where you can find additional learning aids, there are usually tutors available to help in certain subjects, financial aid programs for which you might qualify, and career counseling that offers assistance in determining your major.

And don't forget the professors themselves. Take advantage of their office hours. Most of them are very willing to discuss their courses with you, problems you may be having, or even the grades you receive. Make yourself known to your instructors. If they see you are truly interested in learning, they will be even more willing to help you. But don't wait until you have gotten so confused or far behind that it's impossible for anyone to help you. That's when and why so many students drop out.

When you plan your program of classes, ask students who have been on campus who some of the better instructors are. Instructors develop reputations. Ask around for the names of those who are more likely to be inspirational in their teaching, who make the course exciting. Plan your schedule around their class times, not just any class that fits your preference.

Involvement

The most successful students are those actively involved in their education. Be one of them. Interact with classmates and faculty; participate in activities; become a part of a support group that you can turn to for help. Again, time will determine how active you can get. During your first semester at least, focus more on your academics.

Consider forming or getting into study groups in which you meet regularly with a few classmates to discuss the course material. Ask instructors or the librarian if they have any old examinations you might use from which to study.

Finding Your Major

You may think you already know your major. Maybe not. Don't worry about it too much as a freshman. Think carefully about choosing a career major. College is more than a preparation for a job; it's an opportunity to broaden yourself, to be challenged by new ideas, a preparation for life more than for a career. Many college students do not select their final career path until after they graduate.

Ernest Boyer, president of the Carnegie Foundation for the Advancement of Teaching, says, "When choosing a major, look inside yourself as well as at the economic pattern. If you're genuinely interested in computers, major in them. If you're happiest reading *Beowulf*, don't force yourself to study business." Think carefully before choosing a major. Pick what excites and interests you, not what you think will make you a lot of money.

College can prepare you for a career, but that's not—nor should it be—your purpose for attending. Someone once said that college is a great feast from which you should choose, so don't order the same meal every day. In other words, college offers an opportunity to provide you with experiences you will get nowhere else. Take advantage of all that it offers you in developing yourself as a person, not just as an employee.

COMPREHENSION CHECK

Directions: Answer the following questions without looking back at the article. Don't worry about spelling mistakes.

RECALL

1. About how many students who enter college expecting to get a degree eventually drop out? _____

2. How many hours of study are you expected to do for each hour in class?
_____

3. Does college success require more or less memorization than high school studies do? _____

INTERPRETATION

4. How does the author feel about attending college just to prepare for a career? _____
_____
_____

R: Reading Drill

5. How does this compare with your reasons for attending college? _____

6. Explain why you should not have a class schedule that leaves you no time between classes. _____

7. Why does the author feel that taking a study skills class can be one of the most important classes you can take? _____

APPLICATION

8. If you attended classes twelve hours per week, how many hours of the week would be spent studying and attending classes, based on what is expected of you in study time? _____

9. What support systems does your college have? (If you don't know, what support systems do you feel you should look into?) _____

10. Do you need to take a study skills class? _____ What do you need to learn the most to succeed on campus? _____

E: EXERCISES IN VOCABULARY

In this chapter you will be asked to do some very basic vocabulary work. You will expand words by adding letters of the alphabet or consonant blends to word parts. Such drills may seem unimportant when you have much more difficult vocabulary to deal with in some of your other courses. It's important for you to understand why you are doing these drills.

First, if your reading scores are around the seventh grade level, that does not mean you can't read material at higher levels. Your reading score is an average, meaning you may know some words and comprehension concepts from the eighth to thirteenth grade levels. But you may also not know words or concepts below the seventh grade level, so your score comes out in the seventh grade range—an average. That means you have gaps in your reading skills that need to be filled in. This textbook helps you fill those gaps as well as review concepts you haven't learned or thought about for some time.

Second, many students who don't read much need practice at levels that gradually work up to higher levels. Again, this book provides you with the type of drills that cover a wide range of reading problems, from poor perception of words to poor comprehension.

Do the assigned drills, and you'll find your reading scores quickly increase to the level you want.

DRILLS

DRILL 1: PART A, THE ALPHABET

Directions: In the space that follows, print each letter of the alphabet in correct order. You will use the alphabet list for the next drills.

_____

_____

DRILL 1: PART B, EXPANDING WORDS

Directions: Following are some three-letter words. Use the letters of the alphabet in front of each word to make four-letter words. The first one has been done for you.

1. and *band, hand, land, sand, wand*

2. ear

3. old

4. all

5. ate

6. ail

DRILL 2: CONSONANT BLENDS

Directions: Following are some letters called *consonant blends* and *consonant digraphs*. Consonant blends are two or more letters blended so that *each* letter sound is heard, such as *bl* in *black*, *pl* in *plate*, and *st* in *stamp*. Consonant digraphs are two or more letters that have one sound, such as *th* in *this* and *ch* in *chair*. Try out each consonant blend and digraph with the following words and letter combinations. Write in the words that can be made. Two examples are given for *ear*. You finish them.

bl cl sh sm sp sw br fl
gr qu tr sn st th ch dr

1. ear *clear, shear*

2. ake

3. ill

4. ail

DRILL 3: VOWEL SOUNDS REVIEW

Directions: There are four letters that are always vowels: *a, e, i, o*. There are four letters that are sometimes vowels and sometimes consonants: *u, y, w, h*. U

E: Exercises in Vocabulary

is normally a vowel. But when it follows the letters *g* and *q*, as in *language* and *queen*, it is a consonant because of its sound. *Y* is a vowel when it sounds as it does in *bay* or *boy* and when it ends a word or syllable that does not have a vowel in it, such as *cry* or *happy*. Remember, each syllable has a vowel in it. But *y* is a consonant when it has the sound it has in *you* or *yes*. *W* is usually a consonant. But when it follows a vowel as in *brew*, *crew*, or *crow*, it is a vowel. *H*, like the letter *w*, is a vowel only when it is the second letter following a vowel, as in *ah* or *oh*.

For now, let's deal with only three basic vowel sounds. Read the following examples

Short Vowel Sound (˘)	**Long Vowel Sound (ˉ)**	**Vowels with r Sound**
mat	mate	mark
pet	Pete	pert
bid	bide	bird
rot	rote	stork
cub	cube	curb

Say all the words and listen to the different vowel sounds. Then answer the following questions.

1. One vowel followed by one or more consonants (except *r*) has a _____ sound.

2. One vowel followed by a consonant and final *e* has a _____ sound.

3. One vowel followed by *r* is neither _____ nor _____ but picks up an *r* sound.

4. Check each word that has a long vowel sound:

   hide   brake
   shirt   flop
   child   first
   bold   late

5. Check each word that has a short vowel sound:

   graph   chart
   chorus grab

bid   knot
winter   time

6. Check each word that has a vowel sound controlled by *r:*

chore   bird
wrong   mark
storm   spurt
flurry   ramp

DRILL 4: DOUBLE VOWELS REVIEW

Directions: Read the following rules about double vowels, and then answer the questions that follow.

a. The vowels *ai, ee, oa,* and *ea,* when together in a word and followed by a consonant, usually have the long sound of the first vowel. For example:

     wait   need   road   eat
(There are some exceptions, such as *aisle* and *bear.*)

b. The vowels *ay* (*y* is sometimes a vowel), *ee, ie, ea,* or *oe* at the end of a word have the long sound of the first vowel. For example:

     bay   bee   tie   sea   toe

c. The vowels *ai, ee, oa,* or *ea* followed by the consonant *r* have an *r* controlled sound. For example:

     fair   cheer   roar   year

In the blanks, write in whether each word has a long or short vowel sound.

1. gray _____   6 hope _____

2. meat _____   7. hop _____

3. steam _____   8. bite _____

4. plan _____   9. bit _____

5. plant _____   10. steep _____

Copyright © 1988 Holt, Rinehart and Winston, Inc.

E: *Exercises in Vocabulary*

DRILL 5: HOMONYMS, OR WORDS THAT SOUND ALIKE

Directions: Words that have the same sound and sometimes the same spelling but differ in meaning are called *homonyms*. In the blanks, write the letter of the homonym by the following numbers.

_____	1. weak		a.	see
_____	2. steal		b.	meet
_____	3. meat		c.	deer
_____	4. sea		d.	beat
_____	5. dear		e.	week
_____	6. beet		f.	here
_____	7. fair		g.	fare
_____	8. hear		h.	hole
_____	9. whole		i.	paws
_____	10. pause		j.	steel
_____	11. pain		k.	waste
_____	12. due		l.	tail
_____	13. waist		m.	there
_____	14. tale		n.	sale
_____	15. here		o.	pane
_____	16. their		p.	do
_____	17. sail		q.	male
_____	18. mail		r.	hear

DRILL 6: DEFINITION REVIEW

Directions: Write the letter of the correct definition in the blank by the numbered word. There are more definitions than you need.

_____ 1. plot   a. something that takes your attention away

_____ 2. contacts   b. ideas, beliefs, impressions

_____ 3. assuming   c. a pattern or trend; a leaning toward

_____ 4. preference   d. to draw out graphically; to make a chart

_____ 5. inspire   e. a person whose job requires advanced study or one who earns money from sports

_____ 6. reputation   f. supposing; taking for granted

_____ 7. concepts   g. to stimulate or cause

_____ 8. tendency   h. choice; selection

_____ 9. distraction   i. a large, elaborate meal

_____ 10. feast   j. connections; people you know

                                                                                    k. the beliefs held about someone or something

                                                                                    l. sudden, quick movement

VOCABULARY CHECK

PART ONE

Directions: Underline the vowels in the following words, and in the blank after the word, write in the vowel sound (long, short, silent, or with *r* sound).

1. shake _____
2. flail _____
3. spill _____
4. snail _____
5. quark _____

6. smear _____
7. quick _____
8. chorus _____
9. child _____
10. spurt _____

E: Exercises in Vocabulary

PART TWO

Directions: Circle the consonant blends in the following words.

1. shear
2. grail
3. strong
4. flake
5. shill
6. broil
7. skill
8. drill
9. spoil
10. crank
11. chump
12. smack
13. crack
14. blame
15. shark

PART THREE

Directions: In the blank, write the letter that is not heard in the following words.

1. waist _____
2. waste _____
3. tail _____
4. tale _____
5. pain _____
6. pane _____
7. sail _____
8. sale _____
9. mail _____
10. male _____
11. due _____
12. hear _____
13. here _____
14. fair _____
15. fare _____

PART FOUR

Directions: Write a sentence correctly, using the following homonyms.

1. waist: _____

_____

24   *E: Exercises in Vocabulary*

2. pane: _____

_____

3. pause: _____

_____

4. steel: _____

_____

5. fare: _____

_____

P: PERFECTING READING SKILLS

COMPREHENDING PHRASES

Directions: The following phrases are idiomatic expressions, that is, ways of saying things that mean something other than the literal meaning. Define these phrases in your own words. The first one has been done for you.

1. not in her wildest dreams: *not able to imagine*

2. drive a hard bargain: _____

3. go to bat for him: _____

4. he's a wonder: _____

5. conquered his fear: _____

6. held his tongue: _____

7. in a firm voice: _____

8. shadow of a doubt: _____

9. half out of her wits: _____

10. beat around the bush: _____

_____

COMPREHENDING SENTENCES

PART A

The following set of questions all deal with a famous person. See if you can figure out who it is as you do the drills.

Directions: Read each sentence, and answer the questions that follow.

1. Stevie taught himself to play the piano as quickly as he had once learned the harmonica.

    a. Does this mean Stevie learned to play the piano first? _____

    _____

    b. How do you know? _____

    _____

2. His voice was filled with quiet discovery when he said, "That's it. That's what we'll do."

    a. Does this mean his voice was excited? _____

    b. What does "quiet discovery" mean? _____

    _____

3. "Fingertips" was a smash, topping charts all over the country.

    a. What charts are being referred to? _____

    _____

    b. Was the record successful? _____
4. Stevie felt grown and strong and ready to fly.

    a. What is meant by "ready to fly"? _____

    _____

P: Perfecting Reading Skills 27

    b. Does the sentence say he *is* grown and strong? _____

    _____

5. Stevie fought back from the shadow of death as he had once fought out from the shadow of blindness.

    a. What does the word *shadow* mean in the sentence? _____

    _____

    b. What can we learn about Stevie's personality from this sentence?

    _____

    _____

6. His first worry dissolved in a flurry of public acceptance and critical praise.

    a. Does this mean both the record buyers and the critics liked him?

    _____

    b. Was he worried they wouldn't like him? _____

7. Stevie seemed like an adult genius in a child's body.

    a. Is Stevie a child or an adult? _____

    b. What does the sentence mean? _____

    _____

8. Stevie is a man who conquered his darkness and can bring sunshine to the shadow of other lives.

    a. What do these words mean in the sentence?

    darkness: _____

    _____

    sunshine: _____

    _____

    shadow: _____

    _____

b. Does the sentence mean that Stevie Wonder (did you guess right?) can bring some happiness to people who have problems to overcome? _____

PART B

The following set of sentences deal with—well, you'll see.

9. The moonlight shines into her open window, and a soft breeze gently moves the curtains.

   a. What time of day is it? *Night*

   b. What is the weather probably like? *Hot*

10. He bends over the sleeping woman and sinks two fangs into her neck and drinks her blood.

    a. What words could you use instead of "sinks two fangs"? *bites*

    b. Why did the woman let him do this? _____

11. In 1931, the movie *Dracula* was made from Bram Stoker's novel by the same name.

    a. Which came first, the book or the movie? _____

    b. What was the title of Stoker's book? _____

12. Maria claims that many vampire stories were started by uneducated and superstitious people.

    a. Were all vampire stories started by uneducated and superstitious people? _____

P: Perfecting Reading Skills

    b. What key words tell you this? _____

    _____

13. You can kill a vampire by driving a stake through its heart, by nailing its head to its coffin, or by burning the body—the latter being the best way.

    a. How many ways are there to kill a vampire? _____

    b. Which is the best way? _____

14. They dug up the vampire's body and drove a stake through its heart, but the corpse only laughed and said it would use the stake as a stick to defend itself against dogs.

    a. What method of killing vampires needs to be tried? _____

    _____

    _____

    b. Does the vampire have a sense of humor? _____ How do

    you know? _____

15. At times moviemakers have had to strain to keep up with the people's demand for bigger and ever more terrible monsters, but the human imagination is equal to the job.

    a. Does the sentence mean that people like to be frightened in movies?

    _____

    b. Does the sentence mean that moviemakers will be able to answer the

    demand? _____

COMPREHENDING MAIN IDEAS: PARAGRAPHS

A paragraph is a group of sentences all dealing with a main idea. As you read a paragraph, you should first look for its key idea. The key idea is usually found in its *topic sentence*. The topic sentence of a paragraph is often, though not always, the first one. Sometimes the topic sentence is last, sometimes in the middle, and sometimes there is none. In the latter case, the key idea is suggested or hinted at rather than stated. The other sentences in the paragraph will support or explain the key idea in more detail.

PART A

Directions: Read the following paragraphs, and underline the sentence in each that states the main idea. Then, in the blanks, write the main idea in your own words.

1. (a) <u>The number of hours children spend in front of television is steadily increasing.</u> (b) Preschool children watch about twenty-three hours of television. (c) The average time elementary school children watch television is from twenty-five to thirty-five hours per week. (d) In one study, over half of all twelve-year-olds questioned watched more than six hours a day.

_____

_____

2. (a) <u>The movie *TRON* makes unusual use of film imagery.</u> (b) It offers sights that no eye, no camera has ever seen before. (c) A film about computers, the film was made by computers. (d) Some fifty-three minutes of the film were made mechanically by computers. (e) No pens, no pencils, no brushes were used to create the colorful scenery.

_____

_____

3. (a) <u>Some think that the theater and film are similar.</u> (b) But the differences are greater than the similarities. (c) Film can never be alive. (d) In theater, the audience can accept certain departures from reality. (e) Not so with films. (f) Films rely more on technical skill than the stage.

_____

_____

4. (a) As soon as the film industry invented movie stars, the public caught a case of curiosity about their off-screen lives. (b) Americans began to turn actors into idols. (c) Today, audiences still want to know what they are *really* like. (d) For years, Hollywood made no honest effort to answer the question. (e) Fan magazines made up tales about the stars' private lives. (f) Today, in contrast, there is an outpouring of books by movie personalities who want to "tell it all."

_____

P: Perfecting Reading Skills   31

5. (a) Avon, the paperback giant, has begun publishing a bold new series of Latin-American novels. (b) These new books join Avon's already large list of such books, led by Gabriel García Marquez's *One Hundred Years of Solitude*. (c) It has sold more than 800,000 paperback copies alone. (d) These new listings present serious works by writers unknown to most Americans.

PART B

Directions: Read each of the following paragraphs, and answer the questions that follow.

1. When Henry Aaron was young, he got a job delivering ice. In those days, most people had iceboxes instead of electric refrigerators. A block of ice was kept in the icebox to keep food cool. Henry's job was to mark off a piece of ice the size the customer needed. With a sharp-pointed ice pick, he chopped the piece from a big cake of ice. Usually, the chopped pieces of ice were from twenty-five to fifty pounds. Henry had to carry these blocks of ice from the truck to the customer's icebox. This job may have helped Henry develop his strong wrists that later would bat more home runs than anyone else.

   a. Whom is the paragraph about? _____

   b. When did the events in the paragraph take place? _____

   c. What is the paragraph about? _____

2. When Hank Aaron was eighteen years old, he signed a contract with the Milwaukee Braves C Team. That was in 1952. It was a tough period in his life. It was the first time he had to stay with white people. Being from the South, he knew which places were closed to him there. But new to the North, Hank soon learned that some places where blacks were supposed to be welcome did not want him. He also discovered that some sports reporters and even some of his teammates were biased because of his color. But he stuck it out. Times got better, and so did his playing.

   a. What is the paragraph about? _____

   _____

   _____

   _____

   b. What does this paragraph tell you about Hank Aaron's character?

   _____

   _____

   _____

   _____

   c. How would you feel and what would you do if you were in the same situation Aaron was in 1952? _____

   _____

   _____

   _____

3. On March 14, 1954, Henry Aaron received his big break. The Braves were playing against the New York Yankees. Bobby Thomson, the Braves' left fielder, got a hit. He slid into second base so hard that he broke his ankle. To the surprise of everyone, the Braves manager, Charlie Grimm, picked rookie Henry to fill in. Aaron became the regular left fielder for the Braves.

   a. What sentence in the paragraph sums up the point of the paragraph? _____

   _____

P: Perfecting Reading Skills 33

    b. Why was Bobby Thomson's bad break a good break for Aaron? _____

    ————————————————————————————————

    c. What is a "rookie"? ————————————————————————

    ————————————————————————————————

4. Hank Aaron had a lot to learn his first season. His first few games were not too impressive. Aaron couldn't seem to get a hit. He also made some serious fielding errors. During one game, he was running to base when his hat fell off. Henry made the mistake of going back to get it! But Braves manager Grimm knew Henry was trying too hard. He had faith in Aaron. On April 23, 1954, his faith paid off. Hank hit his first major-league home run. That was the first of a record 715 home runs for Henry Aaron.

    a. Why do you suppose Braves manager Grimm had faith in Aaron? ————————————————————————————

    ————————————————————————————————

    b. What do you think would have happened to Henry Aaron's career if Grimm had not had faith in him? ————————————————

    ————————————————————————————————

    ————————————————————————————————

5. During the 1974 season, the Braves were playing the Los Angeles Dodgers. Almost 54,000 people were crowded into Atlanta Stadium. They were there to see if Henry Aaron was going to break the great Babe Ruth's home-run record. The first time Aaron came to bat, the pitcher walked him. In the fourth inning, Hank was at bat again. He was thrown a fast ball. Aaron snapped his wrists. The bat hit the ball, sending it over a 385-foot sign. His first swing of the game brought him his 715th home run. He broke the Babe's long-standing record.

    a. Where did Aaron break the Babe's home-run record? _____

    ————————————————————————————————

    b. When? ———————————————————————————

    c. Why did the pitcher walk Aaron the first time he went to bat? _____

    ————————————————————————————————

Copyright © 1988 Holt, Rinehart and Winston, Inc.

d. What was Babe Ruth's home-run record? _____

_____

_____

e. How do you think Aaron felt about his record-breaking home run?

_____

_____

_____

COMPREHENDING MAIN IDEAS: ESSAYS

Directions: Sometimes our minds wander when we read. It's usually because we are not ready to concentrate on what we are reading. Earlier in this chapter, you were told to skim over what you are going to read before reading it. Do the same thing here. First, read the title. Then read only the first paragraph. Next, read the headings that divide up the essay. Then come back here, and answer the following questions.

1. What do you think is the main idea of the essay?

_____

_____

2. Does the title help suggest what this essay will probably be about? _____

Explain. _____

_____

_____

3. What do you think you might learn from this essay?

_____

_____

Now read the essay.

Copyright © 1988 Holt, Rinehart and Winston, Inc.

HOW TO USE A LIBRARY

JAMES A. MICHENER

You're driving your car home from work or school. And something goes wrong. The engine stalls out at lights, holds back as you go to pass.

It needs a tune-up—and soon. Where do you go? The library.

You can take out an auto repair manual that tells step-by-step how to tune up your make and model.

Or your tennis game has fallen off. You've lost your touch at the net. Where do you go?

The library—for a few books on improving your tennis form.

"The library!" you say. "That's where my teacher sends me to do—ugh—homework."

Unfortunately, I've found that's exactly the way many people feel. If you're among them, you're denying yourself the easiest way to improve yourself, enjoy yourself and even cope with life.

It's hard for me to imagine what I would be doing today if I had not fallen in love, at the ripe old age of seven, with the Melinda Cox Library in my hometown of Doylestown, Pennsylvania. At our house, we just could not afford books. The books in that free library would change my life dramatically.

Who knows what your library can open up for you?

My first suggestion for making the most of your library is to do what I did: read and read and read. For pleasure—and for understanding.

How to Kick the TV Habit

If it's TV that keeps you from cultivating this delicious habit, I can offer a sure remedy. Take home from the library a stack of books that might look interesting.

Pile them on the TV set. Next time you are tempted to turn on a program you really don't want to see, reach for a book instead.

Over the years, some people collect a mental list of books they mean to read. If you don't have such a list, here is a suggestion. Take from the library some of the books you might have enjoyed dramatized on TV, like Remarque's *All Quiet on the Western Front*, Clavell's *Shōgun*, Tolkien's *The Hobbit*, or Victor Hugo's *Les Misérables*.

If you like what you read, you can follow up with other satisfying books by the same authors.

Some people in their reading limit themselves to current talked-about bestsellers. Oh, what they miss! The library is full of yesterday's best-sellers; and they still make compelling reading today. Some that I've enjoyed: A. B. Guthrie's *The Big Sky*, Carl Van Doren's *Benjamin Franklin*, Mari Sandoz's *Old Jules*, and Norman Mailer's *The Naked and the Dead*.

Reprinted by permission of International Paper Company.

How do you find these or any other books you're looking for? It's easy—with the card catalog.

Learn to Use the Card Catalog

Every time I go to the library—and I go more than once a week—I invariably make a beeline to the card catalog before anything else. It's the nucleus of any public library.

The card catalog lists every book in the library by:
1. author; 2. title; 3. subject.

Let's pick an interesting subject to look up. I have always been fascinated by astronomy.

You'll be surprised at the wealth of material you will find under "astronomy" to draw upon. And the absorbing books you didn't know existed on it.

CAUTION: Always have a pencil and paper when you use the card catalog. Once you jot down the numbers of the books you are interested in, you are ready to find them on the shelves.

Learn to Use the Stacks

Libraries call the shelves "the stacks." In many smaller libraries which you'll be using, the stacks will be open for you to browse.

To me there is a special thrill in tracking down the books I want in the stacks! For invariably, I find books about which I knew nothing, and these often turn out to be the very ones I need. You will find the same thing happening to you when you start to browse in the stacks. "A learned mind is the end product of browsing."

CAUTION: If you take a book from the stacks to your work desk, do not try to return it to its proper place. That's work for the experts. If you replace it incorrectly, the next seeker won't be able to find it.

Learn to Know the Reference Librarian

Some of the brightest and best-informed men and women in America are the librarians who specialize in providing reference help.

Introduce yourself. State your problem. And be amazed at how much help you will receive.

CAUTION: Don't waste the time of this expert by asking silly questions you ought to solve yourself. Save the reference librarian for the really big ones.

Learn to Use *The Reader's Guide to Periodical Literature*

This green-bound index is one of the most useful items in any library. It indexes all the articles in the major magazines, including newspaper magazine supplements.

Thus it provides a guide to the very latest expert information on any subject that interests you.

So if you want to do a really first-class job, find out which magazines your library subscribes to, then consult *The Reader's Guide* and track down recent articles on your subject. When you use this wonderful tool effectively, you show the mark of a real scholar.

Four Personal Hints

Since you can take most books home, but not magazines, take full notes when using the latter.

Many libraries today provide a reprographic machine that can quickly copy pages you need from magazines and books. Ask about it.

If you are working on a project of some size which will require repeated library visits, keep a small notebook in which you record the identification numbers of the books you will be using frequently. This will save you valuable time, because you won't have to consult the card catalog or search aimlessly through the stacks each time you visit for material you seek.

Some of the very best books in any library are the reference books, which may not be taken home. Learn what topics they cover and how best to use them, for these books are wonderful repositories of human knowledge.

Your Business and Legal Advisor

Your library can give you help on *any* subject. It can even be your business and legal advisor.

How many times have you scratched your head over how to get a tax rebate on your summer job? You'll find answers in tax guides at the library. Thinking of buying or renting a house? You'll find guides to that. Want to defend yourself in traffic court? Find out how in legal books at the library.

Library Projects Can Be Fun—and Rewarding

Here are a few ideas:

1. *What are your roots?* Trace your ancestors. Many libraries specialize in genealogy.

2. *Did George Washington sleep nearby?* Or Billy the Kid? Your library's collection of local history books can put you on the trail.

3. *Cook a Polynesian feast.* Or an ancient Roman banquet. Read how in the library's cookbooks.

4. *Take up photography.* Check the library for consumer reviews of cameras before you buy. Take out books on lighting, composition, or darkroom techniques.

Or—you name it!

If you haven't detected by now my enthusiasm for libraries, let me offer two personal notes.

I'm particularly pleased that in recent years two beautiful libraries have been named after me: a small community library in Quakertown, Pennsylvania, and the huge research library located at the University of Northern Colorado in Greeley.

And I like libraries so much that I married a librarian.

Now answer the following questions.

RECALL

1. What is the main idea of the essay?

   _____

   _____

   _____

2. According to the author, there is no way to break the TV habit.

   a. True

   b. False, because _____

   _____

3. How does the card catalog list the books in the library?

   a. _____

   b. _____

   c. _____

4. The shelves where you can find library books are called _____.

5. What information does *The Reader's Guide to Periodical Literature* contain? _____

   _____

P: Perfecting Reading Skills 39

_____

_____

INTERPRETATION

6. We can infer (guess) that reference librarians are too busy to answer questions, so we should know as much about the library as possible before going there.

   a. True

   b. False, because _____

   _____

7. We can infer that Michener thinks parents should take their young children to the library often.

   a. True

   b. False, because _____

   _____

APPLICATION

Note: The last three questions require a trip to your college or local library.

8. Look up the author of the essay you just read in the card catalog. How many books by him are in your library? _____

   How many books about him are in the library? _____

9. Using *The Reader's Guide to Periodical Literature,* look up the subject "women." Explain what you found under that listing. _____

   _____

   _____

Copyright © 1988 Holt, Rinehart and Winston, Inc.

10. Pick one of the magazine listings under the subject "women" in *The Reader's Guide,* and find the article listed. If you need help, ask the reference librarian. In the following space, list the author of the article, the title of the article, the magazine title, the date, and the page numbers of the article.

Name _____ **Section** _____ **Date** _____

Chapter 2

Objectives

P: **PREREADING DRILLS**
Words to Know
Warm-up Drills

R: **READING DRILL**
Reading and Thinking About What You Read
"We Are What We Think We Are" by John Hubris
Comprehension Check

E: **EXERCISES IN VOCABULARY**
Drills
    1: Expanding Words
    2: Expanding Words
    3: Vowel Review
    4: The Schwa (ə)
    5: Homonyms, or Words That Sound Alike
    6: Definition Review
Vocabulary Check

P: **PERFECTING READING SKILLS**
Comprehending Idiomatic Phrases
Comprehending Sentences
Comprehending Main Ideas: Paragraphs
Comprehending Main Ideas: A Chapter From a Psychology Textbook
"The Search for Self-actualization" by Dennis Coon

Objectives

When you are finished working in this chapter, you will

1. Recognize and be able to use at least 90 percent of the vocabulary words presented in the Words to Know section.
2. Have developed your ability to recognize words faster.
3. Know the basic vowel sounds.
4. Know what a schwa is and how it is pronounced.
5. Know how stress marks can help you correctly pronounce words.
6. Know at least ten pairs of homonyms and be able to write sentences using them.
7. Have developed your comprehension of the main ideas in phrases, sentences, and paragraphs by noting how key words and phrases are used.
8. Have experienced answering comprehension questions that help develop your ability to recall main ideas, interpret, and apply what you have read.

P: PREREADING DRILLS

WORDS TO KNOW

Directions: Here are some words that appear in the drills and article you will be reading in this chapter. Read them aloud, and learn the definitions of the ones you don't know. Definitions are based on their use in the article.

1. *psychologists*—those who study emotional and behavioral characteristics.
The psychologists could not agree on the causes of the child's behavior.
2. *impressions*—beliefs or ideas made on the mind.
Terry's impressions of himself were not very good.
3. *unconsciously*—not aware; without thinking.
Our impressions of ourselves are mostly formed unconsciously.
4. *concept*—idea, belief, or thought.
Our concepts of ourselves and others are often wrong.
5. *self-imaging*—the daily practice of picturing oneself doing well at a skill.
Ralph, through self-imaging, developed his tennis serve.
6. *potentialities*—things one is able to do or accomplish but hasn't yet achieved.
Because Steve thought so little of himself, he never discovered his potentialities in school.
7. *vivid*—lifelike; bright; easily seen.
When you practice self-imaging, the pictures in the mind should be as detailed and as vivid as possible.
8. *humiliation*—shame; embarrassment.
Humiliation from mistakes can be useful in learning to overcome such errors.
9. *competent*—properly qualified; capable.
Many students are more competent than they think.
10. *expectations*—things to look forward to; desires; hopes.
Frank's expectations of himself were not very high, so he never felt that he had to try hard.

WARM-UP DRILLS

DRILL 1

Directions: Some words are often misread because they are read too quickly. Read each sentence on the following page, and look carefully at the two words under it. Then, in the blank, write in the correct word.

1. Howard's family _____ has two lions standing on their back legs.
                            crust   crest

2. Dracula spoke with an _____.
   ascent   accent

3. Vampires cannot see their _____ in a mirror.
   reflection   reflective

4. Don't take it seriously; the story is just _____.
   friction   fiction

5. My Aunt Bessie has to buy a new _____ evening gown for the dance.
   formal   former

6. The victim put up a _____ before he passed out.
   straggle   struggle

7. Keep the wooden stake _____ in case we find a vampire in the coffin.
   hardy   handy

8. When she could not see her _____ in the mirror, Ruth was convinced she was a vampire.
   imagine   image

9. Fran is _____ in her job.
   competitor   competent

10. My _____ of her is that she is lazy.
    impressive   impression

DRILL 2

Directions: Move your eyes rapidly across each line. Mark the word by the number each time it appears on the same line. For example:

1. rear   ~~rear~~   roar   ~~rear~~   roar   roar
2. reared roared ~~reared~~ roared roared ~~reared~~

Don't look back on any line. If you make a mistake, don't stop to change your answer. Keep moving on. Try to finish in less than forty seconds. Begin timing.

1. accent   ascent   ascent   accent   ascent   accent
2. stake   stake   steak   stake   steak   steak
3. coffin   coffin   coffin   coffer   coffer   coffee
4. shines   shrines shines   shrines shrines shines
5. formal   formed   formed   formed   formal   formal

P: Prereading Drills

6. connect   correct connect correct connect correct
7. veins   vanes   vanes   veins   vanes   veins
8. image   imagine imagine image   image   imagine
9. struggle straggle struggle struggle straggle struggle
10. bitten   kitten   bitter   bitten   bitter   kitten
11. tales   trails   tails   tales   tales   tails
12. their   there   their   there   their   there
13. since   since   sense   sense   since   sense
14. soul   sole   soul   sole   sole   soul
15. through threw   through thought threw   through

TIME: _____

Now check each line to see if you marked the correct word every time it appears. Make sure you know all the words and their meanings. The words by the numbers appear in the article you will read in the chapter.

TOTAL LINES CORRECT: _____

DRILL 3

Directions: Follow the same directions as for Drill 2. Remember to work quickly. Don't look back on a line. Don't change any mistakes you may make. It takes up time. Try to finish in less than thirty-five seconds this time. Begin timing.

1. fiction   friction fiction friction friction fiction
2. convince   convincing convinced convinced convincing convinced
3. conqueror   conqueror conquer conqueror conquer conqueror
4. mystery   mysterious mysteriously mystery mastery mystery
5. shriek   shriek   shrine   shriek   shrank   shrines
6. shines   shins   shines   shriek   shrink   shines
7. castle   coastal coast   castle   castle   casts
8. reflection reflective reflection reflects reflective reflection
9. creation   creative creates creation creative creatures
10. accident   accent   acidly   accident accident accent
11. corpse   corps   corpse   corps   corpse   corpse
12. disease   disaster disaster disease disease disaster
13. nobleman   nobleman noble   noble   noblewoman nobleman

14. buried   burned buried burned buried burned
15. legend   legion legend logger legion legend

TIME: _____

Check each line to see if you marked the correct word every time it appears. Make sure you can pronounce each word. Learn the meanings of all the words. The words by the numbers appear in the article you are going to read in this chapter.

TOTAL LINES CORRECT: _____

R: READING DRILL

READING AND THINKING ABOUT WHAT YOU READ

Directions: Before reading the article, read the title, the opening paragraph, and the headings. Then answer the following questions.

1. What does the title mean to you?

   _____

   _____

   _____

2. What do you think the main idea of the article will be?

   _____

   _____

   _____

3. What do you think you will learn from reading the article?

   _____

   _____

   _____

Now read the article.

WE ARE WHAT WE THINK WE ARE

JOHN HUBRIS

1   Psychologists tell us that we are what we think ourselves to be. Our self-image defines for us what we believe we can and cannot do. If we think we are failures, we will probably often fail. If we think we are successful, we will prob-

Reprinted by permission of the author.

ably often succeed. Each of us over the years has built up beliefs about ourselves. Unconsciously, our pictures of who we are have been formed by past experiences. Our successes and failures, what others have told us, and what we think people believe about us—all help form impressions of who we think we are. Because the self-image is so important in our growth, it is important to examine our concepts of self in order to reach our full potential.

Effects of Poor Self-images

2   A danger is that we often accept as true the wrong images of self. An example is a student who sees herself as "poor in English." She can be heard to say, "Oh, I've never been good in English classes." So the student avoids English classes that could help her. When she does have to take an English class, she performs poorly and says, "See, I told you I was lousy in English." This makes her self-image all the more real to her. It is also an "excuse" to continue to do poorly in English classes.

3   Chances are the student failed in an English test at one time in the past. Rather than saying, "I failed a test; what can I learn from it?" she began thinking, "I'm a failure; I'll never do well in English." Or perhaps her parents or friends made negative remarks to her about her grades. These are ways that poor self-images develop. In this case, the student became what she thought she was. Unfortunately, many people go through school believing they are poor students when they actually may not be. They've never given themselves a chance to find their true potential.

Self-image Can Be Changed

4   Changing our self-image is possible. Our nervous system does not know the difference between a real experience and an imagined one. It reacts automatically to information it is given. For instance, a man is hiking along a trail and suddenly sees a large rattlesnake coiled in his way. His nervous system reacts automatically. He feels fear without having to say, "Feel fear now." His reactions are based on what he knows about poisonous snakes.

5   But suppose the snake was not real. Suppose it is a rubber one put there as a joke. It still would make no difference in the man's reaction. As long as he *thought* it was a real rattler, he would react exactly as if it *were* a real snake. Only if he knew it to be a fake, or if he were not already afraid of snakes, would he react otherwise.

6   When our ideas and mental concepts of ourselves are not real but we think they are, we are going to act as if they are real. Just imagining ourselves "dumb" will cause us to react to things that way. It becomes our "easy out." The student who thought herself a poor student in English reacted to English classes exactly as she imagined she would—poorly. It never occurred to her to examine her self-image. In fact, her self-concept gave her a good reason not to try very hard.

Changing Self-image

7 Some psychologists suggest we begin to change our self-image by mentally picturing ourselves performing well at some task. Since we presently react to things based on our present images, the suggestion is to replace those with better ones. In many experiments, people were asked to sit quietly for a few minutes each day and imagine themselves doing well at a task. For instance, subjects would sit and imagine themselves throwing darts at a bull's-eye on a target. Over a period of weeks their dart game improved. This has been done with people who wanted to play chess better; throw a ball more accurately; increase their salesmanship, musical talents, and many other skills. In most cases, remarkable improvement is made. That "poor" English student might have found she was much better in the subject than she thought if she had tried seeing herself as a better student.

8 The point of self-imaging is not to develop an image of ourselves that is not real. To try to become something we really aren't is just as wrong as living the unrealistic, inferior image we may have. The aim is to find the "real" self, to bring our mental images of ourselves in line with our true potential. However, it is generally accepted among psychologists that most of us shortchange ourselves. We're usually better than we think we are. Finding that out is the point of self-imaging.

One Method

9 Try this. Set aside about twenty to thirty minutes each day to sit alone quietly and comfortably. Just close your eyes and imagine yourself sitting before a large movie screen. Then picture yourself doing something you want to improve on. This could be schoolwork, test-taking, your backhand stroke in tennis, job interviewing, whatever. Practice seeing yourself doing it correctly and successfully. Make your pictures as real and as vivid as possible. See and hear details, even smells if you can. If you are working on test-taking, for instance, picture the room you are in. Give the room color, furniture, smells. See yourself relaxed at a desk. Picture the clothes you are wearing. Hear the sounds of others writing, moving in their seats. Read the questions on the test and imagine yourself writing answers to them. Make the questions and answers real ones from a real class. Details are considered the most important part of practicing an experience. Such an exercise helps wipe out poor images and gives you new images or pictures of yourself being successful.

Forget Past Mistakes

10 Another important part of changing self-concept is not to think about past mistakes. Don't let failures do harm. Our errors or humiliations over mistakes are necessary steps in learning. It is all right to make mistakes. But when they have taught us what we did wrong, we should forget them and not dwell on

them. Sometimes we keep remembering our failures or mistakes and feel guilty or embarrassed about them. We let them take over us, and then we develop a fear or an excuse to not develop further. That's exactly what the "poor" English student allowed to happen.

11 Currently, many "older" persons are returning to college. At many community colleges the average student age is around twenty-eight years old. Housewives whose children are grown, single mothers, men returning to school for job retraining are all beginning to raise the average age of college students. Many of these people come with poor self-concepts, afraid they aren't good enough for college. But they do come, and most find that they are much brighter and more competent than they ever imagined. In fact, many instructors welcome returning students because they are serious and work hard at learning.

Be Realistic

12 It is important to have realistic expectations of ourselves. Some of our dissatisfaction might come from expecting too much of ourselves. If we demand constant perfection in everything we do, we can be disappointed. Our poor self-concept will continue. If our goal is to reach perfection, we are doomed from the start.

COMPREHENSION CHECK

Directions: Answer the following questions without looking back at the article. Read all the items before selecting an answer.

RECALL

1. The best statement of the main idea of the article is this:
   a. Each of us over the years has built up beliefs about ourselves.
   b. Understanding the power of self-image is important if we are to reach our potential.
   c. If we think we are successful, we will be; if we think we are failures, we will be.
   d. Our self-image defines who we think we are.
2. Changing one's self-image is not possible.

   a. True

   b. False, because _____

   _____

R: Reading Drill 51

3. Define "self-imaging." _____
   _____
   _____

4. When practicing self-imaging, which of the following is very important?
   a. sitting still
   b. being alone
   c. relaxing
   d. picturing details

INTERPRETATION

5. What is the point being made with the story of the snake in the man's path?
   _____
   _____
   _____

6. What point is being made about making mistakes or being embarrassed?
   _____
   _____
   _____

7. Based on this article, it is not psychologically possible to become anything we want.

   a. True

   b. False, because _____
   _____
   _____

APPLICATION

8. Do you think you have a poor self-image in some areas that needs to be changed? _____ Explain. _____

9. How could you use the content of this article to help you personally?

E: EXERCISES IN VOCABULARY

DRILLS

DRILL 1: EXPANDING WORDS

Directions: Below are some three-letter groups. Make four-letter words by putting letters from the alphabet in front of each group. The first one has been done for you.

1. ath *bath, math, path*

2. unk

3. ook

4. ame

5. are

6. ore

7. ing

53

8. ead

DRILL 2: EXPANDING WORDS

Directions: Following are some consonant blends you used in Chapter 1. Try adding each consonant blend to the front of the groups of letters that follow. Write the words that can be made on the lines. One example is given for *ank*, but there are more.

bl cl sh sm cr dr fl pl pr ch
sp st th kn qu sl sn tr wh

1. ank

    blank,

2. ack

3. ump

4. ame

DRILL 3: VOWEL REVIEW

Directions: Following is the vowel sound chart you learned in Chapter 1. Use it to help you answer the questions that follow.

E: *Exercises in Vocabulary*

Short Vowel Sound (˘)	Long Vowel Sound (¯)	Vowels with r Sound
măt	māte	mark
pĕt	Pēte	pert
bĭd	bīde	bird
rŏt	rōte	stork
cŭb	cūbe	curb

1. Check each word that has a long vowel sound in it:

_____ shines   _____ made

_____ formal   _____ bit

_____ connect   _____ bitten

_____ sole   _____ famous

2. Check each word that has a short vowel sound in it:

_____ coffin   _____ victims

_____ struggle   _____ crisp

_____ fangs   _____ legend

_____ tales   _____ accent

3. Check each word that has a vowel controlled by the *r* sound:

_____ formal   _____ superstition

_____ strum   _____ shriek

_____ storm   _____ furies

_____ bright   _____ spurt

4. In the blanks, write in whether each word has a long or short vowel sound in it.

a. soul _____   c. victim _____

b. struggle _____   d. castle _____

Copyright © 1988 Holt, Rinehart and Winston, Inc.

e. veins _____   g. steam _____

f. shriek _____   h. wait _____

DRILL 4: THE SCHWA (ə)

Directions: The schwa is the symbol ə. It is used to show soft vowel sounds, usually like a soft *u* sound. In the dictionary, the schwa (ə) is the sound represented by

a as in *a*bout
e as in tak*e*n
i as in Apr*i*l
o as in lem*o*n
u as in circ*u*s

Here are some words that have the schwa sound. Say them aloud. Notice that the accent mark (′) shows which syllable to stress when you say the word.

hanger (hang′ər)   ancient (ān′shənt)
legend (lej′ənd)   Transylvania (trăn′sĭl vā nē ə)

Following are two columns. In the blanks, write the letter of the word that stands for the word by the number. The first one has been done for you. Some of the words in the second column are not used.

d 1. let′ər   a. hanger

____ 2. mel′ən   b. later

____ 3. lāt′ər   c. color

____ 4. hang′ər   d. letter

____ 5. kol′ər   e. collar

____ 6. pə lēs′   f. melon

____ 7. hun′gər   g. please

____ 8. jen′ər ā′shən   h. hunger

                         i. police

                         j. generator

                         k. generation

E: Exercises in Vocabulary

DRILL 5: HOMONYMS, OR WORDS THAT SOUND ALIKE

Directions: Following are two columns of words. In the blanks, write the letter of the homonym in the blank by the number.

_____ 1. whole   a. weight

_____ 2. knot   b. wood

_____ 3. rap   c. reign

_____ 4. wait   d. hole

_____ 5. piece   e. wrap

_____ 6. would   f. peace

_____ 7. rain   g. not

_____ 8. great   h. corps

_____ 9. isle   i. aisle

_____ 10. core   j. grate

DRILL 6: DEFINITION REVIEW

Directions: The following list of words is from the Words to Know sections in Chapters 1 and 2. Write the letter of the correct definition in the blank by the word. There are more definitions than words.

_____ 1. decade   a. a testing or hearing

_____ 2. wail   b. possible accomplishments

_____ 3. humiliation   c. person who studies emotional and behavioral characteristics

_____ 4. concept   d. a sad, high-toned cry

_____ 5. audition   e. lifelike; real; easily seen

_____ 6. potential   f. an abstract idea or belief

(continued on next page)

_____ 7. vivid   g. a person whose job requires advanced study or one who earns money from sports

_____ 8. professional   h. unlawful

_____ 9. psychologist   i. properly qualified

_____ 10. assuming   j. ten years

                          k. not aware; without thinking

                          l. shame; embarrassment

                          m. taking for granted

VOCABULARY CHECK

PART ONE

Directions: Circle the consonant blends in the words that follow. Some words may not have any.

1. shank
2. crank
3. bank
4. blank
5. slack
6. flame
7. fame
8. knack
9. bead
10. fare
11. flare
12. ting
13. thing
14. plank
15. quick

PART TWO

Directions: In the blank following each word, write in whether the vowel sound is long, short, or controlled by the letter *r*.

1. sole _____
2. fangs _____
3. storm _____
4. shriek _____
5. bright _____
6. struggle _____

E: Exercises in Vocabulary

7. spit _____   9. clang _____

8. crest _____   10. steer _____

PART THREE

Directions: In the blank after the following pronunciation symbols, write what the word is. Remember that the schwa sound is a vowel that sounds like a soft *u*.

1. hung′ər _____   6. mun′ē _____

2. mel′ən _____   7. fūz _____

3. but′ər _____   8. ān′shənt _____

4. dī′ər _____   9. let′ər _____

5. hol′ō _____   10. lĕj′ənd _____

PART FOUR

Directions: In the blank, write in the correct homonym from the words below the sentence.

1. Kathy ate the _____ pie!
                         hole   whole

2. She didn't even save me one _____.
                                             peace   piece

3. It's cold; please get my _____ for me.
                                     wrap   rap

4. Sunday we'll walk down the _____ together.
                                               aisle   isle   I'll

5. Let's rent a boat and go for a _____.
                                               sail   sale

6. José is in the Job _____.
                                 Corps   Core

7. Don't _____ energy; turn off those extra lights.
         waist   waste

8. This is the third window _____ those boys have broken.
         pain   pane

9. The mail is _____ at eleven o'clock.
         do   dew   due

10. It's a _____ day to be alive.
          grate   great

PART FIVE

Directions: Write a sentence correctly, using the following words:

1. competent: _____

2. corps: _____

3. reign: _____

4. expectations: _____

5. grate: _____

6. wail: _____

7. concept: _____

E: Exercises in Vocabulary

8. potential: _____

_____

9. vivid: _____

_____

10. humiliation: _____

_____

Name _____ **Section** _____ **Date** _____

P: PERFECTING READING SKILLS

COMPREHENDING IDIOMATIC PHRASES

Directions: Explain what you think the following phrases mean.

1. finding oneself: _____

_____

2. being bummed out: _____

_____

3. it went over my head: _____

_____

4. doing your own thing: _____

_____

5. down and out: _____

_____

6. get your act together: _____

_____

7. a high-energy experience: _____

_____

8. dig the silence: _____

_____

9. being uptight: _____

_____

P: Perfecting Reading Skills 63

10. he's far-out: _____

_____

COMPREHENDING SENTENCES

Directions: Read for the main idea in each of the following sentences, and answer the questions that follow.

1. Self-discovery involves an element of risk, a willingness to speak your mind, to take chances, to try new things.

    a. Is self-discovery defined? _____

    b. Is self-discovery easy? _____

    c. State in your words what you think the main idea is.

    _____

    _____

2. Many people find that keeping a journal that includes a description of important events, thoughts, feelings, fears, frustrations, and dreams is necessary to personal growth.

    a. Should everyone keep a journal? _____

    b. What sorts of things should a journal contain?

    _____

    _____

    c. How do you suppose keeping such a journal could aid in personal growth? _____

    _____

3. If you feel bored at school, at a job, or in a relationship, consider it a challenge or an indication that you have not taken the responsibility for personal growth.

Copyright © 1988 Holt, Rinehart and Winston, Inc.

a. Is it your own fault when you get bored? _____

b. Does the statement suggest you are in charge of your personal development? _____

c. Do you think you most always accept that responsibility?
_____

4. Parents who don't want to say, "I'm sorry. I made a mistake," to their children are afraid they'll lose face.

    a. State in your own words the main idea.
    _____
    _____

    b. What does "lose face" mean? _____
    _____

    c. Do you think the statement is true? _____

5. The love of one's neighbor is not possible without the love of oneself.

    a. Explain what the sentence means.
    _____
    _____
    _____

    b. What do you think "love of oneself" means? _____
    _____

6. We each have our own mental picture of what the "world out there" is like, a picture shaped by personal experiences, education, and the mass media.

    a. What forms our view of the world? _____
    _____

P: Perfecting Reading Skills 65

    b. Does everyone have the same mental picture of the world?
        _____ Why? _____
        _____

7. It is important to judge ourselves in terms of our own growth, not the growth of others.

    a. Should we compare ourselves with others? _____
        _____

8. Try to experience the world as you did when you were a child; fully, vividly, and directly.

    a. Does this imply we are less open to life as adults? _____
        Explain: _____
        _____
        _____

    b. Does this mean we should be more like children? _____
        Explain: _____
        _____
        _____

COMPREHENDING MAIN IDEAS: PARAGRAPHS

Directions: Read the following paragraphs, and underline the sentence in each that best states the main idea. Then in the blanks, write the main idea in your own words.

1. (a) There are several reasons that some people have a self-concept that others would regard as being unrealistically favorable. (b) First, a self-estima-

tion might be based on obsolete information. (c) Perhaps your jokes used to be funny, but not now. You would be reluctant to give up that self-image. (d) Second, a self-concept might be favorable because of lies people tell you. (e) As a boss, you might receive good impressions of yourself from employees who are buttering you up to keep their jobs. (f) Third, expectations of teachers, parents, and society often demand too much from us. For instance, admitting mistakes is often thought of as a weakness. Couples who "fail" to reach the level of the "perfect couple" don't want to admit they don't have such a relationship. Rather than admit failure, many people engage in self-deception.

_____

_____

2. (a) The way you see yourself isn't always the same as the way others view you. (b) Sometimes the image you hold of yourself might be more favorable than the way others regard you. (c) You might, for instance, see yourself as a witty joke teller when others can barely tolerate your attempts at humor. (d) You might view yourself as highly intelligent although one or more instructors see your scholarship as substandard. (e) Perhaps you consider yourself an excellent worker—in contrast to the employer who wants to fire you.

_____

_____

3. (a) Growing up around overly critical parents is one of the most common causes of negative self-image. (b) In other cases, the remarks of cruel friends, uncaring teachers, overdemanding employers, or even memorable strangers can have a lasting effect. (c) Failing in school work or job tasks without anyone explaining why or how to do it better also contributes to negative self-image. (d) After a while, we begin to believe these put-downs. (e) Such distortions of reality have a strong impact on our self-concept.

_____

_____

4. (a) Many people are caught in a struggle for survival or security. (b) They never get a chance to develop their potentials fully. (c) Others show little interest in personal growth. (d) They are willing to accept who they think they are.

_____

_____

5. (a) Self-actualization is more a process than it is a goal or an end. (b) It requires hard work and patience. (c) Here are some ways to start. (d) Be willing to change. (e) Take responsibility for yourself. (f) Make use of positive experi-

P: Perfecting Reading Skills 67

ences. (g) Be prepared to be different. (h) Get personally involved with whatever you do.

_____

_____

COMPREHENDING MAIN IDEAS: A CHAPTER FROM A PSYCHOLOGY TEXTBOOK

Directions: Skim over the following selection from a psychology textbook before you read. Don't take more than about thirty seconds to read the title, the opening paragraph, and the headings. Then answer the following questions.

1. What do you think is the main idea of the chapter selection?

_____

_____

2. How does the title help suggest what the chapter will deal with?

_____

3. What do you think you might learn from this chapter selection?

_____

_____

4. What questions about the content do you want to answer as you read this selection?

_____

_____

Now read the selection.

Copyright © 1988 Holt, Rinehart and Winston, Inc.

THE SEARCH FOR SELF-ACTUALIZATION

DENNIS COON

Some people fear finding themselves alone—and so they don't find themselves at all (André Gide).

What a man can be, he must be. This need we may call self-actualization (Abraham Maslow).

1   Promoting self-actualization is more difficult than might be imagined. Many people are caught in a struggle for survival or security and never get a chance to develop their potentials fully. Others show little interest in personal growth. . . .

Steps Toward Self-actualization

2   There is no magic formula for leading a more creative life. Knowing or even imitating the traits of unusually effective people cannot be counted on to promote self-actualization. Self-actualization is primarily a *process*, not a goal or an end point. As such, it requires hard work, patience, and commitment. Here are some ways to begin.

Be Willing to Change

3   Begin by asking yourself, "Am I living in a way that is deeply satisfying to me and which truly expresses me?" If not, be prepared to make changes in your life. Indeed, ask yourself this question often and accept the need for continued change.

Take Responsibility

4   You can become an architect of self by acting *as if* you are *personally* responsible for every aspect of your life. Shouldering responsibility in this way is not totally realistic, but it helps end the habit of blaming others for your own shortcomings. This attitude is illustrated by a young woman who realized in a counseling session, "I can't depend on someone else to give me an education. I'll have to get it myself."

Examine Your Motives

5   Self-discovery involves an element of risk. To learn your strengths, limitations, and true feelings, you must be willing to go out on a limb, speak your mind, and take some chances. Fears of failure, rejection, loneliness, or disagreement with others are a tremendous barrier to personal change. If most of your

Reprinted by permission from Introduction to Psychology: Exploration and Application, *3d ed., by Dennis Coon. Copyright © 1983 by West Publishing Company. All rights reserved.*

behavior seems to be directed by a desire for "safety" or "security," it may be time to test the limits of these needs. Try to make each life decision a choice for growth, not a response to fear or anxiety.

Experience Honestly and Directly

6   Wishful thinking is another barrier to personal growth. Self-actualizers trust themselves enough to accept all kinds of information without distorting it to fit their fears and desires. Try to see yourself as others do. Be willing to admit, "I was wrong" or, "I failed because I was irresponsible." This basic honesty can be extended to perception in general. Try to experience the world as you did when you were a child: fully, vividly, and directly. Try to see things as they are, not as you would like them to be.

Make Use of Positive Experiences

7   As a "rule of thumb," growth-promoting activities usually "feel good." Perhaps you have felt unusually alert and alive when expressing yourself through art, music, dance, writing, or athletics. Or perhaps life seems especially rich when you are alone in nature, surrounded by friends, or when you are helping others. Whatever their source, Maslow considered "peak experiences" temporary moments of self-actualization. Therefore, you might actively repeat activities that have caused feelings of awe, amazement, exaltation, renewal, reverence, humility, fulfillment, or joy.

Be Prepared to Be Different

8   Maslow felt that everyone has a potential for "greatness," but most fear becoming what they might. Much of this fear is related to the fact that actualizing potentials may place you at odds with cultural expectations or with others who are important in your life. As part of personal growth, be prepared to be unpopular when your views don't agree with others'. Trust your own impulses and feelings; don't automatically judge yourself by the standards of others. Accept your uniqueness: As one young woman put it, "I've always tried to be what others thought I should be, but now I'm wondering whether I shouldn't just see that I am what I am" (Rogers, 1962).

Get Involved

9   Maslow found with few exceptions that self-actualizers tend to have a mission or "calling" in life. For these people "work" is not done just to fill deficiency needs but to satisfy higher yearnings for truth, beauty, brotherhood, and meaning. Many of the things you do may be motivated by more commonplace needs, but you can add meaning to these activities by endeavoring to work hard at whatever you do. Get personally involved and committed. Turn your attention to problems outside yourself.

Slow Down

10   Try to avoid hurrying or overscheduling your time. Self-awareness takes time to develop, and a certain amount of leisure is essential for contemplation

and self-exploration. Time pressures tend to force a person to rely compulsively on old habits.

Start a Journal

11   Although this suggestion does not come from Maslow's writings, it is a valuable means of promoting self-awareness. Many people find a journal provides the kind of information necessary to make growth-oriented life changes. A journal should include a description of significant events in your daily life. In addition, thoughts, feelings, fears, wishes, frustrations, and dreams should be recorded. Some find it useful to write dialogues in their journal in which they speak to parents, teachers, lovers, objects, and so forth. Review and reread your journal periodically. You will find it is easier to learn from an event after it has "cooled off" and you can view it objectively.

Assess Your Progress

12   Since there is no final point at which one becomes self-actualized, it is important frequently to gauge your progress and to renew your efforts. Boredom is a good sign you are in need of change. If you feel bored at school, at a job, or in a relationship, consider it a challenge or an indication that you have not taken responsibility for personal growth. A situation is only as "boring" as you allow it to be. Almost any activity can be used as a chance for self-exploration if it is approached creatively.

What to Expect

13   As we have already noted, growth-promoting activities are usually personally satisfying.

Question: Are there other signs that one is moving in the right direction?

14   Yes, there should be a noticeable improvement in the quality of your daily life and a greater acceptance of yourself and of others. You should feel more confident and should carry out daily routines with less strain or conflict. These changes do not happen overnight, and your first steps toward self-actualization may be threatening at the same time they are exhilarating. Positive changes can also be quite subtle. An idea of what to expect is provided by the words of Henry David Thoreau. After he had spent two years in the wilderness at Walden Pond, Thoreau had this to say about his experience:

> I learned this, at least, by my experiment: that as one advances confidently in the direction of his dreams, and endeavors to live the life which he has imagined, he will meet with a success unexpected in common hours: He will put some things behind, will pass an invisible boundary; new universal and more liberal laws will begin to establish themselves around and within him.... The laws of the universe will appear less complex, and

solitude will not be solitude, nor poverty, poverty, nor weakness, weakness.

Now answer the following questions.

RECALL

1. What is the main idea of the chapter selection?

_____

_____

_____

2. Name at least five ways or steps toward self-actualization.

_____

_____

_____

_____

_____

3. What is the main idea of paragraph 5?

_____

_____

_____

INTERPRETATION

4. Explain the quote of André Gide at the beginning of the reading selection on page 68.

_____

_____

_____

5. What is the main idea of paragraph 8?

6. Can changing oneself be done quickly? Explain.

7. What does the heading "Experience Honestly and Directly" mean?

APPLICATION

8. In paragraph 7, "growth-promoting activities" are discussed. What activities have you experienced that you could call growth-promoting?

9. Are you living in a way that is deeply satisfying to yourself and that truly expresses who you really are? Why?

10. Do you believe you can be "greater" than you are but are afraid to do anything about it? Explain.

P: Perfecting Reading Skills

Chapter 3

Objectives

P: **PREREADING DRILLS**
Words to Know
Warm-up Drills

R: **READING DRILL**
Reading and Thinking About What You Read
"How to Study-Read" by Michele Learned
Comprehension Check

E: **EXERCISES IN VOCABULARY**
Drills
    1: Dictionary Entry Words
    2: Dictionary Abbreviations
    3: Pronunciation Keys
    4: Word Meanings in Context
    5: Using the Dictionary
    6: Definition Review
Vocabulary Check

P: **PERFECTING READING SKILLS**
Comprehending Sentences: Idioms
Comprehending Paragraphs: Main Ideas and Interpretation
Comprehending Main Ideas: A Textbook Passage
"Mnemonics—Memory Magic" by Dennis Coon

Unit 1   CHECK TEST (CHAPTERS 1-3)
    1: Word Knowledge
    2: Word Usage
    3: Comprehending Paragraphs
    4: Essay Reading Comprehension
       "The Uses of Error" by Isaac Asimov

Objectives

When you are finished working in this chapter, you will

1. Recognize and be able to use at least **90** percent of the vocabulary words presented in the Words to Know section.
2. Have developed your ability to recognize words more rapidly.
3. Understand syllabication and its usefulness in pronouncing words correctly.
4. Know and be able to understand all the information given in a dictionary entry.
5. Know and be able to use dictionary pronunciation keys.
6. Know how to find word entries in the dictionary faster than you do now.
7. Have developed your comprehension skills in recognizing main ideas, details, and idioms in sentences and paragraphs.
8. Have experienced answering comprehension questions that help develop your ability to recall main ideas, interpret, and apply what you have read.
9. Know how to study-read and take notes.

P: PREREADING DRILLS

WORDS TO KNOW

Directions: Here are some words that appear in the drills and the article you will be reading in this chapter. Read them aloud, and learn the definitions of the ones you don't know. Definitions are based on their use in the article.

1. *promote*—to further; to help the progress or growth of something.
Using the study methods described will promote better learning.
2. *retention*—the capacity to remember.
Poor study habits do not aid the retention of what is learned.
3. *skimming*—not reading every word but looking for main points or ideas.
Skimming over a chapter before reading it aids comprehension.
4. *concentration*—the act of keeping the mind focused on a particular subject or area.
Concentration on studies does not come easily for most students.
5. *alien*—not familiar.
Most textbooks have material that is alien to those of us not familiar with the subject.
6. *passages*—parts of a reading selection, not the entire writing.
It is a good idea to read short passages of a chapter, then stop and make certain that you understand what you have read.
7. *elaborate*—thoroughly developed; greatly detailed.
Some note-taking methods are more elaborate than others, but some method should be used for study purposes.
8. *recite*—to repeat or to relate.
Taking notes is one way to recite what was just read.
9. *technique*—the system or way something is done.
A good student will know several study techniques to use with various classes.
10. *review*—to look over or study again.
It's not how long you study that is important but how often you review what has already been covered.

WARM-UP DRILLS

DRILL 1

Directions: Some words are misread because they are read too quickly. Read each of the following sentences. Look carefully at the two words under it. Then write the correct word in the blank. Spell it correctly.

P: Prereading Drills

1. The _____ bought the three minks from him.
    funnier   furrier

2. After her mother scolded her, Carrie _____ for hours.
                                          strewed   stewed

3. Jerry's father is one of the biggest building _____ in town.
                                              contractors   contacters

4. The professor _____ in making us do all the drills in the book.
                  presented   persisted

5. That new, young apprentice has the _____ of an excellent carpenter.
                                       markings   makings

6. Is that the assignment you _____ to yesterday?
                               referring   referred

7. The school _____ caught Jack smoking behind the PE building.
               principle   principal

8. Better not lose those _____, or we won't catch any fish.
                          fries   flies

9. Dad wants me to expose myself to the humanities to _____ my education.
                                                       broader   broaden

10. Ben _____ he could pass without studying, but he's taking the course again this semester.
         taught   thought

DRILL 2

Directions: Move your eyes rapidly across each line. Mark the word by the number each time it appears on the same line. For example:

   1. roar   rear   rear   ~~roar~~   ~~roar~~   rear
   2. struggle   straggle   ~~struggle~~   straggle   ~~struggle~~

Don't look back on any line. If you make a mistake, don't stop to change it. Keep moving. Try to finish in less than forty seconds. Begin timing.

   1. alien   alive   alert   alien   along   alien
   2. marks   marks   makes   marks   makes   makes

Copyright © 1988 Holt, Rinehart and Winston, Inc.

3. change   charge   change   charge   charge   change
4. clearly   cleanly cleanly clearly cleanly clearly
5. politics   political politics polite   political politics
6. bought   brought brought brought bought   bought
7. scraps   scrapes scraps   scrapes scrapes scraps
8. contract   contract contact contact contact contract
9. burst   bust   burst   bust   bust   burst
10. desert   dessert desert   dessert desert   dessert
11. sense   sense   since   sense   sense   since
12. broaden   broader broaden broader broaden broader
13. special   special specially specials specialize special
14. exposed   exposure expose   exposed exposure exposed
15. huge   hug   urge   huge   hug   urge   huge

TIME: _____

Now check each line to see if you marked the right word every time it appears. Make sure you know all the words and their meanings. All the words by the numbers appear in the article you will be reading in this chapter.

TOTAL LINES CORRECT: _____

DRILL 3

Directions: Follow the same directions as for Drill 2. Remember to work quickly. Don't look back on any line. Try to finish in thirty-five seconds or less. Begin timing.

1. stewed   strewed stewed   stewed   strewed   strewed
2. premed   premier premed   preview premed   passages
3. civil   civilian civil   civilly civilian civil
4. admission   admire   admissible admission admission
5. disappoint disappear disappoint disappear disappoint
6. economics   economy economics economy economics
7. sense   since   sense   since   since   sense   since
8. encounter   economics encounter counter economics
9. persist   persist resist   persisted persistent persist
10. opinion   opening opening opinion opening   opinion
11. tussle   tunnel   tunnel   tussle   tunnel   tussle

P: Prereading Drills

12. guarantee   guarantee guaranteed guarantee guaranteed
13. engineer   engine engineer engine engine engineer
14. embarrass   embarrass embarrassed embarrassed
15. humanity   humanly humanly humanity humanly

TIME: _____

Now check each line to see if you marked the right word every time it appears. Make sure you know all the words and their meanings. All the words by the numbers appear in the article in this chapter.

TOTAL LINES CORRECT: _____

R: READING DRILL

READING AND THINKING ABOUT WHAT YOU READ

Directions: Before reading the article, read the title, the opening paragraph, and the headings. Then answer the following questions:

1. What do you think the main idea of the article will be?

   _____

   _____

2. What do you think you will learn from reading the article?

   _____

   _____

3. What part of the article may help you the most?

   _____

   _____

Now read the article.

HOW TO STUDY-READ

MICHELE LEARNED

1. Most students don't know how to study-read. They usually open their textbook to the assigned page and start reading. But before long their minds have wandered off somewhere. Or they read and mark up the pages by underlining everything that seems important. Study-reading is different from regular reading. You are expected to remember more and, in most cases, will be tested on what you read. Here is a four-step method for study-reading textbooks that can help improve comprehension and promote longer retention of what is read.

    Reprinted by permission of the author.

Step One: Reading Preparation

2   Much time can be lost when you try to plunk yourself into reading an assigned chapter if your mind isn't ready. Because you can think faster than you can read, your mind may wander to other thoughts or daydreams if you aren't prepared to read. So, it's important to get yourself ready for the subject you will be reading.

3   Get prepared by skimming over the chapter. Is it short enough to read at one time, or should you divide it up and just study a part of it now? Once that's decided, look carefully at what you will be reading. Let the title of the chapter sink in. Read an opening paragraph or two to see what the chapter will cover. Read the headings and subheadings. Read the summary or the last couple of paragraphs. Much of this may not make sense, but your mind will begin to clear out other thoughts. You'll begin forming questions about the contents of the chapter. What does a particular heading mean? What does that word mean? What will I learn? If there are questions at the end of the chapter, read those. Having questions about what you are reading helps concentration and gives you a purpose for reading.

Step Two: Read

4   After you have prepared yourself, you are ready to read. Often textbooks aren't very exciting reading. They present alien information to us that we are supposed to learn and remember. The best thing to do is not to read too much all at once. Read from one heading to the next and pause for Step Three below. If there are no headings, read only a page or two at the most and then stop for Step Three.

Step Three: Examine What You Read

5   By reading only short passages and then stopping, you stand a better chance of concentrating on the chapter's content. The third step is now to examine what you read. The best way to do that is to take some kind of notes.

6   Much research has been done on note-taking methods. Here is one method most researchers seem to agree is best for courses where the lecture and textbook readings are related. First, use 8½-by-11-inch notebook paper. That's regular notebook size. Second, only write on one side of the page. It may seem wasteful, but it isn't when it's helpful to your learning. If you write on both sides of a page, you can't spread your notes out side-by-side for review-study purposes. Third, use a ruler and divide the page as follows. Make a line about two inches up from the bottom of the page all the way across. Next, about two inches from the left make a line down from the top of the page to the bottom line you drew. You will then have three sections. The two-inch column on the left is for adding key phrases or changing your notes when you look them over

after class. The middle section is for your lecture notes. The bottom section is for your textbook reading notes. If you are taking a course where the lecture and textbook readings are different, then use one notebook page for lecture notes and another for textbook notes.

7   If this method is too elaborate for you, at least write some notes in a notebook for that class. Using a few key words or phrases, write down the major points you just read. Research shows that doing this aids comprehension and retention for future tests.

8   If you don't believe in taking reading notes, at least try to recite to yourself the key points you just read. When you are satisfied you understand what you read, then read from the next heading to the next, stopping every once in a while to take notes or go over what you read. Follow this step until you are finished with the chapter. Though this may seem slow, as you practice this study-reading technique, you'll discover it's really faster because you don't waste time with losing concentration or having to reread what you've read.

Step Four: Plan to Review

9   This last step does not take place immediately after you read, but it's very important for remembering what you read and can mean the difference between a C and an A on a test. You should make a definite plan to review your reading notes every week. As you move through a course, you have more and more to learn. You can't remember it all. In fact, unless we review every week what has been studied before, we can forget over 80 percent of what we read. So plan to review once a week. Go over your notes. If they don't make sense when you review, go back to the chapter and reread what isn't clear. (It's important to write chapter titles and page references to key points in your notes so that you can find things quickly when you review.)

10   Research shows it's not so much how long you study that gets good grades, but how well and how often you study. Try this four-step method (PREP) and watch those grades go up.

COMPREHENSION CHECK

Directions: Answer the following questions.

RECALL

1. The best statement expressing the main idea of the article is:
   a. Most students don't know how to study and do little about it.
   b. There is a method for study-reading textbooks that students should learn to use.

R: Reading Drill

    c. Study-reading and regular reading are very different.
    d. There is a four-step method for study-reading textbooks that can help improve comprehension and retention.
2. List the steps mentioned in the article.

    a. _____

    b. _____

    c. _____

    d. _____

INTERPRETATION

3. How does study-reading differ from "regular" reading, according to the article? _____

_____

_____

4. Why is it important to prepare ourselves to study-read?

_____

_____

_____

5. What is meant by retention?

_____

_____

6. Why is review important to retention?

_____

_____

7. How often is it recommended that you review what you have already studied?

_____

_____

APPLICATION

8. Reread paragraph 6 in the article. Then mark the following sample notebook page as described.

9. What use is the space at the bottom of the page? _____

_____

10. How are each of the two columns to be used for note-taking? _____

_____

_____

Name _____ **Section** _____ **Date** _____

R: Reading Drill

APPLICATION FOLLOW-UP

The following is a sample page of combined lecture and reading notes similar to those described in the previous reading selection. Notice that the notebook page has been divided up as described. For the sake of example, what you read about study-reading is used here as lecture notes. The textbook notes are used to show how a student might bring together both the lecture and reading notes. Of course, it is possible that in some classes you might need less lecture note space and more textbook note space. That would depend on what the course is and what works best for you.

The next time you read an assignment from this book or one from another course you are taking, try this approach. Show it to your instructor, and see if he or she can offer you further advice on study-reading. It may be the most important skill you can learn as a student.

Key phrases from lecture	## Lecture Notes
	A four-step method for study reading
	STEP 1: Reading Preparation
	– skim over chapter; let title sink in
○	– read opening ¶ or 2
SQ3R is like PREP'S 4 steps	– read headings and subheadings
	– read summary or last 2 ¶ s
	STEP 2: Read
	– don't read too much at once
	– read from one heading to next
	– if no headings, read only page or two at once
	STEP 3: Examine What You Read
○	– take notes after reading from heading to next
	– "recite" by writing notes or oral review
learning curve retention better	STEP 4: Plan to Review
	– review notes every week
	– we forget 80% of what we read unless we review regularly
○	## Textbook Notes
	The book chapter was like the lecture, but mentioned SQ3R: Survey, Question, Read, Review, Recite – a mnemonic device(?) (ask instructor what "mnemonic" means)

86

E: EXERCISES IN VOCABULARY

DRILLS

DRILL 1: DICTIONARY ENTRY WORDS

Directions: Study the following dictionary entry. Notice what you can learn from a dictionary entry.

```
                Spelling and        How to pronounce the word
                number of
                syllables          What part of speech
                                                    Different definitions
                        plat·ter (plăt′ər) n. 1. A large, shallow dish or plate, used espe-
                                cially for serving food. 2. A meal or course served on such a
    Entry word                    dish. 3. Slang. A phonograph record. [Middle English plater,
                                from Norman French, from Old French plate, PLATE.]
                                                                            History or
                                                                            origin of
                                        Special meanings                    the word
```

Copyright © 1973 by Houghton Mifflin Company. Reprinted by permission from The American Heritage Dictionary of the English Language.

Now answer the following questions. Don't worry about the questions you can't answer. More exercises will cover these things, and so will your instructor. This drill will let you know what you need to learn about dictionary entries.

1. What is meant by a dictionary entry word? _____

_____

2. How many syllables does the entry word in the preceding example have?

_____

3. Does the first syllable have a long or short vowel sound? _____

4. Can you guess what part of speech the entry word is? _____

5. How many definitions are given for the entry word? _____

6. From what language did the entry word originally come? _____

_____

7. Write a sentence using each of the definitions correctly.

Definition 1: _____

_____

_____

Definition 2: _____

_____

_____

Definition 3: _____

_____

_____

DRILL 2: DICTIONARY ABBREVIATIONS

Directions: All dictionaries use marks and symbols to save space. These keys are explained in the front of dictionaries. Here are a few examples. Study them. Then answer the questions that follow.

Parts of Speech		*Word Origin*	
adj.	adjective	Am.	American
adv.	adverb	A.S.	Anglo-Saxon
conj.	conjunction	Brit.	British
inf.	infinitive verb	D.	Dutch
n.	noun	Fr.	French
pron.	pronoun	G.	German
pl.	plural	Gr.	Greek
v.	verb	L.	Latin
		M.E.	Middle English
		O.E.	Old English

What do these symbols or abbreviations mean?

1. L. _____   4. adv. _____

2. v. _____   5. Am. _____

3. G. _____   6. O.E. _____

Copyright © 1988 Holt, Rinehart and Winston, Inc.

E: Exercises in Vocabulary

7. conj. _____   9. n. _____

8. Gr. _____   10. pl. _____

DRILL 3: PRONUNCIATION KEYS

Directions: All dictionaries have a Pronunciation Key. It is explained in the front of the dictionary. Good dictionaries have sample keys at the bottom of each page or every other page. Study the following key. Then answer the questions that follow.

Pronunciation Key

ā	as in *rate, mail*	ū	as in *fuse, cute*
ă	as in *rat, band*	ŭ	as in *cut, bump*
ē	as in *be, keep*	o͞o	as in *moon, tool*
ĕ	as in *bet, dress*	o͝o	as in *book, look*
ī	as in *bite, pie*	ə	as in *beautiful* (bū′təfəl)
ĭ	as in *bit, ill*	′	accent mark to show which
ō	as in *go, stole*		syllable is stressed
ŏ	as in *rot, plot*		

Part A

Place the correct mark over the vowels in the following words. Draw a line through a vowel not sounded.

1. cute   3. coal   5. gold   7. streak   9. mess
2. clock   4. groan   6. pray   8. bleed   10. toll

Part B

When we pronounce a word with two or more syllables, we accent one syllable. The word *platter* has two syllables (plat′ter). We accent the first syllable when we say the word. Say the word *platter,* and notice where it is stressed. Divide the following words into syllables. Place the accent mark on the syllable that is the accented syllable. The first one has been done for you.

1. hap′pen   7. principal   12. promote   17. exposed
2. letter   8. seven   13. encounter   18. concentration
3. dollar   9. reading   14. apprentice   19. elaborate (v.)
4. alien   10. contact   15. desert   20. contractor
5. skimming   11. retention   16. markings   21. humanities
6. bias

Part C

Sound out the pronunciation symbols in the column on the left. Match each set of symbols with the word it represents from the column on the right. The first one has been done for you.

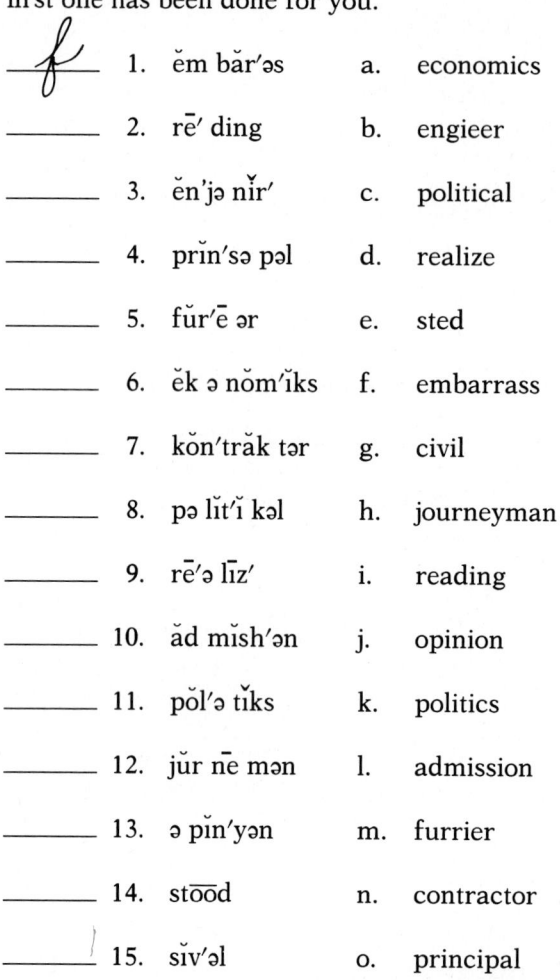

_f_ 1. ĕm băr′əs	a.	economics
_____ 2. rē′ ding	b.	engieer
_____ 3. ĕn′jə nîr′	c.	political
_____ 4. prĭn′sə pəl	d.	realize
_____ 5. fŭr′ē ər	e.	sted
_____ 6. ĕk ə nŏm′ĭks	f.	embarrass
_____ 7. kŏn′trăk tər	g.	civil
_____ 8. pə lĭt′ĭ kəl	h.	journeyman
_____ 9. rē′ə līz′	i.	reading
_____ 10. ăd mĭsh′ən	j.	opinion
_____ 11. pŏl′ə tĭks	k.	politics
_____ 12. jŭr nē mən	l.	admission
_____ 13. ə pĭn′yən	m.	furrier
_____ 14. sto͞od	n.	contractor
_____ 15. sĭv′əl	o.	principal

DRILL 4: WORD MEANINGS IN CONTEXT

Directions: Following is the dictionary entry for *plate*. Notice how many definitions it has. Read each sentence below the dictionary entry. In the blanks, write the number of the definition that best fits the way *plate* is used in the sentence.

E: Exercises in Vocabulary

> **plate** (plāt) *n.* **1.** A smooth, flat, relatively thin, rigid body of uniform thickness. **2. a.** A sheet of hammered, rolled, or cast metal. **b.** A very thin plated coat or layer of metal. **3. a.** A flat piece of metal forming part of a machine: *a boiler plate.* **b.** A flat piece of metal on which something is engraved. **4. a.** A thin piece of metal used for armor. **b.** Armor made of this. **5.** *Abbr.* **pl.** *Printing.* **a.** A sheet of metal, plastic, rubber, paperboard, or other material converted into a printing surface, such as an electrotype or stereotype. **b.** A print of a woodcut, lithograph, or other engraved material, especially when reproduced in a book. **c.** A full-page book illustration, often in color and printed on paper different from that used on the text pages. **6.** *Abbr.* **pl.** *Photography.* A light-sensitive sheet of glass or metal upon which an image can be recorded. **7.** *Dentistry.* A thin metallic or plastic support fitted to the gums to anchor artificial teeth. **8.** *Architecture.* In wood-frame construction, a horizontal member, capping the exterior wall studs, upon which the roof rafters rest. **9.** *Baseball.* Home base, usually a flat piece of heavy rubber. Also called "home plate." **10. a.** A shallow dish in which food is served or from which it is eaten. **b.** The contents of such a dish. **c.** A whole course served on such a dish. **11.** Food and service for one person at a meal: *dinner at a set price per plate.* **12.** Household articles covered with a precious metal, such as gold or silver. **13.** A dish passed among a congregation for the collection of offerings. **14.** *Sports.* **a.** A dish, cup, or other article of silver or gold offered as a prize. **b.** A contest, especially a horse race, offering such a prize. **15.** A thin cut of beef from the brisket. **16.** *Anatomy & Zoology.* **a.** A thin, flat layer or scale. **b.** A platelike part or organ. **17.** *Electronics.* **a.** Any electrode, as in a storage battery or capacitor. **b.** The anode in an electron tube. —*tr.v.* **plated, plating, plates. 1.** To coat or cover with a thin layer of metal. **2.** To armor. **3.** *Printing.* To make a stereotype or electrotype from. **4.** To give a glossy finish to (paper) by pressing between metal sheets or rollers. [Middle English, from Old French, from feminine of *plat*, flat, from Vulgar Latin *plattus* (unattested), from Greek *platus*, broad, flat. See **plat-** in Appendix.*]

Copyright © 1973 by Houghton Mifflin Company. Reprinted by permission from The American Heritage Dictionary of the English Language.

_____ 1. Simon ordered the hot plate for lunch.

_____ 2. Grandpa went to the dentist to get his plate fixed.

_____ 3. The boiler plate was too hot to touch.

_____ 4. The pitcher threw the ball right over home plate.

_____ 5. I was embarrassed at church when they passed the collection plate because I had no money.

_____ 6. The battery plate was cracked.

_____ 7. The book was supposed to have a colored picture on this page, but the printer lost the plate.

_____ 8. It was a cheap cup; the gold plate is already coming off.

_____ 9. Three plates were broken during the earthquake.

_____ 10. The armor plates on the plane made it fly more slowly.

DRILL 5: USING THE DICTIONARY

Directions: For this drill you will need a dictionary. Look up each of the following words, and find the information asked for.

1. *run*

    a. Number of syllables _____

    b. Pronunciation marks _____

    c. Parts of speech _____

    d. List at least four different meanings that you understand.

        1. _____

        2. _____

        3. _____

        4. _____

2. *company*

    a. Number of syllables _____

    b. Pronunciation marks _____

    c. Parts of speech _____

    d. List at least four different meanings that you understand.

        1. _____

        2. _____

        3. _____

        4. _____

E: Exercises in Vocabulary

3. *spirit*

   a. Number of syllables _____

   b. Pronunciation marks _____

   c. Parts of speech _____

   d. List at least four different meanings that you understand.

      1. _____

      2. _____

      3. _____

      4. _____

4. *jam*

   a. Number of syllables _____

   b. Pronunciation marks _____

   c. Parts of speech _____

   d. List at least four different meanings that you understand.

      1. _____

      2. _____

      3. _____

      4. _____

5. *principle*

   a. Number of syllables _____

   b. Pronunciation marks _____

   c. Parts of speech _____

   d. List at least four different meanings that you understand.

      1. _____

2. _____

3. _____

4. _____

6. *personality*

   a. Number of syllables _____

   b. Pronunciation marks _____

   c. Parts of speech _____

   d. List at least four different meanings that you understand.

      1. _____

      2. _____

      3. _____

      4. _____

Discuss your answers in class. Make sure you understand all the definitions.

DRILL 6: DEFINITION REVIEW

Directions: The following list of words is from the Words to Know section. Write the letter of the correct definition in the blank by the word. There are more definitions than words.

_____	1. alien	a.	properly qualified
_____	2. concentration	b.	an abstract idea
_____	3. skimming	c.	parts of a reading selection
_____	4. retention	d.	thoroughly developed
_____	5. promote	e.	to repeat or relate
_____	6. review	f.	a system

E: Exercises in Vocabulary

_____	7.	technique	g.	to look over again
_____	8.	recite	h.	to further
_____	9.	elaborate	i.	capacity to remember
_____	10.	passages	j.	not reading every word
			k.	not familiar
			l.	keeping focused on a particular subject

VOCABULARY CHECK

PART ONE

Directions: In the following space, write at least five things a dictionary entry tells you about a word.

1. _____
2. _____
3. _____
4. _____
5. _____

PART TWO

Directions: Place a stress mark on the syllable in the following words that is most strongly accented or stressed. The first one has been done for you.

1. en gi neer′
2. en coun ter
3. con trac tor
4. ex posed
5. in deed
6. civ il
7. jour ney man
8. hu man i ty
9. bi as
10. o pin ion

PART THREE

Directions: Write a sentence correctly, using each of the following words.

1. decade: _____

_____

2. humiliation: _____

_____

3. concept: _____

_____

4. audition: _____

_____

5. potential: _____

_____

6. vivid: _____

_____

7. professional: _____

_____

8. shinny: _____

_____

9. alien: _____

_____

10. recite: _____

_____

E: *Exercises in Vocabulary*

11. passages: _____
   _____

12. elaborate: _____
   _____

13. promote: _____
   _____

14. retention: _____
   _____

15. concentration: _____
   _____

Name _____ **Section** _____ **Date** _____

P: PERFECTING READING SKILLS

COMPREHENDING SENTENCES: IDIOMS

Directions: Read the following sentences. In the blanks, write what you think the italicized phrase means. If you don't know, guess. Don't spend too much time on any one sentence. These are idiomatic expressions, colorful, sometimes slang, sometimes clichéd, ways of saying things.

1. The doctor said Mickey will be *back on his feet* in a week or so.
   _____

2. You can't *back out* on me now! You promised you'd go.
   _____

3. Mac's got a lot of *hang-ups*.
   _____

4. When she turned me down, I felt really *bummed out*.
   _____

5. *Eat your heart out*, Hank; I'm taking Juana to the dance.
   _____

6. *Keep your chin up;* maybe she'll go with you the next time.
   _____

7. I told my husband that if he'd *foot the bill*, I'd go to college.
   _____

8. Takaka never seems to know when I'm *putting him on*.
   _____

P: Perfecting Reading Skills

9. Judy really has been *getting her act together* lately.

_____

10. I borrowed money from a loan shark, and now I'm *paying through the nose.*

_____

11. What Peg said really *rubbed me the wrong way.*

_____

12. When I see Peg, I'm going to give her a *piece of my mind.*

_____

COMPREHENDING PARAGRAPHS: MAIN IDEAS AND INTERPRETATION

Directions: Read the following paragraphs, and answer the questions that follow them.

1. In the past fifteen years, every state in the union has passed a law against child-beating. Now many states are also passing laws against wife-beating. Wife-beating is a bigger problem than most people think. A bill has been sent to Congress that would set up centers to help the beaten wife.

    a. What is the paragraph's main idea?

    _____

    _____

    b. Does the paragraph tell what states have laws against wife-beating?

    _____

2. Helping wives who have been beaten by their husbands is not easy. Beaten

wives don't like to give information or discuss their problems with their doctors or the police. But a recent issue of the *Journal of the American Medical Association* has a report that shows battered wives are afraid to tell the truth about how they are hurt by their husbands.

   a. Is it easy to help a woman who has been beaten by her husband?

   _____

   b. Why? _____

   _____

   c. Why do you think beaten wives don't often tell their doctors or the police? _____

3. Doctors say these are the early signs of alcoholism. One is what they call "pattern drinking." That means the person has, for example, a drink every night when he or she gets home. Or maybe the person drinks only on weekends. The time of drinking has a pattern to it. Two, the drinker can't stop the habit even when he or she tries. Third, the drinker changes from one drink to another. Fourth, the drinker argues with family and friends. Fifth, the drinker loses interest in things that don't involve drinking.

   a. What is the main idea of the paragraph?

   _____

   _____

   b. If a person fits several of the five points listed, what does that mean?

   _____

   _____

4. The page boys who work for the House of Representatives are angry. They say that the page girls who work with them get to quit work at 6 P.M., even when the House has night sessions. But the page boys have to work until the House quits no matter how late. It is explained that the page girls leave early because Washington, D.C., is not a safe city at night. It is feared that the girls will get mugged. But the page boys refuse to accept this argument because three page boys have already been mugged in the city.

P: Perfecting Reading Skills 101

    a. What is the main idea of the paragraph? _____

_____

_____

    b. Where is this taking place? _____

    c. What do you think the page boys want? _____

_____

_____

    d. Why do you agree or disagree with the page boys? _____

_____

_____

5. The need for secretaries has not dropped. Secretaries know that jobs are easy to find just about everywhere. Because of this, they are being more aggressive on their jobs. Secretaries are no longer letting their bosses just send them for coffee, have them empty ashtrays, or do other such jobs. Ellen Cassedy, head of a Boston group called "9 to 5," says, "We hope to embarrass businessmen into not doing this kind of stuff any more and to encourage women to refuse."

    a. What is this paragraph about? _____

_____

    b. Why are secretaries being more aggressive on the job? ____

_____

_____

    c. What does the name of the group "9 to 5" mean? _____

_____

_____

    d. Can you guess what the "9 to 5" group does or wants to do for its

Copyright © 1988 Holt, Rinehart and Winston, Inc.

members? _____

_____

_____

6. (a) When taking notes during a lecture, learn to abbreviate words. (b) Don't try to write a word such as *psychology*. (c) Use something like *psych* instead. (d) Use the symbol & for *and*, the letter *g* for *ing* words, and so forth. (e) Listen for key words such as *first, second, next,* or *in summary.* (f) Good notes don't require as much writing as they do good listening and then jotting down words or phrases that will trigger your memory later. (g) As soon as possible when a class is over, read over your notes. (h) Then correct or add to your notes. (i) That's why it's important to divide your notebook paper into columns for reading notes, lecture notes, and changes or additions when you review.

    a. What is the main idea of the passage?

_____

_____

    b. Is there a topic sentence? _____ Which one? _____

_____

    c. Into how many columns does this paragraph suggest you should divide your notebook paper for notes? _____

    d. How soon should you go over your lecture notes when the class period is over?

_____

7. "The temptation of the educator is to explain and describe, to organize a body of knowledge for the student, leaving the student with nothing to do. I have never been able to understand why educators do this so often especially where books are concerned. Much of the time they force their students to read the wrong books at the wrong time, and insist that they read them in the wrong way. That is, they lecture to the students about what is in the books, reduce the content to a series of points that can be remem-

P: Perfecting Reading Skills 103

bered, and if there are discussions, arrange them to deal with the points. . . . There is only one way to read a book, to give yourself up to it, alone, without instruction as to what you should be finding in it, without the necessity of making it into a series of points, but enjoying it, coming to know in personal terms what is in the mind of the writer. Only after that should there be discussion, criticism, comment by the educators. Otherwise education becomes too much like another kind of real life, the kind in which nobody reads the book, everyone reads the reviews, and everyone talks as if he knew the book."

(From "The Private World of the Man with a Book," by Harold Taylor. Saturday Review, *Sept. 9, 1961.)*

a. What is the main idea here? _____

_____

_____

_____

b. Explain the last sentence in the paragraph. _____

_____

_____

c. Do you agree with the author? _____

   Why or why not? _____

_____

_____

_____

COMPREHENDING MAIN IDEAS: A TEXTBOOK PASSAGE

Directions: Skim the following selection from a textbook before you read. Don't take more than about thirty seconds to read the title, the opening paragraph, and the headings. Then answer the following questions.

1. What is the passage about? (Don't just answer "memory.")

_____

2. What do you think you might learn from this passage that could help you in your studies?

_____

_____

3. What questions do you have in your mind now that you want answered as you read?

_____

_____

_____

4. How long do you think it will take you to read the selection? _____

As you read the selection, take some notes either in your book or on a separate sheet. Read a few paragraphs, then stop. Make some notes in your own words about what you read. Then read some more, stopping again to take notes. See if this doesn't help you concentrate better as you read.

MNEMONICS—MEMORY MAGIC
DENNIS COON

Various "memory experts" entertain by giving demonstrations in which they memorize the names of everyone at a banquet, the order of all the cards in a deck, long lists of disconnected words, or other seemingly impossible amounts of information. These tricks are performed through the use of mnemonics (nee-MON-iks). A mnemonic is any kind of memory system or aid.

Some mnemonic systems have become so common that almost everyone

Reprinted by permission from Introduction to Psychology: Exploration and Application, *3d ed., by Dennis Coon. Copyright © 1983 by West Publishing Company. All rights reserved.*

knows them. If you are trying to remember how many days there are in a month, you may find the answer by reciting, "Thirty days hath September...." Physics teachers often help their students remember the colors of the spectrum by giving them the mnemonic "Roy G. Biv": *r*ed, *o*range, *y*ellow, *g*reen, *b*lue, *i*ndigo, *v*iolet. The budding sailor who has trouble telling port from starboard may remember that port and left both have four letters or may remind himself, "I *left port*." And what beginning musician hasn't remembered the notes represented by the lines and spaces of the musical staff by learning "face" and "*every good boy does fine*"?

Mnemonic techniques are ways of avoiding *rote* learning (learning by simple repetition). The superiority of mnemonic learning as opposed to rote learning has been demonstrated many times. For example, Bower (1973) asked college students to study 5 different lists of 20 unrelated words. At the end of a short study session subjects were asked to recall all 100 items. Subjects using mnemonics remembered an average of 72 items, whereas a control group using simple or rote learning remembered an average of 28.

Stage performers rarely have a naturally superior memory. Instead, they make extensive use of memory systems to perform their feats. Few of these systems are of practical value to the student, but the principles underlying mnemonics are. By practicing mnemonics you should be able to greatly improve your memory with little effort.

The basic principles of mnemonics are:

1. **Use mental pictures.** There are at least two kinds of memory, *visual* and *verbal*. Visual pictures or images are generally easier to remember than words. Turning information into mental pictures is therefore very helpful (Paivio, 1969).
2. **Make things meaningful.** Transfer of information from short-term to long-term memory is aided by making it meaningful. If you encounter technical terms that have little or no immediate meaning for you, *give* them meaning, even if you have to stretch the term to do so. (This point is clarified by the examples below).
3. **Make information familiar.** Connect it to what you already know. Another way to get information into long-term memory is to connect it to information already stored there. If some facts or ideas in a chapter seem to stay in your memory easily, associate other more difficult facts with them.
4. **Form bizarre, unusual, or exaggerated mental associations.** When associating two ideas, terms, or especially mental images, you will find that the more outrageous and exaggerated the association, the more likely you are to remember it later.

A sampling of typical applications of mnemonics should make these four points clear to you.

Example 1 Let's say you have 30 new vocabulary words to memorize in Spanish. You can proceed by rote memorization (repeat them over and over until you begin to get them) or you can learn them with little effort through mnemonics. To remember that the word *pájaro* (pronounced pa-ha-ro) means bird, you can give the word familiar meaning and use mental images. *Pájaro* (to me) sounds like "parked car-o." To remember that *pájaro* means bird, I will visualize a parked car jam-packed full of birds. I will try to make this image as vivid and exaggerated as possible. I will picture the birds flapping and chirping and feathers flying everywhere. Perhaps I will also visualize my own car parked with a giant bird peeking out from inside. If you form similar images for the rest of the words on the list, you may not remember them all, but you will get most without any further practice. As a matter of fact, if you have formed the *pájaro* images just now, it is going to be almost impossible for you to ever see the word *pájaro* again without remembering that it means bird.

Question: What if I think pájaro *means "parked car" when I take my Spanish test?*

This is why you should form one or two extra images so that the important feature (bird, in this case) is repeated.

Example 2 Let's say you have to learn the names of all the bones and muscles in the human body for biology. You are trying to remember that the jawbone is the *mandible*. This one is easy because you can associate it to a *man nibbling*, or maybe you can picture a *man dribbling* a basketball with his jaw (make this image as ridiculous as possible). If the muscle name *latissimus dorsi* gives you trouble, familiarize it by turning it into *"the ladder misses the door, sigh."* Then picture a ladder glued to your back where the muscle is found. Picture the ladder leading up to a small door at your shoulder. Picture the ladder missing the door. Picture the ladder sighing like an animated character in a cartoon.

Question: This seems like more to remember, not less; and it seems as if it would cause you to misspell things.

Mnemonics are not a complete substitute for normal memory; they are an aid to normal memory. Mnemonics are not likely to be helpful unless you make extensive use of *images*. Your mental pictures will come back to you easily. As for misspellings, mnemonics can be thought of as a built-in hint in your memory. Often when taking a test, you will find that the slightest hint is all you need to remember correctly. A mnemonic image is like having someone leaning over your shoulder who says, "Psst, the name of that muscle sounds like ladder misses the door, sigh."

Here are two more examples to help you appreciate the flexibility of a mnemonic approach to studying.

Example 3 Your art history teacher expects you to be able to name the artist when you are shown slides as part of exams. Many of the slides you have only seen once before in class. How will you remember them? As the slides are shown in class, make each artist's name into an object or image. Then picture the object in paintings done by the artists. For example, Van Gogh you can picture as a *van* (automobile) *going* through the middle of each Van Gogh painting. Picture the van running over things and knocking things over. Or, if you remember that Van Gogh cut off his ear, picture a giant bloody ear in each of his paintings.

Example 4 If you have trouble remembering history, try to avoid thinking of it as something from the dim past. Picture each historical personality as a person you know right now (a friend, teacher, parent, and so on). Then picture these people doing whatever the historical figures did. Also try visualizing battles or other events as if they were happening in your town or make parks and schools into countries. Use your imagination.

Question: How can mnemonics be used to remember things in order?

Here are three techniques that are helpful.

> 1. **Form a chain.** To remember lists of ideas, objects, or words in order, try forming an exaggerated association (mental image) connecting the first item to the second, then the second to the third, and so on. To remember the following short list in order: elephant, doorknob, string, watch, rifle, oranges, picture a full-sized *elephant* balanced on a *doorknob* playing with a *string* tied to him. Picture a *watch* tied to the string, and a *rifle* shooting *oranges* at the watch. This technique can be used quite successfully for lists of 20 or more items. Try it next time you go shopping and leave your list at home.
> 2. **Take a mental walk.** Mnemonics were well known to ancient Greek orators, who would take a mental walk along a familiar path to associate ideas they wanted to cover in a speech to the images of statues found along the walk. You can do the same thing by "placing" objects or ideas along the way as you mentally take a familiar walk.
> 3. **Use a system.** Many times the first letter or syllables of words or ideas can be formed into another word that will serve as a reminder of order. "Roy G. Biv," just cited, is an example. As an alternative, learn the following: 1 is a bun, 2 is a shoe, 3 is a tree, 4 is a door, 5 is a hive, 6 is sticks, 7 is heaven, 8 is a gate, 9 is a line, 10 is a hen. To remember in order, form an association between bun and the first item on your list, then form an association between shoe and the second item, and so on.

If you have never used mnemonics, you may still be skeptical, but give this approach a fair trial. Most people find they can greatly extend their memory through the use of mnemonics. You may want to discuss these ideas further with your instructor and classmates.

Review your notes and then answer the following questions.

RECALL

1. What is the main idea of the reading passage?

   _____

   _____

   _____

2. What is a "mnemonic"? _____

3. What are the four basic principles of mnemonics?

   a. _____

   b. _____

   c. _____

   d. _____

INTERPRETATION

4. Why is it important to use visual images to remember things better?

   _____

   _____

   _____

5. What example is given for remembering the jawbone *mandible*?

   _____

   _____

   _____

   _____

Copyright © 1988 Holt, Rinehart and Winston, Inc.

P: Perfecting Reading Skills

APPLICATION

6. Think of something you need to remember for a test you are going to be taking (maybe a word from this unit). Make up a mnemonic device you can use to remember it.

   _____

   _____

7. Make up a mnemonic device that will help you memorize all the words in Drill 6, pages 94–95.

   _____

   _____

Name _____ **Section** _____ **Date** _____

UNIT 1
CHECK TEST (CHAPTERS 1–3)

PART ONE: WORD KNOWLEDGE

A. Directions: Mark the vowels in the following words as long (ā), short (ĕ), or controlled by *r* (ⓘr).

1. hide
2. grab
3. time
4. chore
5. first
6. ramp
7. spurt
8. storm
9. chorus
10. flop
11. tail
12. smear
13. child
14. mail
15. male

B. Directions: In the following blanks, write the letter of the word that stands for the symbols by the number.

_____ 1. pə lēs

_____ 2. mel'ən

_____ 3. lāt'ər

_____ 4. hang'ər

_____ 5. kol'ər

a. letter
b. later
c. melon
d. mellow
e. please
f. police
g. hanger
h. hunger
i. collar
j. color

110

Unit 1 Check Test (Chapters 1–3) **111**

C. Directions: In the blanks, write each of the following words in syllables. Then place the accent mark on the syllable that gets stressed. For example, contractor: *con'trac tor*

1. principal: _____

2. encounter: _____

3. bias: _____

4. apprentice: _____

5. humanities: _____

PART TWO: WORD USAGE

Directions: Write a sentence using the following words correctly.

1. waste: _____
_____

2. pause: _____
_____

3. fare: _____
_____

4. wail: _____
_____

5. decade: _____
_____

6. core: _____
_____

Copyright © 1988 Holt, Rinehart and Winston, Inc.

7. frustration: _____

_____

8. audition: _____

_____

9. concept: _____

_____

10. potential: _____

_____

11. superstitious: _____

_____

12. ancient: _____

_____

13. bias: _____

_____

14. vivid: _____

_____

15. humiliation: _____

_____

16. competent: _____

_____

17. retention: _____

_____

Unit 1 Check Test (Chapters 1–3) 113

18. elaborate: _____

_____

19. technique: _____

_____

20. recite: _____

_____

PART THREE: COMPREHENDING PARAGRAPHS

Directions: Read the following short selections on studying, and answer the questions that follow each selection. Try not to look back for an answer unless you have to. You will have only twenty minutes to read and answer all questions.

A. Almost every job requires the use of tools and skills. Carpenters, mechanics, plumbers, painters, to name just a few, develop their skill with tools. Doctors, artists, teachers, sports people all have certain tools and skills they must learn to use well. Students are no different. They, too, have tools and skills they must develop to do well in school. These are known as "study skills." Study skills include managing study time, listening, note-taking ability, good reading comprehension, and knowledge on how to take tests. Though many students try to do well in college, they do not have the proper skills. They don't know how to study, and they don't take time to develop study skills.

1. What is the main idea of the paragraph? _____

_____

_____

2. What study skills do students need to develop? _____

_____

_____

Name _____ **Section** _____ **Date** _____

3. Why do some students not do well in school even though they try? _____

_____

_____

4. Would the author probably be for or against study skills classes being taught at colleges? _____ Why? _____

_____

B. Managing study time is a big problem with many students. Here are some hints that may help. First, try to study a subject at the same time and place each day. If, for example, you study English at the same hour and place each day, you soon will be in the habit of thinking about English at that time. You will get in the mood to study English more quickly that way. Do this with each of your subjects. Second, don't spend more than an hour in one sitting on a subject. Studies show that more is learned in four one-hour sessions over a four-day period than one long six-hour study session. The mind can only soak up so much at one time. Third, take rest periods often. Don't sit and cram a lot in at once. A five-minute break whenever you feel tired or restless is best. Then study until you need another break. Fourth, don't study when you are tired. In fact, studies prove that the best learning technique is to review what you have already learned a few minutes before a class begins. Then study the new material learned in class as soon afterward as possible.

5. What is the main idea of the paragraph? _____

_____

_____

6. Why should you study a subject at the same time and place each day if possible? _____

_____

7. Why should you not study one subject for more than an hour at a time with breaks? _____

_____

_____

Unit 1 Check Test (Chapters 1–3)

8. What is the method suggested as the best learning technique? _____

_____

_____

PART FOUR: ESSAY READING COMPREHENSION

Directions: Read the following essay, and then answer the questions that follow. Apply all the skills on vocabulary and comprehension that you have practiced in this unit. Try to finish in ten minutes or less.

THE USES OF ERROR

ISAAC ASIMOV

In less than seven years we will be celebrating the 500th anniversary of the discovery of the American continents by Christopher Columbus. It's not too soon to try—once again—to set the record straight on that achievement.

In the first place, the common belief—which children pick up from elders who are as ignorant as they are—is that Columbus believed the world was round (the proper word is *spherical*) while everyone else thought it was flat.

This is ridiculous. To be sure, uneducated people in ancient and medieval times thought the world was flat, but so do uneducated people in most parts of the world today. Educated Europeans have known that the world is spherical ever since the time of Aristotle in the Fourth Century B.C.

This, then, was not a matter of dispute between Columbus and his opponents. The point in question was this: Given that the earth is a sphere, how large is it?

The first person we know of who tried to determine the size of the earth was a Greek geographer named Eratosthenes. About 240 B.C. he noted that at noon at the summer solstice, the sun was directly overhead at Syene (now Aswan) in Egypt, while it was seven degrees from the zenith at Alexandria. From this, and by use of simple geometry, he decided the earth was 25,000 miles in circumference—and he was correct.

Reprinted by permission of American Way, *inflight magazine of American Airlines, copyright © 1985 by American Airlines.*

Name _____ Section _____ Date _____

However, this seemed uncomfortably large to the Greeks. The land they knew of would fill only a small corner of such a huge world, and the thought of all that emptiness bothered them. About 150 years later, another Greek scholar, Poseidonius, repeated Eratosthenes's work and came up with a circumference of 18,000 miles. This was wrong, but the lower figure was more comforting, and the Greeks accepted it.

What's more, the Greek geographers had estimated the Mediterranean Sea to be longer east and west than it really was, and based on that and the meticulous account of Marco Polo, the eastern edge of Asia was considered to be substantially farther east than it really was.

In Columbus's time the Portuguese were trying to reach India by going around the African continent, a long and arduous voyage of some 10,000 miles. Columbus, assuming the small circumference of the world and the eastern overextension of Asia, maintained that one could achieve the same result by sailing 3,000 miles westward.

He approached the Portuguese with this idea, but the Portuguese geographers—the best in the world at that time—were convinced the earth was larger than Columbus thought and that the trip around Africa was the shorter route to India. Columbus, they said, would never reach any part of Asia.

Columbus got Spanish backing and sailed westward. What he didn't know, and what none of his European contemporaries knew, was that a vast, unknown continent blocked the way to Asia, and it was that new land that he reached—not India, even though we speak of native Americans as Indians to this day.

There are some other points.

First, Columbus did not prove that the earth was round. Those who wanted to believe it was flat could still do so, provided the flat earth was large enough to hold the Americas as well as Europe, Asia, and Africa. It wasn't until the voyage headed by Ferdinand Magellan (although he died en route) 40 years after Columbus that anyone actually sailed westward all the way to Asia and then continued onward back to Europe.

Second, Columbus did not truly discover America; he was not the first human being to set foot on it. Indeed, human beings met him on the shore. Human beings had discovered the American continents when the first Siberian hunters crossed the Bering land bridge into North America about 25,000 years ago, and they settled the continents to the southernmost tip before Columbus arrived.

Columbus wasn't even the first European to arrive, since Norsemen had reached North America 500 years before him. Columbus was, however, the first person to publicize the discovery so effectively that Europeans explored and settled the new world and went on to dominate the whole world for a period of 450 years.

So you see the uses of error. If Columbus had not been wrong, if he had known the truth—that 12,000 westward miles separated him from Asia—he

Unit 1 Check Test (Chapters 1-3) 117

would not have made the voyage, and the history of the world would have been different.
   Who knows what mistaken scientific beliefs today may serve to lead us to great discoveries in the future.

Now answer the following questions.

1. What is the main idea of the essay? _____
   _____

2. Columbus and his opponents both believed the earth was round, but what was it they questioned about the earth? _____
   _____
   _____

3. For how long have educated people known the earth was round? _____
   _____

4. About 240 B.C., the Greek geographer Eratosthenes was able to determine the correct size of the earth, which is _____.

5. Why did the Greeks not accept this distance as correct?
   _____
   _____

6. What error did Columbus make regarding the size of the earth? _____
   _____
   _____

7. Why are native Americans called Indians? _____
   _____
   _____

Copyright © 1988 Holt, Rinehart and Winston, Inc.

8. Columbus proved the earth was round.

    a. True

    b. False, because _____

    _____

    _____

9. Columbus discovered America.

    a. True

    b. False, because _____

    _____

10. What mistake did Columbus make that changed the history of the world?

    _____

    _____

    _____

Name _____ **Section** _____ **Date** _____

UNIT 2

Chapter 4

Objectives

P: **PREREADING DRILLS**
Words to Know
Warm-up Drills

R: **READING DRILL**
Reading and Thinking About What You Read
"Reading the Social Sciences" by Scott Forbes
Comprehension Check

E: **EXERCISES IN VOCABULARY**
Drills
    1: Root Words
    2: Prefixes
    3: Suffixes
    4: Syllables and Vowels
    5: Context Clues and Dictionary Definitions
    6: Definition Review
Vocabulary Check

P: **PERFECTING READING SKILLS**
Comprehending Sentences: More Idioms
Comprehending Paragraphs: Main Ideas and Interpretation
Comprehending History Textbook Passages: Marking and Underlining
"The Kennedy Administration" by George E. Frakes and W. Royce Adams

Objectives

When you have finished with this chapter, you will

1. Recognize and be able to use at least 90 percent of the vocabulary words listed in the Words to Know section.
2. Know what root words are and how to identify them.
3. Know how to use the prefixes *dis, im, in, ir,* and *un.*
4. Know how to use the suffixes *able, ly, ic, ful, ness,* and *less.*
5. Have reviewed syllabication and know what makes a syllable.
6. Be able to define the term *context clues.*
7. Know how to use context clues to help you select the proper dictionary definition of a word that has more than one meaning.
8. Have developed your reading comprehension skills in the areas of identifying main ideas, inferences, and sequence of events.
9. Know how to mark and underline as you study-read.

P: PREREADING DRILLS

WORDS TO KNOW

Directions: Read the following words aloud. Study the definitions and sample sentence. These words appear in the article you are about to read.

1. *carburetor*—a device used in gasoline engines that sends fuel and air to the engine.
A carburetor in a Ford is not the same as one in a VW.
2. *dismantle*—to take apart.
A good mechanic knows which parts to dismantle first.
3. *parasite*—a life form that lives on or in another life form.
The tapeworm spends its adult life as a parasite in the intestines of another organism.
4. *obscure*—out of sight; hidden; hard to understand.
The meaning of the poem is obscure.
5. *anarchy*—disorder; confusion; loss of governmental control.
When anarchy visited Nicaragua, President Coolidge had no choice but to send in marines.
6. *token force*—a symbolic or superficial pledge of power to show good faith.
Coolidge withdrew a token force of marines from Nicaragua.
7. *literal*—word for word; the exact meaning.
In poetry, words become symbols of other meanings besides their literal definitions.
8. *altered*—changed; modified.
The president made a decision that altered the course of history.
9. *concession*—something given up in an agreement.
Who made greater concessions at the conference?
10. *discrepancies*—disagreements; differences in facts.
Discrepancies in social science writings are common.

WARM-UP DRILLS

DRILL 1

Directions: Select the correct word from the list you just studied, and write it in the blanks in the following sentences. You may need to add a letter or letters to the word from the list to make it fit the sentence, such as *ed* to change the word into the past tense.

1. The teacher _____ the directions to the test once we pointed out the errors.

2. Jack's father called him a _____ and told him to get out of the house and get a job.

3. Once the government collapsed, there was _____.

4. There were not too many _____ in the two reports of the accident.

5. Sara found many of the words _____, thus making the reading difficult.

6. The entire machine will have to be _____ in order to find the problem.

DRILL 2

Directions: Move your eyes quickly from left to right. Mark the word by the number every time it appears on the same line. Don't look back on a line. Don't change mistakes. Work rapidly. Try to finish in thirty seconds or less. Begin timing.

1. soldier   sold solder soldier solid soldier
2. shoulder   should shoulder shudder should shoulder
3. protect   protected protecting protect protected protects
4. flaming   farming flaming flame flamed flaming
5. wrist   waist write wrist waist wrist
6. breast   beast breast beast breast beast
7. courage   courage courageous courage cougar court
8. church   chance churned church church chunk
9. cannon   canon canon cannon canon cannon
10. stack   stack stock stack stock stock
11. shawl   shame shawl shame shame shawl
12. surround   surround surrounds surround surrounds
13. whipped   whopped whipped wiped whopped whipped
14. adopted   adapted adopted adapted adopted adopted
15. charged   charged changed charged changed changed

TIME: _____

P: Prereading Drills

Check each line to see if you marked the correct word every time it appears. Make sure you know all the words in the drill. The words by the numbers appear in the article in this chapter.

TOTAL LINES CORRECT: _____

DRILL 3

Directions: Move your eyes quickly from left to right. Mark the word by the number every time it appears on the same line. Don't look back on a line. Don't change mistakes. Work rapidly. Try to finish in thirty seconds or less.
Begin timing.

1.	natural	nature natural nation national natural
2.	difficulty	differ different difference difficulty
3.	mechanic	mechanic mechanism mercury machine
4.	courses	coarse course courses cause courses
5.	organism	organ origin organism organic original
6.	fertile	futile fertilizer fertile fritter
7.	capable	captain captain capable credible carp
8.	alter	altar alter alter altar already also
9.	dismantle	disregard dismantle discover dismayed
10.	anarchy	anarchy anagram analyze archery anarchy
11.	literal	lateral little listen literal limitless
12.	social	society society social sassy socialize
13.	token	taken total token tacked taught token
14.	parasite	paragraph parachute paramedic parasite
15.	concession	confusion countered concession concede

TIME: _____

Check each line to see if you marked the correct word every time it appears. Make sure you know all of the words in the drill. The words by the numbers appear in the next article you will read.

TOTAL LINES CORRECT: _____

R: READING DRILL

READING AND THINKING ABOUT WHAT YOU READ

Directions: The following selection deals with reading the social sciences—history, anthropology, sociology, political science, economics, and the like. Look at the title and the headings; then answer the following questions.

1. What do you think this reading selection will be about?

   _____

2. Do you think that reading social science textbooks is easier or more difficult than reading science books?

   _____ Why? _____

   _____

   _____

3. What do you think you might learn from reading the following passage?

   _____

   _____

   _____

   _____

   _____

Now read the following selection.

READING THE SOCIAL SCIENCES
SCOTT FORBES

Reading isn't a natural thing. Like all skills, it needs practice and training. Auto mechanics, for instance, will know what a carburetor is and how it works. But the carburetor on a Ford is not the same as one on a VW. Good mechanics will not have difficulty working on either one. The more experience a mechanic

Reprinted by permission of the author.

R: Reading Drill 127

has in working with different models, the faster and easier a job can be done. Mechanics learn tricks of the trade, which tools work best on certain jobs, which parts to dismantle first, and which parts need more attention than others.

Reading skills are much the same. The reading you do in social science courses is different from the reading you do in science or English courses. Look at the following three selections and decide if you would read them all in the same way.

> A single tapeworm contains both male and female organs. The egg and sperm from the same animal unite to form a new tapeworm. In other words, the tapeworm is self-fertilizing. There is a good reason why the tapeworm reproduces by this means. Because the tapeworm spends its adult life as a parasite in the intestines of another organism, the chances that it will ever meet another adult of its species are very slim. Tapeworms would have disappeared from the earth long ago if they had not been capable of self-fertilization.

> Below the surface-stream, shallow and light,
> Of what we *say* we feel—below the stream,
> As light, of what we *think* we feel—there flows
> With noiseless current strong, obscure and deep,
> The central stream of what we feel indeed.
>
> *(Matthew Arnold)*

> When anarchy visited Nicaragua, President Coolidge had no choice but to act unilaterally. First, in 1925, he withdrew a token force of marines from that nation which then seemed capable of servicing its foreign debt and preserving its internal stability. But the appearance was deceptive. Almost at once, revolution broke out, and Coolidge again landed the marines, in time some five thousand.
>
> *(John Blum,* The National Experience, *Harcourt Brace Jovanovich, 1973.)*

The first selection is obviously about a science topic. But how does it differ from the other two selections? The passage about the tapeworm deals with fact. It explains how and why a tapeworm reproduces as it does. Another science text would probably explain this process the same way because the facts are well established and agreed on by scientists.

This explanation of a process is only one commonly used pattern found in science writing. If you examine a science text, you will find that a classification pattern is also used. That is, everything that exists is divided into types—living things, objects, minerals, gases, liquids, and so forth. These may even be subdivided into smaller classes. Other scientific writing patterns include the use of instructions for doing experiments, problem-solving patterns, and the use of abbreviations and equations. These patterns are seldom, if ever, found in social science texts.

The second selection, the poem, differs most from the others. Unlike a science selection, a poem does not deal with facts. It deals with sound, images, mood, and feeling. Although the poem is short, it probably takes longer to read and understand than the science passage. The poem has to be read several times. Words become symbols of other meanings besides their literal definitions. In other words, the reading skills required by poetry and science are completely different.

Each of the types of literature you read in English classes demands a different reading skill. When you read a short story, you do not use the same skill you use in reading a poem or an essay. Each literary form requires its own special reading skill.

The third selection is taken from a history text—one of the social sciences. The sample passage is typical of the social sciences. It tries to deal with facts. But in that attempt, human events and human beings must also be considered. Why people behave a certain way, why a president made a certain decision that altered the course of history, or why the population voted a particular individual into office—such questions cannot be handled in the same way as questions about scientific facts. So in social sciences, opinions are often mixed with facts. As a reader, you need to be able to tell fact from opinion.

The Characteristics of Social Science Writing

The social sciences all have one thing in common: They attempt to discover facts. But there are not as many proved facts in the social sciences as in science. For there is no way to get positive proof about many social science events. But you may think, "What about cut-and-dried facts such as Columbus and the discovery of America?"

If a historian stated what he knew for certain about the discovery of America, it might sound like this:

> On a day conveniently labeled October 12, 1492, a group of sailors under the command of a man known in English as Christopher Columbus landed on an island which was apparently the one now called Watling Island.

These are the types of "facts" that social scientists have to work with. Nevertheless, the social scientists *are* concerned with facts, but often the facts of the social sciences cannot be proved like those of a scientific experiment. For instance, the date Columbus discovered America is uncertain because other dating systems than the calendar we now use were in use during Columbus' time. Other "facts" show that Columbus was not necessarily the first to discover America. You have probably heard of the Viking, Leif Ericsson, who is given credit by some historians for discovering America first. Some historians also claim that Columbus did not land on the mainland, but on an island, and which island is not agreed upon. And still other historians claim there is some uncertainty about Columbus' nationality. There are many such problems in history that may never be answered because the facts are lost in the past.

Scientific Facts vs. Historical Facts

Scientists can conduct controlled experiments to get the facts. Obviously, it is impossible to conduct controlled experiments on whole countries, governments, or entire civilizations. Most of the information historians gather cannot be scientifically tested.

History is probably the least scientific of the social sciences. Therefore, it is sometimes classed as one of the humanities, along with literature, philosophy, and art. You may have noticed that at times history reads more like a novel than a factual account.

However, social scientists make every attempt to deal with facts. In economics, for instance, mathematics, accounting, and statistics are important in presenting facts. But economists, like all social scientists, cannot use scientific experiments to test their theories. For example, by studying what happened in this country in 1929, economists think they can predict pretty well what would happen if another Great Depression happened. But they can't prove what they believe. They can't experiment with the economy of the country and cause a depression just to see if they are right.

Scientists can be detached from their experiments; historians usually are not. A scientist wants to define a problem, collect data, classify it, guess what will happen, then set up an experiment to see what happens. A historian, on the other hand, selects information that he or she is personally interested in, then develops his or her opinion. Notice the difference in these two historical accounts of the Yalta Conference that took place in February 1945:

> The second conference of the Big Three, held at Yalta in February 1945, represented the high point of Soviet diplomatic success and correspondingly the low point of American appeasement [giving in].
> *(W. H. Chamberlin,* America's Second Crusade, *Henry Regnery, 1950.)*

> The record of the Conference shows clearly that the Soviet Union made greater concessions at Yalta to the United States and Great Britain than were made to the Soviets. The agreements were, on the whole, a diplomatic triumph for the United States and Great Britain.
> *(Edward Stettinius, Jr.,* Roosevelt and the Russians, *Doubleday, 1950.)*

The writers of both these passages studied the Yalta Conference, the men involved, the results, and the points discussed. But each writer came to a different conclusion. One says that Russia came out ahead; the other feels the United States and Great Britain were more successful. Such discrepancies are typical of social science writings.

Don't get the idea, however, that you cannot accept as fact anything you read in social science books. Most books agree on the basic facts of history. You, as a reader, should be aware when you read the social sciences that facts are presented and then interpreted according to the author. Your job is to learn to recognize fact, opinion, and interpretation.

How do fact, opinion, and interpretation fit together? It might help to think of them as three separate levels of information:

1. *Fact*—basic information that can be proved.
2. *Interpretation*—a writer's attempt to help or explain a reader's understanding of the facts.
3. *Opinion*—a writer's personal feelings about the facts.

Facts provide you with information, interpretations increase your understanding of what the facts mean, and opinions tell you how a writer feels about the information.

All three are important and serve three different purposes. Reading can be like eating a bowl of chicken noodle soup. Sometimes you may feel like eating only the meat, sometimes you want only the noodles, and sometimes you want only the broth. But most of the time you eat it all together. As a good reader, you must be prepared to sort out all three, or you will read interpretation and opinions as truth.

COMPREHENSION CHECK

Directions: Answer the following questions without looking back unless the question requires you to do so.

RECALL

1. The main idea (thesis) of this essay is that the particular writing patterns found in the social sciences require different reading skills from those required in other types of writing.

    a. True

    b. False, because _____

    _____

2. Science writing is basically based on _____.
3. Why can a poem when read take longer to understand than a chapter in

R: Reading Drill **131**

   a social science text? _____

   _____

   _____

4. What is it that all social science writings have in common?
   a. they attempt to discover facts
   b. they deal in facts
   c. they can't be accepted as truth
   d. none of the above

INTERPRETATION

5. Why can scientists deal more easily with facts than social scientists?

   _____

   _____

   _____

6. Two passages from social science books that deal with the 1945 Yalta Conference are presented. What point is being made by showing us these? _____

   _____

   _____

   _____

7. What three things must you be alert to when you read in the social sciences? _____

   _____

   _____

8. Explain the difference between interpretation and opinion. _____

   _____

   _____

   _____

Copyright © 1988 Holt, Rinehart and Winston, Inc.

APPLICATION

9. Explain the difficulty in discussing who discovered America. _____

10. Summarize the essay in your own words in one paragraph.

E: EXERCISES IN VOCABULARY DRILLS

DRILL 1: ROOT WORDS

Directions: Many words are made by adding endings, prefixes, and suffixes to root words. A root word is a word from which others are formed. For example:

create	s		creat	ion		un	creat	ive
(an ending)		(a suffix)		(a prefix and a suffix)

The root word is *create*. Sometimes, as in the case of *create*, the final letter of a root word is dropped when a suffix is added. In the blank following each of the following three word groups, write the root word. Sometimes you may need to add a letter to the root because it was dropped when the suffix was added, as in *creation (create)*. The first one has been done for you.

1. artist, artistic, unartistic *art*
2. conventions, conventional, unconventional _____
3. unreal, realist, realistic _____
4. dependable, dependent, independent _____
5. personality, impersonal, personalities _____
6. impractical, practically, practicalness _____
7. unenjoyable, enjoyable, enjoys _____
8. ordinarily, extraordinary, ordinariness _____
9. accountant, accountable, accounts _____
10. conservation, conservative, conserving _____

DRILL 2: PREFIXES

Directions: Prefixes, like *un*, *in*, and *dis*, are word parts that are added to the beginning of a word to make a new word. For example, the prefix *un* placed in front of *creative* makes the word *uncreative*. The following prefixes generally mean "not" or "opposite of."

    dis im in ir un a

Here are a few clues that might help you decide which prefix to use:

1. Root words that begin with *r* usually use the prefix *ir*.
2. Root words beginning with *p*, *m*, and *b* usually use the prefix *im*.
3. Root words that begin with *l* usually take the prefix *il*.
4. Root words beginning with *m* often take the prefix *im*.

See how many of the following words can be changed to new words by adding one of the preceding prefixes. Write the correct prefix in the blank.

1. ___*im*___ practical
2. _____ patience
3. _____ sensitive
4. _____ social
5. _____ replaceable
6. _____ typical
7. _____ regular
8. _____ personal
9. _____ artistic
10. _____ legal
11. _____ dependable
12. _____ mobile

DRILL 3: SUFFIXES

Directions: Suffixes, like *y*, *ness*, and *ic*, can be added to the end of a word to make a new word. For example, the suffix *ness* added to the end of the word *shrewd* makes the word *shrewdness*. Add the correct suffixes from the following list to the following words. There may be more than one answer for some.

    able ly ic ful ness less

1. sensitive _____
2. sociable _____
3. depend _____
4. doubt _____
5. point _____
6. personal _____

E: Exercises in Vocabulary 135

4. practical _____   9. realist _____

5. impatient _____   10. creative _____

DRILL 4: SYLLABLES AND VOWELS

Directions: Every word has at least one vowel in it. The vowels, remember, are *a, e, i, o, u,* and sometimes *y, w,* and *h.* Every syllable in a word also has at least one vowel in it. For example:

Art is a one-syllable word with the vowel *a.*
Artist has two syllables (ar′-tist); the vowel *a* is in the first syllable; the vowel *i,* in the second syllable.

Artistically has five syllables (ar-tis′-ti-cal-ly); the vowel *a* is in the first syllable; *i,* in the second; *i,* in the third; *a,* in the fourth; and *y,* in the fifth because the *y* sounds like the vowel *e.*

In the blanks after each of the following words, divide the words into syllables, and underline the vowels in each syllable. The first one is done for you.

1. conventional *c<u>o</u>n-v<u>e</u>n-t<u>io</u>n-<u>a</u>l*

2. independent

3. uncommonly

4. impersonal

5. conversation

6. impractical

7. accountant

8. probability

9. curiousness

10. realistic

DRILL 5: CONTEXT CLUES AND DICTIONARY DEFINITIONS

Part A

Following are some dictionary entries. Notice that more than one definition is given for each word entry. For instance, *conservative* has ten definitions.

---

con·ser·va·tive (kən-sûr'-və-tiv) *adj.* **1.** Tending to favor the preservation of the existing order and to regard proposals for change with distrust. **2.** *Capital* **C.** Adhering to or characteristic of the Conservative Party of the United Kingdom. **3.** *Capital* **C.** Adhering to or characteristic of Conservative Judaism. **4.** Moderate; prudent; cautious; *a conservative estimate* **5.** Traditional in manner or style, not showy: *a conservative suit.* **6.** Tending to conserve; conserving; preservative. —*n.* **1.** A conservative person. **2.** *Capital* **C.** *Abbr.* **C.** A member or supporter of the Conservative Party of the United Kingdom. **3.** *Capital* **C.** *Abbr.* **C** A member or supporter of the Progressive-Conservative Party of Canada. **4.** A preservative.

con·ven·tion·al (kən-vĕn'shən-əl) *adj.* **1.** Developed, established, or approved by general usage: customary. **2.** Conforming to established practice or accepted standards. **3.** Marked by or dependent upon conventions, to the point of artificiality. **4.** *Art.* Represented in simplified or abstract form. **5.** *Law.* Based upon consent or agreement; contractual. **6.** Of or having to do with an assembly. **7.** Using means other than nuclear weapons or energy; —**con·ven'tion·al·ism'** *n* —**con·ven'tion·al·ist** *n.* —**con·ven'tion·al·i·za'tion** *n.* —**con·ven'tion·al·ly** *adv.*

im·pres·sion (im-prĕsh'ən) *n.* **1.** The act or process of impressing. **2.** The effect, mark, or imprint made on a surface by pressure. **3.** An effect, image, or feeling retained as a consequence of experience. **4.** A vague notion, remembrance, or belief. **5.** *Printing.* **a.** All the copies of a publication printed at one time from the same set of type. **b.** A single copy of this printing **6.** *Dentistry.* An imprint of the teeth and surrounding tissue in material such as wax or plaster, used as a mold in making dentures or inlays. —See Synonyms at **opinion**.

sen·si·tive (sĕns'sə-tiv) *adj.* **1.** Capable of perceiving with a sense or senses. **2.** Responsive to external conditions or stimulation. **3.** Susceptible to the attitudes, feelings, or circumstances of others. **4.** Quick to take offense; touchy. **5.** Easily irritated; *sensitive skin* **6.** Readily altered by the action of some agent: *sensitive to light.* **7.** Registering very slight differences or changes of conditions. Said of an instrument. **8.** Fluctuating or tending to fluctuate, as stock prices. **9.** Dealing with classified governmental information, usually involving national security: *a sensitive post in the State Department.*

so·cial (sō'shəl) *adj* **1. a.** Living together in communities. **b.** Characterizing such communal living. **c.** Of or pertaining to society. **2.** Living in an organized group or similar close aggregate: *social insects.* **3.** Involving allies or members of a confederacy. **4.** Of or pertaining to the upper classes. **5.** Sociable; fond of the company of others. **6.** Intended for convivial activities. **7.** Pertaining to or occupied with welfare work: *a social worker* —*n.* An informal social gathering, as of the members of a church congregation. Also called "sociable."

Copyright © 1973 by Houghton Mifflin Company. Reprinted by permission from The American Heritage Dictionary of the English Language.

Read each of the following sentences. Write in the blanks the number of the dictionary definition that best fits the way the *italicized* word is used in the sentence.

E: Exercises in Vocabulary

_____ 1. The army was told to use only *conventional* weapons.

_____ 2. For a superstar, her dress seems rather *conventional*.

_____ 3. My sister Ellen mixes with a higher *social* class than I do.

_____ 4. Gorillas are very *social* animals.

_____ 5. Harry's hearing is very *sensitive*, and he can hear sounds I can't.

_____ 6. Harry is also very *sensitive* about his big ears.

_____ 7. Because he is so *conservative*, I bet he does not approve of the tax reform bill.

_____ 8. Susan's new dress is very *conservative*.

_____ 9. The dentist took a wax *impression* of my teeth.

_____ 10. After the meeting, I got the *impression* Helen was angry.

Part B

Directions: Look up the following familiar words in the dictionary, and find the information requested.

1. *cross*
   a. Number of syllables _____

   b. Pronunciation _____

   c. Parts of speech _____

   d. Write at least five different meanings.

      1. _____

      2. _____

      3. _____

      4. _____

      5. _____

2. *pump* a. Number of syllables _____

   b. Pronunciation _____

   c. Parts of speech _____

   d. Write at least five different meanings.

      1. _____

      2. _____

      3. _____

      4. _____

      5. _____

3. *pocket* a. Number of syllables _____

   b. Pronunciation _____

   c. Parts of speech _____

   d. Write at least five different meanings.

      1. _____

      2. _____

      3. _____

      4. _____

      5. _____

4. *field* a. Number of syllables _____

   b. Pronunciation _____

   c. Parts of speech _____

   d. Write at least five different meanings.

      1. _____

E: Exercises in Vocabulary 139

        2. _____

        3. _____

        4. _____

        5. _____

5. *company*   a. Number of syllables _____

        b. Pronunciation _____

        c. Parts of speech _____

        d. Write at least five different meanings.

            1. _____

            2. _____

            3. _____

            4. _____

            5. _____

6. *give*   a. Number of syllables _____

        b. Pronunciation _____

        c. Parts of speech _____

        d. Write at least five different meanings.

            1. _____

            2. _____

            3. _____

            4. _____

            5. _____

Discuss your answers in class.

DRILL 6: DEFINITION REVIEW

Directions: The following words are from the Words to Know sections in this and the last chapter. Write the letter of the correct definition in the blank in front of the word. There are more definitions than words.

_____ 1. obscure   a. thoroughly developed

_____ 2. anarchy   b. foreign; unfamiliar

_____ 3. literal   c. to take apart

_____ 4. carburetor   d. disorder; confusion

_____ 5. dismantle   e. hidden; hard to understand

_____ 6. parasite   f. word for word

_____ 7. altered   g. device on gasoline engines

_____ 8. concessions   h. a life form living off another life

_____ 9. discrepancies   i. changed; modified

_____ 10. token   j. disagreements; differences

k. things given up

l. symbol of good faith

VOCABULARY CHECK

PART ONE

Directions: Write a sentence using each of the following words. You may change endings to fit the context of your sentence.

1. obscure: _____

_____

2. anarchy: _____

_____

E: Exercises in Vocabulary

3. literal: _____

_____

4. carburetor: _____

_____

5. dismantle: _____

_____

6. parasite: _____

_____

7. token: _____

_____

8. altered: _____

_____

9. concession: _____

_____

10. discrepancy: _____

_____

PART TWO

A. Directions: Cross out any prefixes or suffixes on the following words, and define the root word only. Sometimes the final letter of the root word has been dropped when a suffix is added.

1. uncreative _____

2. unrealistic _____

3. unsociable _____

4. impatient _____

5. shrewdly _____

B. Directions: Use the correct prefix to change the following words to mean the opposite of what they mean.

   dis   il   im   in   ir   un

1. _____ sensitive   6. _____ conventional

2. _____ artistic   7. _____ accountable

3. _____ legal   8. _____ typical

4. _____ dependable   9. _____ appoint

5. _____ perfect   10. _____ replaceable

P: PERFECTING READING SKILLS

COMPREHENDING SENTENCES: MORE IDIOMS

Directions: Read each sentence, and answer the questions that follow. Try not to use the words in the sentences when you write your answers. Most sentences use idiomatic expressions. Underline the words or phrases you feel are idiomatic.

1. The ownership of the company will change hands next month unless the present owners come up with the money.

    a. What might happen next month? _____

    b. Why? _____

2. Get in touch with a lawyer, Mort; you've been given a raw deal.

    a. What is Mort being told to do? _____

    b. Why? _____

3. After our date last week, Ed has been giving me the cold shoulder.

    a. Did Ed probably have a good time on his date? _____

    b. Why? _____

4. The way Ed treats Joan makes my blood boil; I'd love to give him a piece of my mind.

    a. How does Ed treat Joan? _____

143

b. How do you know? _____

_____

5. Look, Ed and Joe are supposed to be bosom friends; Ed didn't need to bite his head off like that!

   a. What is the relationship between Ed and Joe? _____

   _____

   b. Did Ed kill Joe? _____

   c. How do you know? _____

   _____

6. Men, leave no stone unturned; I want the killer found.

   a. What are the men supposed to do? _____

   _____

   b. Where are they supposed to look? _____

   _____

COMPREHENDING PARAGRAPHS: MAIN IDEAS AND INTERPRETATION

Directions: Read the following paragraphs, and answer the questions that follow.

1. Some historians say that the end of the Plains Indians occurred at Wounded Knee Creek, South Dakota. In December 1890, soldiers had gathered the Sioux Indians in order to take their guns from them. Most of the Indians stacked their guns as they were told to do. But when one Indian refused, shooting started. It suddenly got out of hand. When the shooting stopped, over 300 Indians, mostly women and children, had been senselessly killed. After this, there were no more major Indian wars in the plains areas.

P: Perfecting Reading Skills 145

    a. What is the main idea of this paragraph? _____

_____

    b. What is meant by the phrase "end of the Plains Indians"? _____

_____

_____

_____

    c. What is fact, and what is interpretation in this paragraph? _____

_____

_____

_____

2. When he was young, Curly had a vision. He dreamed and went into the world where there is nothing but the spirits of all things. He was on his horse in that vision. The horse, himself, the tree, the grass, the stones—everything was made of spirit. Nothing was hard. Everything seemed to float. His horse was standing there. Yet it danced around like a horse made only of shadow. This is how Curly got his name, Crazy Horse. It does not mean that his horse was crazy or wild, but that in his vision the horse danced around in a strange way.

    a. What is the main idea of the paragraph? _____

_____

_____

    b. Do you believe there is a "world where there is nothing but the spirits of all things"? _____

_____

_____

    c. Can you guess how many Indians got their names? _____

3. Crazy Horse had many followers because of his vision and his belief that he could not be killed in battle. Though not an official chief, his followers loved him because he was concerned with his people and not with gaining wealth. He refused to accept many gifts or to own many horses, a sign of wealth. He often went without food when it was scarce. When he went into a fight, he always put himself in danger. He was never wounded in battle.

Zuñi Indian Kachina Dolls

P: Perfecting Reading Skills

    a. What is the main idea of the paragraph? _____

_____

_____

    b. What was the Plains Indian's idea of wealth? _____

_____

    c. Plains Indians believed strongly in visions. Do you? _____

Why? _____

_____

4. The white man's desire for land and gold was to destroy still another Indian life-style. In 1863, the Nez Percé signed a treaty. But the Indians did not really understand the treaty they signed because it took away three-fourths of their land. The treaty left them with only a small reservation in Idaho. Confused, some of the Indians refused to leave their homes. In 1873, they asked President Grant if they could stay. He let them stay, but two years later he changed his mind. The reason was that too many white settlers and businessmen were putting pressure on Grant for the land. In 1877, he sent an army to move the Indians to a reservation.

    a. Whom is this paragraph about? _____

_____

    b. Where did the events take place? _____

_____

    c. What is the main idea of the paragraph? _____

_____

_____

    d. How would you feel if you were told you must leave your home and go to live where the government told you to? _____

5. The Nez Percé peacefully started toward the reservation area. Their leader was a great man named Chief Joseph. One night during the move, some angry Indians killed eleven white men. The army outnumbered the Nez Percé two to one. When they learned of the murder of the whites, the army attacked the Indians. Chief Joseph and his small band managed to kill one-third of the soldiers and escaped into the mountains. Chief Joseph led his people over 1,300 miles trying to escape to Canada. Battles were constant during the long march. For months, Chief Joseph and fewer than 300 warriors and 400 women and children kept the entire Northwest army on the move. Finally, Chief Joseph accepted a truce offering. But he was tricked and learned, as many Indians did, that the white soldier was not to be trusted.

   a. What is the main idea of the paragraph? _____

   b. What do you think of Chief Joseph? _____

   c. Is the author of the paragraph on the side of the whites or the Indians in this report? _____ How do you know? _____

COMPREHENDING HISTORY TEXTBOOK PASSAGES: MARKING AND UNDERLINING

In the last chapter you learned how to take notes as you read. Some students find it helpful to mark and underline in their books as they read. Then, during a review, they use their markings to write their notes in a notebook. Marking and underlining as you read are fine. Just don't mark everything. Be selective and mark only main ideas and supporting points.

Observe how the passage at the top of page 149 is not overmarked. It highlights only the main ideas.

Notice that notes and comments are written in the margin. Only main ideas and major points are underlined.

Copyright © 1988 Holt, Rinehart and Winston, Inc.

the point > Most history books consider the problems of Reconstruction from a white perspective. In recent years, attempts have been made to understand <u>the impact of Reconstruction on the Negro</u>. As early as 1866, Blacks realized that <u>unless their rights were guaranteed by laws and by the army, their lives, freedom, and property would not be safe</u>. With white ill will sometimes obviously present, the Blacks <u>had to</u> ① <u>become politically active</u>. They had no <u>choice but to</u> ② <u>join the Republican party</u> and particularly its radical wing. Blacks also began <u>to organize themselves</u> ③ <u>politically</u>. Negro <u>newspapers</u> such as the *Colored American* and the *Loyal Georgian* <u>began to inform</u> ④ their Black audiences of the key political issues of that day. By 1870, <u>massive voter registration drives</u> ⑤ <u>had given the vote</u> to many of the 3,800,000 Blacks of the old Confederacy.

5 results on Blacks

Marking forces you to keep your mind on what you are reading. Then when you transfer your markings into your notes, they might look something like this:

During Reconstruction, blacks had to do something to guarantee their rights.
They: 1. Got involved in politics.
2. Joined the Republican Party.
3. Organized themselves politically.
4. Kept blacks informed with black newspapers.
5. Pushed black voter registration.

Marking as you read and then taking notes during a review session serve as a strong aid in comprehension and retention.

DRILL 1: READING AND MARKING

Part A

Read the following paragraph from a history book, and mark the most important points. You may need to read it more than once. It's typical of many textbook passages you will encounter.

When anarchy visited Nicaragua, Coolidge had no choice but to act unilaterally. First, in 1925, he withdrew a token force of marines from that nation, which then seemed capable of servicing its foreign debt and preserving its internal stability. But the appearance was deceptive. Almost at once revolution broke out, and Coolidge again landed the marines, in time some five thousand. Regrettably, in its quest for order, the United States chose to support the reactionary faction, whose identification with large landowners and foreign investors had helped provoke the revolution in the first place.

(From The National Experience *by John Blum et al., Harcourt Brace Jovanovich, 1973, p. 617.)*

Part B

Read the following paragraph, and mark the most important points. It deals with the same subject as the previous paragraph. It's from a different textbook, however.

The United States, despite the current anti-war sentiment, was reluctantly forced to adopt warlike measures in Latin America. Disorders in Nicaragua, perilously close to the Panama Canal jugular vein, had jeopardized American lives and property, and in 1927 President Coolidge felt compelled to dispatch over 5000 troops to this troubled banana land. His political foes, decrying mailed-fist tactics, accused him of waging a "private war," while critics south of the Rio Grande loudly assailed *Yanqui* imperialism.

(From The American Pageant, *2d ed., by Thomas A. Bailey, D. C. Heath & Co., 1961, p. 803.)*

Part C

Answer the following questions about the two passages you just read.

1. What is the main idea in both passages?

2. How do the two passages differ in the reporting of the incident?

P: Perfecting Reading Skills

DRILL 2: READING AND MARKING A HISTORY TEXTBOOK PASSAGE

Directions: The following passage is from a history textbook similar to the type of books you will be required to read in college. Use what you have learned so far:

1. Prepare to read by surveying first.
2. Read from one heading to the next.
3. Use context clues to understand words you may not know.
4. Examine what you've read by marking or taking notes as you read.
5. Review the passage before answering the questions that follow.

THE KENNEDY ADMINISTRATION

GEORGE E. FRAKES AND W. ROYCE ADAMS

Personal Background

John Fitzgerald Kennedy was the youngest man to be elected president in the history of America. His political education began at an early age because his maternal grandfather and his millionaire father, Joseph Kennedy, were both deeply involved in political life. Born to a family loaded with money and talent, "Jack" Kennedy followed the pattern of many eastern aristocrats: education at private schools; further studies at Princeton, Harvard, London School of Economics, and Stanford Business School; extensive travel abroad; and opportunities to meet the influential people of America. Kennedy lived with the inconvenience and pain of Atkinson's disease, old athletic injuries, and a poor back. Although he was eligible for exemption from military service, he successfully trained to pass the physical examination.

Early Career

He emerged from World War II as a combat hero and a man who valued personal courage. His Irish name, good looks, wealth, and ability enabled him to be elected to Congress from the Irish-American section of Boston in 1946. His marriage to the beautiful, young heiress, Jacqueline Bouvier, added to his glamour in an age that highly valued youth and good looks. As a senator, Kennedy had never been a member of the inner circle of powerful senators. He seemed

Reprinted by permission of the authors.

too aggressive, too reform oriented, and too ambitious to be a cooperative member; instead, he seemed determined to be a spokesman for the have-nots in America. Kennedy's book, *Profiles in Courage*, which dealt with senators who chose to make difficult political decisions, won him a Pulitzer Prize in history, and he developed a reputation as an intellectual in politics. All this was training for the most demanding job in the world, the presidency. As president he found there were plenty of old and new problems that awaited his concern: poverty, racism, disease, inadequate education, and the Cold War.

The New Frontiersman

Part of the excitement of the Kennedy years was generated by a group of new, hard-working, talented people who came to Washington to help Kennedy solve these problems. President Kennedy asked able men and women from business, law, and the academic circles to advise him and to act as government leaders. This administration came armed with many new ideas and hoped to shake the American public from its comfortable, satisfied values. Many of these advisers, such as John Kenneth Galbraith, Dean Rusk, Arthur M. Schlesinger, Jr., Robert McNamara, Theodore Sorensen, Arthur Goldberg, Pierre Salinger, Lawrence O'Brien, George McGovern, and others, continued to be active in political and intellectual circles throughout the 1960s and 1970s. These leaders of the New Frontier brought a sense of mission, combined with wit and excitement, that made Washington, D.C., a greatly different place from what it had been under Eisenhower.

Problems with the New Frontier

Even though John Kennedy and his advisers brought new ideas, enthusiasm, and talent to Washington, their batting average of successful laws was not very high. Many Kennedy leaders were inexperienced in their relations with Congress. The Democratic majority Kennedy had in Congress was also misleading, because many southern Democrats voted with Republicans to oppose the New Frontier. Also, some of the early programs that were passed were not well run, which prejudiced legislators against Kennedy's ideas. The biggest problems that stood in the way of Kennedy's programs were a lack of enthusiastic support by the general public and real reservations, even hostility, toward his ideas among many business leaders. The country was prosperous and many people did not share the president's concern for the elderly, the sick, the poor, and the minorities.

Early Successes

Even though there were legislative failures, Kennedy had notable successes also. His inaugural address, in which he made his famous statement, "Ask not what your country can do for you, but what you can do for your country...."

set a high standard of dedication for many Americans. Young Americans responded by actively participating in the Peace Corps' efforts to help underdeveloped nations. Kennedy's Alliance for Progress offered hope, at least for the short run, that Hispanic-American nations would be able to solve their problems. Other notable successes were in tax reform, education, and space research. One of Kennedy's chief objectives was to reduce unemployment and increase the rate of economic growth in America.* This objective was achieved after several months of negotiating for legislation.

Kennedy and Big Business

The president was determined to stop the inflation that had been an unpleasant part of American life since 1946. He tried a variety of methods to accomplish this end: (1) guidelines to limit raises for labor union members, (2) tax law changes, and (3) attempts to urge business to hold the line on price increases. In 1962, a domestic problem developed. When steelworkers received a very slight increase in benefits, the major steel manufacturing companies announced price increases that exceeded the president's inflationary guidelines. Prior to this action, Vice President Lyndon Johnson had urged that attempts be made to seek the cooperation of business leaders with the Democratic administration. The president had assumed business would cooperate. When the steel producers ignored his request, John Kennedy believed he had been tricked and began to put pressure of government and of public opinion upon the steel men. Steel prices were reduced, but the stock market dropped, costing investors millions of dollars. Businessmen, as a result of 1962, believed more firmly than ever that Kennedy was hostile to their interests. In 1963, stock prices rebounded and the price of steel rose, but this time Kennedy did not oppose the increase. As a result, inflation started spiraling upward again.

Kennedy's Foreign Policy

Cuban Problems, Act 1

Since Fidel Castro had won control of Cuba by revolution during the Eisenhower administration, that island nation had been a thorn in America's side. A plan of the Joint Military Chiefs of Staff and the CIA (Central Intelligence Agency) for invasion of Cuba had been developed in 1960, and was set to go when Kennedy took over in 1961. The new president accepted the recommendation of the Joint Chiefs, and 1,200 Cuban exiles, trained and armed by America, invaded southern Cuba at the Bay of Pigs. In order for the plan to succeed, air superiority was needed. Unfortunately for the exiles, their air forces were not effective, and Kennedy was not willing to use the United States Air Force to provide air cover. Castro's force soon destroyed the expedition. Later, success-

---

* Today, ecologists are having afterthoughts about the desirability of this objective. Rapid economic growth is closely related to problems of pollution and waste.

ful efforts were made to rescue the imprisoned Cuban invaders through ransom payments of bulldozers, farm equipment, and money.

As a result of this disastrous attempt, the American image as the defender of freedom was somewhat bruised. Unlike many leaders, John Kennedy did not place the responsibility for failure on any *scapegoats* (someone picked to take blame); instead, he accepted full blame for the disaster. Kennedy was determined to make sure similar mistakes would not happen again, so he enlarged his staff of presidential advisers in order to have better sources of information before he took any major steps.

Cuba, Act 2

After the failure of the Bay of Pigs, the Russian Premier, Nikita Khrushchev, severely criticized the United States. Russia began to provide military help to Cuba, including sophisticated military equipment. In October 1962, aerial photographs from our spy planes showed that Russian technicians in Cuba had secretly constructed a number of guided missile sites, some of which could hit and damage the United States. Evidently the Russians hoped to pressure the United States into backing down in Berlin, the Middle East, and Indochina.

Kennedy and Nuclear Showdown

Rather than risk another Bay of Pigs, President Kennedy decided to take a different line of action—a naval and aircraft blockade or quarantine of Cuba to put pressure upon Russia in return. After building up the military in a way that looked as if he might invade Cuba, Kennedy began to secretly negotiate with the Russians from a position of strength. After a few nervous weeks, a compromise was worked out that satisfied both sides. The Russians dismantled their missiles in Cuba and the United States removed their obsolete Thor missiles from Turkey. Many Americans were dissatisfied with Kennedy for not taking stronger action and driving Castro and his Russian supporters out, but the Democratic gains in the election of 1962 indicated that most people were pleased by the president's action. In addition to the Cuban crisis, another crisis was bubbling on the back burner—Berlin.

Berlin

Following the pattern of many postwar leaders who are in political trouble, John Kennedy left for Vienna, Austria, in June 1961, for a summit conference about Berlin with Russia's Nikita Khrushchev. At that conference there was a severe confrontation between the Russians and Kennedy. As a result of that difficult meeting, the young president responded to Russian threats to take over Berlin by calling thousands of reservists to active duty. The Soviets responded in August 1961 by constructing the Berlin Wall, which was to cut off all communications between the two Germanies and prevent many people from escaping from behind the Iron Curtain for nearly a decade. The Berlin Wall was, of course, a monument to the failure of communism, but its very existence was a

P: Perfecting Reading Skills 155

symbol of oppression that bothered many Americans who felt Kennedy should have used force to eliminate this barrier.

After a quick review of your notes or markings, answer the following questions.

RECALL

1. What is the main idea of the passage regarding Kennedy's administration as president?

___

2. What made Kennedy so appealing to many voters?

___

3. Name three major problems Kennedy had to deal with early in his presidency.

___

4. What were some early successes Kennedy had?

___

INTERPRETATION

5. Does the author treat Kennedy in a favorable or nonfavorable way? Explain.

APPLICATION

6. What words did you learn from using context clues? (Skim back if necessary.)

7. Pick one of the following and write a short answer.
    a. Discuss ways Kennedy tried to stop inflation.
    b. What was the Bay of Pigs episode? What effect did it have on Kennedy's image?
    c. Discuss Kennedy's early career before becoming president.

8. Select a textbook from another class you are taking. Apply the following to your next reading assignment from it:
    a. Prepare to read by surveying first.
    b. Read from one heading to the next, marking the passage as you were shown.
    c. When finished, summarize the chapter on a separate sheet and turn it in to your instructor for this class.

Name _____ Section _____ Date _____

Chapter 5

Objectives

P: **PREREADING DRILLS**
Words to Know
Warm-up Drills

R: **READING DRILL**
Reading and Thinking About What You Read
"Computers and Work" by Arthur Luehrmann and Herbert Peckham
Comprehension Check

E: **EXERCISES IN VOCABULARY**
Drills
      1: Prefixes
      2: More Prefixes
      3: Suffixes
      4: Compound Words
      5: Homonym Review
      6: Words in Context
      7: Definition Review
Vocabulary Check

P: **PERFECTING READING SKILLS**
Comprehending Sentences Using Idioms
Comprehending Paragraphs: Main Ideas
Comprehending Health Textbook Passages: Applying Study-Reading Techniques
"Do Large Doses of Vitamin E Retard the Aging Process?" by Eva May Hamilton and Eleanor Noss Whitney

Objectives

When you have finished with this chapter, you will

1. Recognize and be able to use at least 90 percent of the vocabulary words listed in the Words to Know section.
2. Be able to name and use at least six pairs of homonyms used in this chapter.
3. Know the various meanings of the prefix *in* and name at least six words using it.
4. Know the meanings of the prefixes *ante, anti, mis, mal,* and *post.*
5. Know the meanings of and how to use the suffixes *ish, er, or, ful, able,* and *ible.*
6. Know at least five compound words.
7. Know how to define the term *compound words.*
8. Know how to use context clues in sentences to define key words.
9. Have developed your reading comprehension skills in drawing inferences and understanding idiomatic expressions.
10. Have developed your reading comprehension skills by applying study-reading techniques to textbook selections.

P: PREREADING DRILLS

WORDS TO KNOW

Directions: Read the following words aloud. Make sure you know their meanings. All the words are defined as they appear in the essay you will read in this chapter.

1. *dramatic*—full of excitement; unexpected, interesting conflict.
We have seen three rapid, dramatic changes in the type of work that most people do.
2. *vast*—large; great in size.
There was a vast movement of people from the farms to factory towns.
3. *trend*—a movement in a certain direction; a tendency to follow.
Today half the workers in the United States are information workers, and the trend is continuing.
4. *simulation*—imitation; pretending to be the real thing.
They run simulation programs and study the effects of a decision before they make it.
5. *pesticides*—chemicals used to kill pests, insects.
You need to know whether or not to use pesticides.
6. *on-line data base*—a large amount of information stored in such a way that a computer can take input or send output to the data base.
Real estate agents use an on-line data base to help clients find the house they want.
7. *repetitive*—over and over again.
A robot can do dull, repetitive work on an assembly line.
8. *programmers*—people who write special programs for computer use.
Application programming and systems programming are just two of the types of work computer programmers do.

WARM-UP DRILLS

DRILL 1

Directions: Read each of the following sentences. Write in the correct word from the choices under each sentence.

1. The computer plays a big _____ in the changes happening today.
   roll   role

2. Big _____ are under way for the farmer.
         charges changes

3. To be a successful farmer, you need more than good

   _____.
   weather whether

4. Robots are very _____ to factory owners because
         attraction attractive
   they never get bored or sloppy on the job.

5. A factory robot is a _____, such as a mechanical hand or
         devise device
   arm, that performs various motions.

6. Memos are entered _____ into a computer message
   system.   direct directly

7. Computers are _____ our work habits.
         changing charging

8. Experts _____ that the demand for people with computer
         prefer predict
   skills will remain for a long time.

9. We need to _____ many people on the job.
         refrain retrain

10. Our educational system is short of _____ and teachers
    needed to handle new computer courses. funs funds

DRILL 2

Directions: Move your eyes quickly from left to right. Mark the word by the number every time it appears on the same line. Work rapidly. Don't look back on a line, and don't change any mistakes. Try to finish in thirty-five seconds or less.
Begin timing.

1. ever   every   even   ever   even   ever   every
2. though   though   through   though   through   through
3. leaves   leave   leaf   leaves   leave   leaves

P: Prereading Drills

4.	stepped	stopped	stopped	stepped	stopped	stepped	
5.	ashore	ashes	ashore	ashame	ashame	ashore	
6.	amaze	amuse	amuse	amaze	amuse	amaze	
7.	brought	brought	bought	bought	bought	brought	
8.	chewing	chew	chewed	crewing	chewing	chewing	
9.	cheap	cheep	cheap	cheap	cheap	cheaply	
10.	fad	fade	fad	fad	fade	fade	
11.	expensive	expensive	expansive	expansion	expensive		
12.	quit	quite	quiet	quit	quite	quiet	quit
13.	industry	industrial	industry	industrious	industrial		
14.	blend	blond	blown	blend	blender	blended	
15.	crops	corpse	cops	crops	corpse	cops	crops

TIME: _____

Check each line carefully. Make certain you underlined the correct word on each line. Learn any words you don't know.

TOTAL LINES CORRECT: _____

DRILL 3

Directions: Follow the same directions as in the last drill. The only difference here is that you will be looking for a two-word phrase, not a single word. For example:

1. green leaves   green eyes   green leaves   green house
2. new custom   new costume   new candy   new custom

Try to finish in forty seconds or less.
Begin timing.

1. vile odor   file order   vile aroma   vile odor
2. curious mind   curious mink   curious mind   curious cat
3. dried leaves   dead leaves   dried lunch   dried leaves
4. not accepted   now accepted   not accepted   not expected
5. next crop   next corpse   next cop   next crop
6. tripled sales   tripled sales   tripled sails   tripled sales
7. published report   published book   published report

Copyright © 1988 Holt, Rinehart and Winston, Inc.

8. tobacco blend   tobacco blend   tobacco book   tobacco crop
9. old habit   old hobby   old habit   old house   old habit
10. new situation   nice situation   now situated   new situation
11. milder taste   milky taste   milder taste   milder touch
12. quite vile   quit now   quite mild   quite vile
13. nicotine fit   nicotine fad   nicotine fit   nicotine time
14. cheaply made   cheap maid   cheaply run   cheaply made
15. brought ashore   brought home   brought ashore   brought

TIME: _____

Check each line carefully. Some lines may have the phrase more than once. Learn any words or phrases you don't know.

TOTAL LINES CORRECT: _____

DRILL 4

Directions: Follow the same directions as in the last drill. Work quickly. Try to finish in thirty seconds or less.
Begin timing.

1. beautiful scenery   beautiful hills   beauty   beautiful scenery
2. clever situation   clever fellow   clever situation   clever mind
3. even desirable   every desire   even decide   even desirable
4. probably due   probably dew   probably due   probably do
5. some smoke   some smoke   some stuff   some smokers
6. don't want   don't wait   don't want   don't waste
7. receive millions   receive much   receive   receive millions
8. cancer-causing   cancer-caused   cancer   cancer-causing
9. related to   relieved to   related two   related to   related to
10. beat faster   beat slower   beat faster   beat fast
11. was published   was published   was perished   published
12. more cases   more causes   more cases   more causes
13. the nonsmokers   the nonsmokers   the nun smokers
14. federal taxes   federal tacks   federal tax   federal taxes
15. blood pressure   blood relative   blood pressure   block pressure

TIME: _____

P: Prereading Drills **163**

Check each line for mistakes. Some lines may have the phrase more than once. Learn any words you don't know.

Total lines correct: _____

DRILL 5

Directions: Before you go on, make certain you know all the words in the first two drills.

R: READING DRILL

READING AND THINKING ABOUT WHAT YOU READ

Directions: Take a minute to look over the following essay. Don't read it. Just answer these questions:

1. Based on the title, what do you think the essay is about? _____

   _____

   _____

2. Write in the titles of each of the four major headings in the essay.

   1st heading: _____

   2d heading: _____

   3d heading: _____

   4th heading: _____

3. Now what do you think the essay will be about? _____

   _____

   _____

   _____

4. Do you think the essay will be *for* or *against* computers? _____

   Why? _____

   _____

   _____

   _____

Now read the following chapter from a computer literacy textbook.

COMPUTERS AND WORK

ARTHUR LUEHRMANN AND HERBERT PECKHAM

A Century of Working

In the last hundred years, we have seen three rapid, dramatic changes in the type of work that most people do. The computer plays a big role in the change happening today.

100 Years Ago

Your great-great-great-grandparents probably lived on a farm. A century ago, more than half of all American workers were still farmers, but big changes were under way. Farm machinery was making it possible for fewer and fewer people to grow more and more food. The factories that made farm machinery and other products needed workers. So there was a vast movement of people from the farms to the factory towns.

50 Years Ago

Your grandparents probably grew up and worked at jobs in a city. Fifty years ago the majority of work was in manufacturing trades: welding, sewing garments, operating looms, building houses, and working on an assembly line. Only two people out of every ten were farmers then. People in cities had money to spend and needed new services: grocery stores, laundries, department stores, entertainment, and education. Jobs in service industries grew rapidly.

Today

Even fewer people work on farms today; less than one job in 30 is a farm job now. The number of manufacturing jobs is also shrinking: There are more jobs in service industries today than in manufacturing. The biggest new growth today is in the number of information workers—people whose main work is handling and processing information: secretaries, bank clerks, office managers, accountants, lawyers, and teachers. Fifty years ago, only two people in ten were information workers. Today, half the workers in the United States are information workers, and the trend is continuing.

Computers and Jobs

Farm machines made farm work easier and more efficient. Factory machines made factory work easier and more efficient. It should not come as a surprise that information machines—computers—are making information work easier and more efficient. But computers are also changing farm work and factory work.

From Computer Literacy, *by Arthur Luehrmann and Herbert Peckham, McGraw-Hill Book Co., copyright © 1983, pp. 358–362. Reprinted by permission.*

The Modern Farmer

To be a successful farmer, you need more than land, good weather, and machinery. You also need information. You need to know what risks you run by planting too early or too late, how much to spend on fertilizer, when to apply it, whether to use pesticides, and so on. To get help with decisions such as these, many farmers are buying small computers. They run simulation programs and study the effect of a decision before they make it.

Factory Robots

Many jobs on a factory assembly line, such as inserting bolt number 37 into hole number 23 and tightening it, are repetitive and boring. These mechanical jobs can often be done better and more cheaply by **robots.** Factory robots are different from the robots you see walking around in movies. A factory robot is a device, such as a mechanical hand or arm, that performs various motions. A computer is programmed to send output signals that tell the robot what to do. Some robots also send back information about what the robot is touching to the computer. Robots are very attractive to factory owners because they never get bored or sloppy, they work 24 hours a day in unheated rooms with no lights, and they never stay home sick.

The Modern Office

The people who work in an office do little or no physical labor. They do not grow food or build things. Instead, they work almost entirely with information: letters, memos, reports, budgets, and expenses. Computers are now essential tools for handling office information. Letters are typed on a **word-processing system,** a computer used mainly for writing, editing, and typing letters and papers. Memos are entered directly into a computer **message system.** The person getting the memo can read it immediately on the computer screen in her or his office. Computer software helps people plan budgets, estimate expenses, and study reports.

The Computer on the Desk

More and more workers have computers at their fingertips. The bank teller checks your bank account on a computer screen. The travel agent uses a computer system to reserve tickets on an airline or rooms at a hotel. The checkout clerk at the supermarket uses a cash register connected to a computer. Real estate agents use an on-line data base to help clients find the house they want. Newspaper reporters search data bases for news information and then write their stories on a computer system. Mail-order and telephone-order clerks enter each order into a computer system.

Computer Jobs at Home

Why do office workers have to go to the office? Until now, the main reason has been that the information they needed was at the office. Networks of computers now make it possible to do most office work wherever there is a computer and a telephone. For this reason, many people today can work at home; they use computers to get and send information. Handicapped people, parents of young children, and other homebound people now are able to enter the work force.

Problems for Society

Computers are changing our work habits in both good and bad ways. Computers create opportunities, but they also pose problems that must be solved.

Boring Work

Not all computer applications lead to exciting jobs. Data entry is an example. Thousands of people spend all day reading numbers from sheets of paper and entering them into a computer. This work is often necessary, but it does not make people happy.

Loss of Jobs

We should be happy that a robot can keep a human being from having to do dull, repetitive work on an assembly line. But what happens to the person who used to do that dull job? Does another job automatically appear? If not, what should such a person do? Most studies show that new technologies create about the same number of jobs that they replace. Farm machines replaced farmers but created new jobs in farm-machinery factories. Computers replace some workers but create new jobs for programmers. Unfortunately, the person who loses a job to a computer system is not usually the same person who gets a job as a programmer.

Need for Education

Experts predict that the demand for people with computer skills will remain far ahead of the supply for many years to come. Schools and colleges, therefore, are under strong pressure to teach more computer courses to more students. We also need to retrain people who lose their jobs to computer systems. Yet our educational system is short of funds and teachers able to handle the new computer courses.

Unequal Opportunity

Computers do not affect everyone in the same way. Not everyone has the same chance to benefit from the computer revolution. A child in a neighborhood where parents are unemployed or work in manual jobs has a much lower chance of learning about computers than a child in a neighborhood where parents work in information jobs. The first child is likely to grow up with only manual skills at a time when there are fewer and fewer manual jobs. The second child is likely to be ready for the new information jobs. This inequality is a problem for the whole society.

Computer Careers

As we said, demand for people with computer skills is far ahead of the supply. Now is a good time to think about a career in computing. In this section, we look at careers that involve close work with computers and at the education needed for each career.

Office Information Systems

As offices and small businesses make greater use of computers for word processing, messages, and data processing, they usually need someone to manage the entire information system. Such a person needs to understand the work of the office or the business as well as the role of the computer. A general knowledge of word processing and computer accounting is important.

Application Programming

People who write special-purpose programs for other people are called **application programmers.** They usually know two or three computer languages, such as BASIC, COBOL, Pascal, or FORTRAN. A college degree in computer science or a business degree with four or five computer courses is good preparation for this work. You will need a good math background for either degree.

System Programming

As you know, BASIC on your computer is itself a set of computer programs: the LIST program, the RUN program, and so forth. These are called system programs, and people who write them are called **system programmers.** They also design data bases and the programs that use data bases. System programmers need to know the same things that application programmers know. In addition, they need a stronger computer-science background, including knowledge of machine languages and computer design.

Computer Engineering

The people who design and build computer hardware are called **computer engineers.** They usually prepare for this work by studying electrical engineering and computer science in a five-year college program.

COMPREHENSION CHECK

Directions: Answer the following questions without looking back.

RECALL

1. What was the main type of job in the United States one hundred years ago? _____

R: Reading Drills

2. What was the main type of job in the United States fifty years ago? ____

3. Today half the workers in the United States are ____

4. How are computers used in factories? ____

5. How does a computer make it possible for an office worker to work at home? ____

INTERPRETATION

6. Are all computer jobs interesting and exciting? Explain.

7. Do computers take away jobs from people? Explain. ____

8. Why is it a problem if too many people in a society have only manual skills? _____

_____

_____

_____

APPLICATION

9. Which of the computer careers discussed hold some interest as a possible career for you? Explain. _____

_____

_____

_____

10. What did you learn from reading this selection? _____

_____

_____

_____

Name _____ Section _____ Date _____

E: EXERCISES IN VOCABULARY

DRILLS

DRILL 1: PREFIXES

Directions: In the last chapter you learned the prefixes *dis, im, in, ir,* and *un.* They all mean "not" or "opposite of." The prefix *in* can also mean "in" or "into," as in *indoors.* In the blank in front of the following words, write whether the prefix *in* means "not" or "in." The first one has been done.

1. __*not*__ inactive
2. _____ infield
3. _____ independent
4. _____ ingrown
5. _____ informal
6. _____ indirect
7. _____ insane
8. _____ inhale
9. _____ insecure
10. _____ inside
11. _____ inexact
12. _____ inland
13. _____ inexpensive
14. _____ inhuman
15. _____ indent
16. _____ inexact
17. _____ incapable
18. _____ inspect
19. _____ invisible
20. _____ invade

DRILL 2: MORE PREFIXES

Directions: Study the following prefixes and their meanings. Then define the words that follow on the next page.

Prefix	Definition
ante	before
anti	against or opposite
mis	wrongly
mal	badly
post	after

1. antedate _____

2. antiballistic missile _____
_____

3. misbehave _____

4. malfunction _____

5. postdate _____

6. anteroom _____

7. antifreeze _____

8. mispronounce _____

9. maladjusted _____

10. postwar _____

DRILL 3: SUFFIXES

Directions: Study the following suffixes and their meanings. Then answer the questions that follow.

Suffix	Definition	Examples
able, ible	can be done	enjoyable, inducible
ance, ence	state of being	acceptance, dependence
tion, ion	state of being	protection, collection
ful	full of	skillful, peaceful
er, or	degree; person	greater, inspector
ish	like; belong to	childish, Spanish

A. Make the following words mean "people" by adding the correct suffix from the preceding list.

1. sail _____   6. conduct _____

2. farm _____   7. swim _____

E: *Exercises in Vocabulary*

3. employ _____   8. teach _____

4. act _____   9. visit _____

5. wait _____   10. govern _____

B. Make the following words mean "full of" by adding the correct suffix from the list of suffixes just given.

1. peace _____   6. success _____

2. pain _____   7. hand _____

3. doubt _____   8. distrust _____

4. bash _____   9. purpose _____

5. skill _____   10. mind _____

C. Change the following words to mean "like" or "belong to" by adding the correct suffix.

1. self _____   6. Jew _____

2. fool _____   7. shrew _____

3. Scot _____   8. fever _____

4. style _____   9. wolf _____

5. green _____   10. sheep _____

D. Change the following words by adding the correct suffix. (Don't use *ed* or *ing*.)

1. accept _____   6. differ _____

2. assist _____   7. protect _____

3. deliver _____   8. perish _____

4. convert _____   9. reverse _____

5. depend _____   10. response _____

DRILL 4: COMPOUND WORDS

Directions: Compound words are words made up of two or more words. Following are some compound words. Fill in the blanks in the sentences with the correct compound word.

sailboat overcook
mailman nightgown
password seaman
bathroom tablecloth
newspaper handbag

1. Tibb is in the room where you take a bath (_____).

2. Do you want to buy a powerboat or a boat that sails (_____)?

3. You'll need to be a good man of the sea (_____) in order to sail that one.

4. Mom bought a new covering for the table (_____) when she went shopping.

5. While shopping, she almost had the bag she carries her money in (_____) stolen.

6. Mom also bought me a new gown to sleep in (_____) because mine was ruined in the washer.

7. I was left to finish dinner, but I am afraid I let the meat cook too long (_____).

8. The sentry wanted the soldier to give the word that allowed him to pass through the gate (_____), but the soldier forgot it.

9. The man who brings the mail (_____) is late today.

10. The daily paper that contains news (_____) is going up to thirty cents a copy.

E: Exercises in Vocabulary

DRILL 5: HOMONYM REVIEW

Directions: Read each sentence that follows. In the blank, write the correct homonym from under the sentence. Use the dictionary if necessary.

1. I needed to borrow _____ dictionary.
   there   their   they're

2. The police were on the _____ of the accident five minutes after the call.
   seen   scene

3. Please don't take the _____ on my desk.
   stationary   stationery

4. Thelma doesn't know _____ or not her horse will get well.
   weather   whether

5. She needs a new _____ for her horse.
   bridal   bridle

6. As the song says, "Nobody knows the trouble I've _____."
   scene   seen

7. _____ one should he buy?
   Witch   Which

8. The dog was on the _____ of the escaped convict.
   cent   scent

9. Because Terry was a _____, the man in the liquor store would not sell him any booze.
   minor   miner

10. Mr. Diaz did not have enough _____ to start his own business.
    capital   capitol

11. I confess my story was not _____ correct.
    holy   wholly

12. The cat tore the _____ on my skirt.
    seem   seam

13. The convict was caught and sent back to his _____.
    sell   cell

14. It's not nice to _____ at someone.
    stair   stare

15. Look in that _____ brown box in the corner.
    plane   plain

DRILL 6: WORDS IN CONTEXT

Directions: Following are some words with more than one definition. In the blanks, write in the definition that fits the way the sentence uses the word.

1. *meet:* to gather together; to pay; to be introduced to; to come face to face.

    a. The club will meet every Tuesday. _____

    b. The teacher wanted to meet my parents. _____

    c. The company is afraid he won't meet his debts. _____

2. *cross:* angry; mix or mingle; a symbol; to go from one side to another.

    a. The little girl was afraid to cross the street. _____

    b. In the lab, we crossed a cat with a fish and got a catfish! _____

    c. What's Al so cross about? _____

3. *heavy:* weighty; intense; severe; sad; boring.

    a. Late last night we got a heavy rain. _____

E: Exercises in Vocabulary

    b. The heavy snow on the limb of the tree caused it to break. _____

    c. The movie was so heavy to bear that I wanted to leave. _____

4. *form:* (as a verb) to instruct; to develop; to shape; to take shape; (as a noun) type; shape; paper; document.

    a. The clouds began to form over the mountains. _____

    b. Parents have much to do with forming a child's attitude about life.

    c. Please sign this form on the broken line. _____

5. *spirit:* mood or feelings; ghost; energy.

    a. We need to show the team our school spirit. _____

    b. My spirits have been high ever since Jan said she'd go out with me.

    c. Some say an evil spirit still lives in that old house. _____

DRILL 7: DEFINITION REVIEW

Directions: Match the letter of the definition in the right column with the word in the left column. There are more definitions than words.

_____ 1. dramatic   a. nasty

_____ 2. vast   b. large

_____ 3. trend   c. full of action, conflict, or changes

_____ 4. simulation   d. dangerous chemicals

_____ 5. pesticides   e. hidden

_____ 6. data base   f. one who writes computer input data

_____ 7. repetitive   g. imitation

_____ 8. programmer   h. over and over

_____ 9. discrepancies   i. invitation

_____ 10. obscure   j. tendency to follow

                                                     k. information stored on computer

                                                     l. differences; disagreements

VOCABULARY CHECK

Part A

Directions: Write a sentence for each of the following words.

1. scene: _____

_____

2. stationery: _____

_____

3. antisocial: _____

_____

4. capital: _____

_____

E: Exercises in Vocabulary 179

5. misrepresent: _____

_____

Part B

Directions: In the blanks, write the prefix *in* if it can change the following root words.

1. _____ formal   6. _____ dent
2. _____ payable   7. _____ secure
3. _____ dependence   8. _____ resent
4. _____ lunge   9. _____ field
5. _____ variable   10. _____ capable

Part C

Directions: Circle the suffixes in the following words. Draw a line under any compound words.

1. selfish   6. distrustful   11. careless   16. timetable
2. painful   7. powerful   12. waiter   17. misread
3. homemade   8. preference   13. conductor   18. maladjusted
4. wolfish   9. securely   14. deliverance 19. unknown
5. tenderness   10. tiptoe   15. handful   20. antiwar

Part D

Directions: Answer the following questions.

1. What prefix can mean "in" or "not"? _____

2. What suffixes are used to make words mean "people"? _____

_____

3. What suffix is used to mean "full of"? _____

_____

Copyright © 1988 Holt, Rinehart and Winston, Inc.

4. What suffix is used to mean "like" or "belong to"? _____

_____

5. What is a compound word? _____

_____

6. What is meant by the contextual meaning of a word? _____

_____

_____

7. What prefix means "bad" or "badly"? _____

8. What prefix means "before"? _____

9. What prefix means "after"? _____

10. What does the prefix *mis* mean? _____

Name _____ Section _____ Date _____

P: PERFECTING READING SKILLS

COMPREHENDING SENTENCES USING IDIOMS

Directions: Read each sentence, and answer the questions that follow it to see if you understand the idiomatic expressions used. Idiomatic expressions are colorful, sometimes slang, ways of saying things.

1. Pablo's work is a far cry from that of his brother's.

    a. Does the sentence mean Pablo's work is better than his brother's? _____

    b. What does "a far cry" mean? _____

2. Look, Gino, just be honest; tell them you did it, and face the music.

    a. Is Gino guilty of something? _____

    b. How do you know? _____

3. Gino is afraid he will get a raw deal if he tells them because they never liked him in the first place.

    a. What does "raw deal" mean? _____

    b. Why is Gino afraid of them? _____

4. Follow my advice, Gino, and I'll stick by you through thick and thin.

    a. Is the person talking to Gino a friend? _____

    b. How do you know? _____

5. Grandpa was under the weather last week, but he says he's fit as a fiddle now.

181

a. What was wrong with Grandpa last week? _____

_____

b. Is he feeling well now? _____
6. You must learn to keep your nose to the grindstone, or you'll never get your work done.

   a. What does the sentence mean? _____

   _____

   b. What picture or image do you get in your mind when you read "keep your nose to the grindstone"? _____

   _____

7. Bill, will you just lay off! Going out with you is out of the question.

   a. Is Bill "bugging" someone for a date? _____

   b. Does it sound as though he will get a date with that person? _____

   c. Why? _____

   _____

8. Lee loaned Janet the money, but she skipped town and left him holding the bag.

   a. Does Janet sound like a good friend to have? _____

   b. Is it likely that Lee will get his money back? _____
9. The first day of class Curt felt like a fish out of water.

   a. Does the sentence mean Curt was taking swimming lessons?

   _____

   b. Did Curt like the first day of class? _____

   c. How do you know? _____

   _____

10. My son monkeyed around with something under the hood, and the engine started right up.

P: *Perfecting Reading Skills* 183

a. What was the son doing? _____

_____

b. Does it seem that the son knew what he was doing? _____

_____

c. How do you know? _____

_____

COMPREHENDING PARAGRAPHS: MAIN IDEAS

Directions: Practice underlining main ideas as you read the following paragraphs, and answer the questions that follow each.

1. Usually, you can spot smokers even when they are not smoking. The odor of smoke is on their clothes. Sometimes tiny burn holes from ashes appear on their clothing. Their fingers are often yellow or brown from holding cigarettes. Teeth also show stains from nicotine. And some smokers have developed a "smoker's hack" or cough.

    a. What is the main idea of the paragraph? _____

    _____

    _____

    b. What word or words could be used in the first sentence to replace

    "spot smokers"? _____

    _____

    c. Could this paragraph be used in a cigarette ad? _____ Why?

    _____

    _____

2. Some smokers get what is called "hairy tongue." This is a brown or black furlike coating on the tongue. "Hairy tongue" is caused by chemicals in smoke that keep the dead cells of the tongue's surface from wearing away

as they normally would. The little bumps on the tongue (papillae) grow longer than normal if you smoke. Food gets caught in the papillae and causes bad breath.

    a. What is the main idea of the paragraph? _____

_____

_____

    b. Why do smokers often have bad breath? _____

_____

3. One of the dangers of smoking mentioned in the Surgeon General's report is lung cancer. It has been found that the lung cancer rate for smokers is ten times higher than for nonsmokers. A person who smokes a pack of cigarettes a day is twenty times more likely to die of cancer than the nonsmoker. The cancer is caused by the tar and nicotine in cigarettes. These change and destroy lung cells. The new cells that develop become cancerous. Since cancer cells grow rapidly, they destroy normal cells. Soon the cancer cells take over. They then can enter the bloodstream. The result is often damage to the liver and brain.

    a. What is the main idea of the paragraph? _____

_____

_____

    b. Why does smoking cigarettes cause lung cancer? _____

_____

_____

_____

_____

    c. Do you believe the information in this paragraph? _____

        Why? _____

P: Perfecting Reading Skills 185

4. Smoking is also dangerous to your circulatory system. Your circulatory system is made up of your heart, arteries, and veins. Your heart is a muscle that pumps blood through your body. The blood that flows through your arteries brings food and oxygen to all the cells in the body. The veins carry away the cells' waste matter. Nicotine in cigarette smoke makes the heart beat faster. This raises the pressure of the blood in your arteries, causing high blood pressure.

   a. What is the main idea of the paragraph? _____

   b. How does the circulatory system work? _____

   c. Why can cigarette smoking cause high blood pressure? _____

5. In many places, requests to limit smoking in public places are being made. For example, in both Arizona and Connecticut, smoking in public meetings is against the law. The New York City Council banned smoking in certain public places, such as classrooms, supermarkets, and elevators. Right now the fine is fifteen days in jail and a $50 fine. But once the law is better known, the penalty will be one year in jail and a $1,000 fine. Because of the difficulty in enforcing the law, the rules are always being broken.

   a. What is the main idea of the paragraph? _____

b. Do the laws mentioned in the paragraph seem fair to you? _____

Why? _____

_____

_____

c. Do you think smoking should be illegal in public places? _____

Why? _____

_____

_____

COMPREHENDING HEALTH TEXTBOOK PASSAGES: APPLYING STUDY-READING TECHNIQUES

Directions: The following passage is from a health textbook similar to one you may use in a health class. Apply the skills you have learned:

1. Prepare before you read.
2. Read from heading to heading.
3. Use context clues to understand unfamiliar words.
4. Examine each section read by marking, underlining, or taking notes.
5. Review the passage before answering the questions that follow it.

DO LARGE DOSES OF VITAMIN E RETARD THE AGING PROCESS?

EVA MAY HAMILTON AND ELEANOR NOSS WHITNEY

What Vitamin E Does

1   It acts as an antioxidant, protecting red cell (and other) membranes from being destroyed by oxygen. In premature infants, whose immature lungs are

Reprinted by permission from Nutrition: Concepts and Controversies, *2d ed., by Eva May Hamilton and Eleanor Noss Whitney. Copyright © 1982 by West Publishing Company. All rights reserved.*

especially vulnerable to oxidation, this effect is especially important. It is only at the very end of pregnancy that the mother's blood concentration of vitamin E rises so that the infant will receive protective amounts; the premature baby is born without this extra vitamin E and so has a deficiency. Without supplemental doses, such a baby will develop anemia from breakage of the red blood cells (hemolytic anemia).

2   The lungs experience a higher oxygen concentration than any other part of the body except the skin. Many of the recently confirmed effects of vitamin E have to do with the antioxidant protection of lung cells and red blood cells (as they pass through the lungs):

- Preventing human red blood cells from the damage done by oxidizing air pollutants (at doses up to 200 IU per day but not higher).
- Promoting survival of infants born with severe respiratory distress.
- Helping to keep the red blood cells from assuming abnormal shapes and losing their usefulness in sickle-cell anemia.
- Improving red cell survival in other rare disorders.

3   Other cells of the blood may also be dependent on vitamin E for some of their functions. The white cells, which are responsible for fighting off the challenge of infection, function better when they have enough vitamin E—at least, judging from experiments with animals. And the cells of the liver, which are damaged by certain kinds of poisons, can also be protected by vitamin E.

4   Three other tissues have been seen to respond to vitamin E under very special circumstances. One is the lens of the eye in rats that were made diabetic-like: large vitamin doses given by injection prevented them from getting cataracts, as they would otherwise have done. This may have no application to any human situation but may lead to useful research showing how vitamin E works. The second is the tissue of the human breast. Some women develop lumps which are not cancerous but are composed of fibrous tissue, and this unexplained symptom can be relieved in some cases by large doses (600 IU) of vitamin E. The third is the muscles of the calves, in which cramping can sometimes be relieved by administration of vitamin E.

5   Finally (while still on the subject of what vitamin E *does*), it is important to remember that any vitamin deficiency causes symptoms that that vitamin can relieve. Vitamin E deficiency in humans is very, very rare, but it does turn up occasionally. It has been seen, as already mentioned, in premature infants, in sickle-cell anemia, and other rare lung and blood disorders. It is also seen in cases where hospital patients (babies and even adults) are fed formulas that don't contain the vitamin, or when people can't absorb fats, or when they have been exposed to poisons that destroy it. Under these conditions, disorders of the brain, the muscles, the eyes, and the heart have occasionally been seen.

What It Doesn't Do

6	During the 1960s and 1970s some tremendous claims were made for vitamin E. It was said to improve athletic endurance and skill, to increase potency and enhance sexual performance, to prolong the life of the heart, and to reverse the damage caused by atherosclerosis and even heart attacks. An immense amount of experimentation has discredited these and many similar claims. To give one example: Doses of 1600 IU a day given to forty-eight patients for six months had no effect on chest pain (angina), exercise capacity, heart function, or other factors related to heart disease. Vitamin E also does not help with:

- Lowering high blood lipids, including cholesterol.
- "Hot flashes."
- Bladder cancer.

Nor does it have any effect on other processes of aging, such as the graying of the hair, wrinkling of the skin, and reduced capacity of body organs to perform their functions.

What Vitamin E Megadoses Do

7	It has been said that, even though the vitamin may not do all that is claimed for it, there can be no harm in taking supplements because it has no harmful effects even in very large doses. In fact, vitamin E does remain one of the few vitamins for which reports of toxicity are rare. There are isolated reports in the medical literature of adverse effects on laboratory animals and of nausea, intestinal distress, and other vague complaints in human beings. However, the impression remains that "for most individuals daily doses below 300 IU are innocuous." But with the recent interest in new research have come new reports of toxicity even for "harmless E."

8	In one study, 300 IU per day of vitamin E given to men and boys impaired the ability of their white blood cells to respond to a challenge by infection with bacteria. Too high a ratio of vitamin E to vitamin K may interfere with the clotting action of the latter, cause uncontrolled bleeding, and decrease the rate of wound healing. In animals, where more informative experiments can be conducted, vitamin E megadoses have dramatic effects on many body organs including the bones and the heart, effects which the investigators concluded were clearly harmful. Dr. Victor Herbert, whose conscientious research into the nonexistence of "vitamin B_{15}" was described in Controversy 9, has reminded *Nutrition Reviews* readers that, now that so many people are taking megadoses of vitamin E, we are beginning to see cases where damage is real and severe. That damage involves the very same areas people want to improve with their self-dosing; their vision, sex organs, skin, muscles, blood, and nerves.

Personal Strategy

9   It probably remains true that people taking large doses of vitamin E have a better chance of escaping unharmed than they would with many other vitamins and with most of the minerals. For most people, there may be few hazards associated with taking vitamin E supplements other than those to the pocketbook—and if a psychological boost results from the dose, it may be worth the price. Only in one situation is there certain danger: If taking vitamin E lulls a user into postponing a trip to the doctor for correct diagnosis and treatment of a serious condition, then it may cost more than anyone can afford to pay.

10   But if you actually want to remain young, there are some far more effective strategies than playing games with vitamin pills, and they require taking a broader perspective. Good nutrition is one—but not the only—factor involved in prolonging the body's health and vigor into the later years. It's a matter of lifestyle—all elements relating to health.

11   A study designed by Belloc and Breslow probed the question of what aspects of lifestyle promote good health and came up with some informative answers. Their study explored the relationship of a number of personal health practices to the state of health in a sample of almost 7000 persons in California. Those who followed all of the "good" practices were in better health at every age than those who followed none or a few.

12   And what were these health practices? Taking vitamin E capsules was not one of them. They were:

- Getting adequate sleep.
- Eating regular meals.
- Maintaining desirable weight.
- Not smoking.
- Drinking alcohol moderately or not at all.
- Getting regular exercise.

13   These answers are not surprising. But it is fitting to end this book's presentation by putting nutrition back into perspective as part of a larger picture. The six practices listed here lay the groundwork for the ability to enjoy, in good health, "the best years of life for which the first were made."

14   A ninety-year-old landscape gardener at his annual checkup asked the doctor, "How am I doing?" Truthfully, the doctor replied, "Well, old man, you're not getting any younger." "But doctor," the old man countered, "I don't ask to get younger. I only ask to get older! I have more trees to plant."

Review your notes or markings before answering the following questions.

RECALL

1. Large doses of vitamin E slow the aging process.
   a. true
   b. false
2. Which of the following does vitamin E do in humans?
   a. prevents red blood cell damage from oxidizing air pollutants
   b. helps reduce severe respiratory distress in infants
   c. helps keep red blood cells from forming abnormal shapes
   d. improves red cell survival in some rare disorders
   e. all of the above
3. Which of the following does vitamin E *not* do in humans?
   a. helps lower high blood lipids
   b. prevents "hot flashes"
   c. retards bladder cancer
   d. improves athletic endurance
   e. none of the above
4. Too much vitamin E (megadoses) can be harmful.
   a. true
   b. false
5. What strategies are suggested if you want to remain in better than average health? (Each answer counts as one.)

   a. _____

   b. _____

   c. _____

   d. _____

   e. _____

   f. _____

INTERPRETATION

6. Do the authors believe everyone should take vitamin E? Explain.

_____

_____

_____

P: Perfecting Reading Skills

APPLICATION

7. Are you interested in taking vitamin E after reading the passage? Explain. _____

_____

8. What did you learn from reading this selection that will help your health? _____

_____

_____

_____

Name _____ Section _____ Date _____

Chapter 6

Objectives

P: **PREREADING DRILLS**
Words to Know
Warm-up Drills
R: **READING DRILL**
Reading and Thinking About What You Read
"On Teaching the First Grade" by Carl Sagan
Comprehension Check
E: **EXERCISES IN VOCABULARY**
Drills
       1: Words Often Confused
       2: Prefix Review
       3: More Prefixes
       4: Suffix Review
       5: More Suffixes
       6: Compound Words
       7: Words in Context
       8: Definition Review
Vocabulary Check
P: **PERFECTING READING SKILLS**
Comprehending Sentences
Comprehending Paragraphs
Comprehending Science Textbook Passages: Applying Study Reading Techniques
"Origin of the Earth" by Arthur Beiser and Konrad B. Kranskopf

UNIT 2   CHECK TEST (Chapters 4–6)
       1: Word Knowledge
       2: Word Usage
       3: Comprehending Paragraphs
       4: Essay Reading
"Big Business: Selling Cancer" by Walter Raleigh

Objectives

When you have finished this chapter you will

1. Recognize and be able to use at least 90 percent of the vocabulary words listed in the Words to Know section.
2. Have learned or reviewed at least thirty words that are often confused, such as *accept* and *except*, *breath* and *breathe*, and *decent* and *descent*.
3. Know the definitions of and how to use the prefixes *pre, de, dis,* and *re*.
4. Know how to use the suffixes *al, ive, ment, est, er,* and *ous*.
5. Know how to use compound words to shorten phrases and sentences.
6. Know how to use various context clues to define unfamiliar words.
7. Have developed your reading comprehension skills in recognizing main ideas, drawing inferences, comparing and contrasting, and interpreting what you read.

P: PREREADING DRILLS

WORDS TO KNOW

Here are some words that are in the article you will be reading in this chapter. Learn the definitions of the ones you don't know.

   1. *astronomy*—the scientific study of the universe beyond earth. (*astronomical*—[a] pertaining to astronomy; [b] a huge amount)
The ancient Greeks considered *astronomy* one of the half dozen or so subjects required for the education of free people.
   2. *astrology*—studying the stars to predict their influence on humans.
Most newspapers in America have a daily syndicated *astrology* column.
   3. *nebulae*—plural of nebula, a wide mass of interstellar dust or gas.
Scientists believe that stars develop when *nebulae* contract and condense.
   4. *cherubic*—chubby; rosy; innocent.
I looked at their bright-eyed, cherubic faces.
   5. *initial*—first; beginning.
Dr. Sagan *initially* underestimated the first-graders when he talked about astronomy.
   6. *reverently*—feeling respect or showing devotion to.
For most of the history of humankind, it was *reverently* held that the earth was flat.
   7. *coup de grace*—the final stroke.
As the *coup de grace,* one pinafored little girl casually inquired about the Foucault pendulum experiment.
   8. *regimenting*—organizing; systematizing.
I very much hope these children can survive twelve to twenty years of our *regimented* "education."
   9. *cosmic perspective*—a view of the relationship between earth and the cosmos; a wide-ranging view of things.
We should make an effort to learn more about science and technology and to see ourselves in a more *cosmic perspective* if we are to insure our survival.
10. *confrontation*—a conflict; a face-to-face disagreement.
Most students can pass from the first to the twelfth grade without any *confrontation* with the cosmic perspective.
11. *pervades*—spreads throughout.
Astrology pretends to describe an influence that *pervades* people's lives.
12. *sham*—phony; not true or real.
Most scientists believe astrology is a *sham*.

P: Prereading Drills

WARM-UP DRILLS

DRILL 1

Directions: Read each sentence that follows. Under each sentence are two words. Write in the correct word in the blank. Spell it correctly.

1. The rumor about the instructor's heart attack proved to be a _____; he's quite well.
      sham   shame

2. The _____ Sue had with her husband ruined her day.   confronting   confrontation

3. Some feel that our educational system is too _____
regimentation regimenting
and does not teach students to think for themselves.

4. Doe always did what she was told _____ and without question.   reverently reverent

5. The _____ dive into the water is always the worst.
           initially initial

6. The children's _____ faces touched the woman deeply.
           cherub cherubic

7. Astrology pretends to describe an influence that _____ people's lives.   prevents pervades

8. _____ is the scientific study of the universe beyond earth.   Astrology Astronomy

9. At midnight tomorrow there will be an _____ of the moon.
           ellipse eclipse

10. There is an enormous untapped _____ of interest and excitement in things astronomical.   reserves reservoir

DRILL 2

Directions: Move your eyes rapidly across each line. Mark the word by the number each time it appears on the same line. Don't look back on any line. If

Copyright © 1988 Holt, Rinehart and Winston, Inc.

you make a mistake, don't stop to change your answer. Try to finish in less than thirty seconds.
Begin timing.

1. regiment   recent revere recent regiment recent regiment
2. pockets   pockets pocket pocket pockets pocket
3. concern   concert concert concern concert concern
4. initial   initials invite initial initiate initial
5. great   grate great grate great grate
6. pitter   patter pitter patter patter pitter
7. sham   shame sham shame share sham
8. waist   waste waste waste waist waist
9. stagger   swagger stagger swagger stagger swagger
10. applaud   applause applied applaud applause applied
11. charged   charged charged changed changed change
12. since   sense sense since since sense
13. astronomy   astronomic astrology astronomy astrology
14. super   super supper super supper supper
15. field   filed filed filed field field

TIME: _____

Check each line to see if you marked the correct word every time it appears. Make sure you can pronounce *all* the words and know their meanings. Some of the words by the numbers appear in the article in this chapter.

TOTAL LINES CORRECT: _____

DRILL 3

Directions. Follow the same directions as in the last drill. Move quickly. Don't look back on a line. Don't stop to change mistakes. Try to finish in thirty seconds or less.
Begin timing.

1. dominate   dominate dominated dominate dominoes
2. champ   champ chump champion champ chump
3. trying   frying trying frying frying trying
4. aspects   aspire aspects aspire aspire aspects

P: Prereading Drills

5. cosmic   cosmos   cosmic   cosmos   cosmic
6. belt   felt   belt   belt   felt   felt   felt
7. shuffle   shuffle   swagger   swagger   shuffle   shudder
8. reverent   reverse   reverent   reverently   revere
9. seem   seam   seam   seam   seem   seem
10. nebulae   nebula   nebulous   nebula   nebulae
11. worth   worry   worry   worth   worry   worth
12. pervades   provides   pervert   pervades   prevent
13. bench   bunch   bunch   bench   bench   bunch
14. break   brake   brake   break   brake   break
15. ankles   angles   ankles   angles   ankles   angles

TIME: _____

Check each line to see if you marked the correct word every time it appears. Make sure you know all the words. Some of the words by the numbers appear in the article in this chapter.

TOTAL LINES CORRECT: _____

DRILL 4: RAPID PHRASE RECOGNITION

Directions: Move your eyes straight down the following columns. Every time the key phrase **send the mail** appears, mark it. Do not begin until you are told to do so. Try to finish in thirty seconds or less.

under the hill   over the rainbow
the large park   send the mail
mail the letters   near the mailbox
males and females   write it all down
send the males   in the agreement
send the letter   send the mail
that he is   a big argument
not so much   remember your eyes
big brown eyes   send it airmail
send the mail   place it near here
half the price   plenty of confusion
around the corner   cram for it
send the militia   put it together
proved to be it   what is the letter
gather together   send the mail
the whole portion   the large area

(continued on next page)

Copyright © 1988 Holt, Rinehart and Winston, Inc.

take a horse	brand new chairs
send the mail	across the horizon
that is nice	put in the mail
put in the mail	that is nice
across the horizon	send the mail
brand new chairs	that is nice
the large area	the whole portion
send the mail	gather together
what is the letter	proved to be it
put it together	send the militia
scream and shout	around the corner
plenty of confusion	half the price
place it near here	send the mail
send it airmail	send the militia
remember your eyes	males and females
a big argument	send the toys
send the mail	on the way
in the agreement	under the couch
write it all down	mail the letters
near the mailbox	send the males
send the mail	send the militia
over the rainbow	send the mail

TIME: _____

Carefully check each line. Make sure you marked **send the mail** every time it appears. It appears eleven times.

R: READING DRILL

READING AND THINKING ABOUT WHAT YOU READ

Directions: The article you are about to read was written by Carl Sagan, director for Planetary Studies at Cornell University. You may have seen Dr. Sagan's program "Cosmos" on television. Knowing that Carl Sagan is an astronomer, see if you can answer these questions without looking at the article.

1. Read only the title of the article. What do you think the essay will be about?

_____

_____

2. What subject matter (English, history, science) do you think the author will discuss?

_____

_____

3. What do you think his point will be regarding the teaching of first grade?

_____

_____

_____

ON TEACHING THE FIRST GRADE

CARL SAGAN

A friend in the first grade asked me to come to talk to his class, which, he assured me, knew nothing about astronomy but was eager to learn. With the approval of his teacher, I arrived at his school in Mill Valley, California, armed

"On Teaching the First Grade" by Carl Sagan from The Cosmic Connection. Copyright © 1973 by Carl Sagan and Jerome Agel. Reprinted by permission of Doubleday & Company, Inc.

with twenty or thirty color slides of astronomical objects—the Earth from space, the Moon, the planets, exploding stars, gaseous nebulae, galaxies, and the like—which I thought would amaze and intrigue and, perhaps to a certain extent, even educate.

But before I began the slide show for these bright-eyed and cherubic little faces, I wanted to explain that there is a big difference between stating what science has discovered and describing how scientists found it all out. It is pretty easy to summarize the conclusions. It is hard to relate all the mistakes, false leads, ignored clues, dedication, hard work, and painful abandonment of earlier views that go into the initial discovery of something interesting.

I began by saying, "Now you have all *heard* that the Earth is round. Everybody *believes* that the Earth is round. But *why* do we believe the Earth is round? Can any of you think of any evidence that the Earth is round?"

For most of the history of mankind, it was reverently held that the Earth is flat—as is entirely obvious to anyone who has stood in a Nebraska cornfield around planting time. The concept of a flat Earth is still built into our language in such phrases as "the four corners of the Earth." I thought I would stump my little first-graders and then explain with what difficulty the sphericity of Earth had come into general human consciousness. But I had underestimated the first grade of Mill Valley.

"Well," asked a moppet in the sort of one-piece coverall worn by railroad engineers, "what about this business of a ship that's sailing away from you, and the last thing you see is the master, or whatever it's called, that holds up the sail? Doesn't that mean that the ocean has to be curved?"

"What about when there's an *ellipse* of the Moon? That's when the Sun is behind us and the shadow of the Earth is on the Moon, right? Well, I saw an *ellipse*. That *shadow* was round, it wasn't straight. So the Earth has to be round."

"There's better proof, much better proof," offered another. "What about that old guy who sailed around the world—Majello? You can't sail *around* the world if it isn't round, right? And people today sail around the world and fly around the world all the time. How can you fly around the world if it isn't round?"

"Hey, listen, you kids, don't you know there's *pictures* of the Earth?" added a fourth. "Astronauts have been in space, they took pictures of the Earth; you can look at the pictures, the pictures are all round. You don't have to use all these funny reasons. You can *see* that the Earth is round."

And then, as the *coup de grace*, one pinafored little girl, recently taken on an outing to the San Francisco Museum of Science, casually inquired, "What about the Foucault pendulum experiment?"

It was a very sobered lecturer who went on to describe the findings of modern astronomy. These children were not the offspring of professional astronomers or college teachers or physicians or the like. They were apparently ordinary first-grade children. I very much hope—if they can survive twelve to twenty years of regimenting "education"—that they will hurry and grow up and start running things.

Astronomy is not taught in the public school, at least in America. With a few notable exceptions, a student can pass from first to twelfth grade without ever encountering any of the findings or reasoning processes that tell us where we are in the universe, how we got here, and where we are likely to be going; without any confrontation with the cosmic perspective.

The ancient Greeks considered astronomy one of the half dozen or so subjects required for the education of free men. I find, in discussions with first-graders and hippie communards, congressmen and cab drivers, that there is an enormous untapped reservoir of interest and excitement in things astronomical. Most newspapers in America have a daily syndicated astrology column. How many have a daily syndicated astronomy column, or even a science column?

Astrology pretends to describe an influence that pervades people's lives. But it is a sham. Science really influences people's lives, and in only a slightly less direct sense. The enormous popularity of science fiction and of such movies as *2001: A Space Odyssey* is indicative of this unexploited scientific enthusiasm. To a very major extent, science and technology govern, mold, and control our lives—for good and for ill. We should make a better effort to learn something about them.

COMPREHENSION CHECK

Directions: Answer the following questions without looking back at the article.

RECALL

1. The author's main idea is best expressed in which of the following statements?
   a. Because of the influence of science and technology on our lives, we should learn more about them.
   b. Teaching first-graders is more difficult than the author thought.
   c. Astronomy should be taught in our schools.
   d. Because there are syndicated daily astrology columns, there should be daily syndicated astronomy columns.
2. The author overestimated the first-graders he visited.

   a. True

   b. False, because _____
   _____
   _____

3. The children in the first grade were mostly offspring of professional people, such as doctors, lawyers, and so on.

   a. True

   b. False, because _____

   _____

   _____

4. Which of the following did the children mention as reasons we know the earth is round?
   a. a ship sailing away disappears on the horizon
   b. people who sail or fly around the earth
   c. the Foucault pendulum experiment
   d. pictures from space
   e. all of the above

INTERPRETATION

5. When a student mentioned an *ellipse* of the moon, what was really meant?

   _____

6. A *bias* is a leaning toward, or a strong preference for or against, something. Is Sagan biased for or against astrology in schools? _____Why?

   _____

   _____

7. When Sagan says he hopes the first-graders "can survive twelve to twenty years of regimenting 'education,'" what can we infer or guess his opinion

   of schooling in America is? _____

   _____

   _____

8. If you could discuss the issue of science with Carl Sagan, what would you

   like to ask him and why? _____

   _____

R: Reading Drill 203

APPLICATION

9. Restate Sagan's views on science as shown in the essay. Do you agree or disagree with him? _____ Why? _____

10. Name some areas of science that "govern, mold, control our lives—for good or ill." _____

Name _____ Section _____ Date _____

E: EXERCISES IN VOCABULARY

DRILLS

DRILL 1: WORDS OFTEN CONFUSED

Directions: Following are some sentences. Under each sentence are words that are often confused or misused. Write the correct word in the blank.

1. Margaret was not there to _____ her scholarship award. accept (ăk-sĕpt′)   except (ĕk-sĕpt′)

2. The smoke was so thick we could hardly

   _____ .
   breath (brĕth)   breathe (brēth)

3. The diver cut herself on the _____ while looking for pearls.   coral (kor′əl)   corral (kə-ral′)

4. We all watched as the hang glider made its

   _____ toward us.
   decent (dēs′ənt)   descent (dĭ-sent′)

5. The blankets they gave the Indians had been used by _____

   _____ persons, and the Indians, too,
   diseased (dĭ-zēzd′)   deceased (dĭ-sēst′)
   became sick.

6. The court _____ will probably last for weeks.
   trial (trī′əl)   trail (trāl)

7. Hitler's _____ did not last very long.
   empire (ĕm′-pīr)   umpire (ŭm-pīr)

8. Sadie grew up to be _____ a remarkable woman.   quiet (kwī′ĭt)   quite (kwīt)   quit (kwĭt)

9. _____ going to be a nice day.
   Its (ĭts)   It's (ĭts)

E: Exercises in Vocabulary

10. The shirt was too _____, so he returned it.
   lose (lōōz)   loose (lōōs)

11. Everyone may leave _____ you, John.
   accept (ăk-sĕpt′)   except (ĕk-sĕpt)

12. Let me catch my _____.
   breath (brĕth)   breathe (brēth)

13. He seems like a _____ guy.
   descent (dĭ-sent′)   decent (dēs′ənt)

14. Lillie has tried very hard to _____ smoking.
   quite (kwīt)   quit (kwĭt)

15. Don't _____ that book; _____ the
   loose (lōōs)   lose (lōōz)   its (ĭts)   it's (ĭts)
only copy I have.

DRILL 2: PREFIX REVIEW

Directions: Before learning some new prefixes, review the ones you've already learned by circling the prefixes in the following words. Then define the word in the blank. The first one has been done for you.

1. independent   *not dependent*
2. illegal   _____
3. misrepresent   _____
4. antitoxin   _____
5. maladjusted   _____
6. inhuman   _____
7. postwar   _____
8. disbelieve   _____
9. impractical   _____
10. unlikely   _____

DRILL 3: MORE PREFIXES

Directions: Following are some more of the prefixes you should learn. Use them to fill in the blanks in front of the following words. Some words may take more than one prefix. The first one has been done for you.

pre = before
de = down, away
dis = no longer
re = repeat, do again

1. *pre/re* view
2. _____ own
3. _____ fix
4. _____ grade
5. _____ paid
6. _____ appear
7. _____ feat
8. _____ do
9. _____ caution
10. _____ allow
11. _____ planning
12. _____ able
13. _____ open
14. _____ agree
15. _____ throne
16. _____ fresh
17. _____ form
18. _____ lay
19. _____ like
20. _____ code

DRILL 4: SUFFIX REVIEW

Directions: Before learning some new suffixes, review the ones you've learned. Underline the suffixes in the following words, and define the word in the blanks. The first one has been done for you.

1. enjoy<u>able</u> *can enjoy*
2. skillful _____
3. instructor _____
4. childish _____
5. protection _____
6. waiter _____
7. deliverance _____
8. distrustful _____

E: Exercises in Vocabulary

DRILL 5: MORE SUFFIXES

Directions: Following are some suffixes you should know. Use them to fill in the blanks after the following words. Some words may take more than one suffix.

-al -ment -er
-ive -est -ous

1. act _____
2. music _____
3. light _____
4. move _____
5. clean _____
6. protect _____
7. content _____
8. poison _____
9. select _____
10. renew _____
11. express _____
12. treat _____
13. electric _____
14. strong _____
15. assign _____
16. murder _____
17. near _____
18. impress _____
19. politic _____
20. agree _____

DRILL 6: COMPOUND WORDS

Directions: Read the following sentences. In the blank that follows the sentence, write in a compound word that could be used in place of the part of the sentence that is underlined. For example:

The light of the moon was shining in the window. *moonlight*

1. Make a ball of snow, and throw it at your sister. _____
2. Mom is decorating my bedroom with some pretty paper that goes on the walls. _____
3. On her day of birth, Jeanne will be twenty-five years old.

_____

4. When that tree is <u>grown to its full size</u>, it will be about thirty feet high. _____

5. The Indians cut <u>holes for their eyes</u> in the sheets. _____

6. The boss thinks he'll make a good <u>hand with the cows</u>. _____

7. When the <u>men in the cavalry</u> rode up the hill, they were met by the Indians. _____

8. The <u>walking place along the side of the road</u> was almost covered with weeds. _____

9. Tell Jerry, the <u>boy who brings the newspaper</u>, to stop delivery until we come back from vacation. _____

10. The <u>room where we have school</u> needs cleaning. _____

DRILL 7: WORDS IN CONTEXT

Directions: Following are some sentences. In each sentence there is an underlined word. See if you can figure out what the underlined word means by the way it is used in context. Write your answers in the blanks.

1. The jeweler <u>appraised</u> the diamond necklace at $60,000.

2. My friends seemed <u>incredulous</u> and laughed when I told them I had seen a flying saucer.

3. The police were unable to <u>elicit</u> the truth from the criminal.

4. A <u>dirge</u> was sung at the man's burial.

5. Mary will not be <u>eligible</u> for graduate school unless she passes her Chemistry III class.

6. Ellen made several <u>vain</u> attempts to stop smoking.

E: Exercises in Vocabulary 209

7. When we ran out of food, we began to look for some <u>edible</u> berries.

_____

8. They need to <u>dredge</u> the mouth of the harbor because boats can't get through.

_____

9. The lake was so <u>placid</u> it looked as though you could walk on the water.

_____

10. Gasoline is highly <u>flammable</u> and should be used with care.

_____

DRILL 8: DEFINITION REVIEW

Directions: Write the letter of the correct definitions in the blanks in front of the words that follow. There are more definitions than words.

_____	1. astrology	a.	wide mass
_____	2. cherubic	b.	final blow
_____	3. confrontation	c.	beginning
_____	4. regimenting	d.	spreads throughout
_____	5. coup de grace	e.	scientific study of the universe
_____	6. reverently	f.	face-to-face meeting
_____	7. initial	g.	chubby; rosy
_____	8. pervades	h.	phony
_____	9. astronomy	i.	showing respect
_____	10. sham	j.	study of the stars' influence on humans
		k.	systematizing
		l.	cosmic perspective

Copyright © 1988 Holt, Rinehart and Winston, Inc.

VOCABULARY CHECK

PART A

Directions: Following are some pronunciation key spellings of words in this chapter. In the blank, write what the word is.

1. brēth _____
2. ăk-sĕpt' _____
3. lo͞oz _____
4. kwī'-ĭt _____
5. dēs'ənt _____

6. trī'əl _____
7. kwĭt _____
8. lo͞os _____
9. disēst' _____
10. kor'əl _____

PART B

Directions: Circle the prefixes in the following words.

1. preschoolers
2. insertion
3. deflate
4. removed
5. prepaid
6. relearn
7. degrading
8. disown
9. remained
10. disband
11. deformed
12. pretend
13. reporters
14. disarmament
15. defeat

PART C

Directions: Write the correct suffix for the underlined word in each of the following sentences. Correct spelling is required.

1. My grandmother is very act_____ for her age.
2. Sally has music_____ talents that should be developed.
3. This box is light_____ than that one.
4. The contents of the bottle are very poison_____.
5. Be more select_____ the next time you buy a car.
6. The electric_____ shock almost killed him.

E: Exercises in Vocabulary

7. Bill's service record is very impress_____.

8. How many assign_____ did you complete?

9. Willie proved he is the strong_____ of all of them.

10. When is the renew_____ date on your driver's license?

PART D

Directions: Draw a line between the words that make up the following compound words.

1. inside
2. sometimes
3. rainbow
4. buckskin
5. daybreak
6. outstretched
7. cavalrymen
8. horseback

PART E

Directions: Write a sentence correctly using each of the following words. You may add suffixes if you need to.

1. appraise: _____

2. vain: _____

3. elicit: _____

4. edible: _____

5. placid: _____

6. confrontation: _____

7. astrology: _____

_____

8. initial (not letters): _____

_____

9. eligible: _____

_____

10. pervades: _____

_____

Name _____ **Section** _____ **Date** _____

P: PERFECTING READING SKILLS

COMPREHENDING SENTENCES

Directions: Read each sentence and answer the questions that follow it.

1. The train was delayed ten hours because of heavy snow on the tracks.

    a. Does the sentence mean the train will be late? _____

    b. What one word tells you this? _____

2. If you are practical, Mario, don't plan to enroll in more classes than you can handle with your present twenty-five-hour workweek.

    a. Does the sentence mean that Mario is enrolled in school now? _____

    b. Is Mario working now? _____

3. It is never a good idea to repeat rumors because they may not be true.

    a. Does this mean you should repeat only true rumors? _____

    b. Does this mean you should not repeat gossip? _____

4. After his fall, Carlos was more cautious on his skateboard.

    a. Did Carlos probably get hurt when he fell? _____

    b. Why? _____

5. Very few intellectuals are ever elected president of the United States.

    a. Does this mean few intellectuals ever become president? _____

    b. Does this mean few intellectuals ever run for the office of president?
    _____

    c. Could this mean voters don't want an intellectual for a president?
    _____

6. Shortly after the Zuñi Indians finished their rain dance, thunder was heard and lightning flashed.

    a. Who did the dancing? _____

213

b. What type of dance was it? _____

c. When was the thunder heard? _____

d. Did it rain right after the dance? _____

7. The Skytrain DC-10 lifted high into the sky and began its polar flight to London.

    a. What is a Skytrain DC-10? _____

    b. Where is it going? _____

    c. What route is it taking? _____

    d. How long has the flight been so far? _____

    _____

8. Maria was so sensitive about the burn hole in her skirt that she kept her hand over it so no one could see it.

    a. Was Maria embarrassed? _____

    b. What was burned? _____

    c. How was it burned? _____

    _____

    d. Does Maria smoke? _____

COMPREHENDING PARAGRAPHS

Directions: Read each paragraph and answer the questions that follow it.

1. Whereas I thought with my head, Jack seemed to think with his hands. I believed his way of thinking was inferior. I was wrong. For instance, on camping trips, he saved me from disaster many times. Jack would have no trouble building fires or a shelter. My wife said that if she were stranded on a desert island, she'd rather have Jack along than me.

    a. Whom is the paragraph about? _____

    b. What is the paragraph about? _____

    _____

P: Perfecting Reading Skills

    c. Does the "I" think he is better than Jack? _____

2. Most food would be usable after a nuclear attack. Radiation passes through food and does not hurt it. The danger would be swallowing fallout particles that were on the food itself or on the can or package. These can be wiped or washed off.

    a. Would it be all right to eat canned food after a nuclear explosion?

    _____

    b. Why? _____

    c. What is the real danger with food after a nuclear attack? _____

    _____

3. Most people speak at about 125 words per minute. Yet we think about four or five times faster. It's like a speaker's being in the slow lane and the listeners being in a fast lane on a highway. Often we want to leave the speaker behind. That's why we need to learn listening concentration.

    a. How fast do we speak? _____

    b. How fast do we think? _____

    c. Why does this sometimes cause listening problems? _____

    _____

4. The *Dictionary of Occupational Titles* (or *DOT*) is a two-volume book that describes and classifies all the different jobs in America today. *DOT* is a good aid to students, counselors, employers, and others. It lists all job fields, the tasks they involve, and the skills needed for the job. Looking through *DOT* can help people be aware of jobs available and what skills or training they should get in order to qualify for a particular job.

    a. What does *DOT* stand for? _____

    b. What kind of book is *DOT*? _____

    _____

    c. Why is it helpful? _____

    d. To whom is it helpful? _____

    _____

5. Mrs. Gomez was tired. It seemed like weeks since she had slept. Her

twelve-year-old daughter, Alicia, was resting quietly now. Mrs. Gomez knew from experience that she would sleep well for hours. She got up from her chair by the bed. She checked Alicia's breathing once more, then went to bed for some rest.

    a. Why was Mrs. Gomez tired? _____

    b. What time of day is it? _____

    c. Is this the first time Alicia has been so ill? _____

    d. What's wrong with Alicia? _____

6. A college student has trouble concentrating when trying to study for an exam. She thumbs through the pages of her books and daydreams. When a friend interrupts her, she responds immediately, as if relieved to turn away from the task in front of her. When she returns to her books, her mind wanders to thoughts of Christmas vacation and what she has planned for all that free time. In two hours she actually studies for only about fifteen minutes. After biofeedback training, she is not easily interrupted in her study when friends stop by, and daydreams do not distract her. She can concentrate steadily for an hour, and a short break is all she needs to refresh herself before she tackles her next subject.

    a. What is the student like in the first half of the paragraph? _____

    _____

    b. What is she like in the latter part of the paragraph? _____

    _____

    c. What caused the change? _____

    _____

7. What is *biofeedback?* The simplest definition is this: It is information about an individual's biological functions. Actually, each of us has been receiving some information of this sort all our lives. For example, every time you use a simple bathroom scale you get direct feedback on your own weight control. When you think you may have a fever and put a thermometer in your mouth, the thermometer reading (the biological feedback) tells you something about what is going on inside you. When you count your pulse before, during, and after jogging, you get feedback about your physiological reactions, which can help you "see" the effects that jogging has on

(From Biofeedback: An Introduction and Guide, *by David Danskin and Mark Crow, Mayfield Publishing Co., 1981, pp. 2–3)*

your body. And how about the doctor's blood pressure cuff or stethoscope? If you were to read the blood pressure meter or listen to your heartbeat through a stethoscope, you would receive the same biological feedback as the doctor.

Note that none of the instruments does anything *to* you. The scale, the thermometer, the jogger's fingers for feeling a pulse, the blood pressure cuff, and the stethoscope only give you information about something inside you. Each instrument acts as an external mirror for your internal states. Simply stated, this is biofeedback.

a. This passage defines biofeedback. What is it? _____

_____

_____

b. Give some examples of instruments that give us biological feedback.

_____

_____

8. *Biofeedback training* is using instrument feedback to learn how to make changes *voluntarily* in whichever process is being monitored. By watching an instrument give continuous measurements of a body function, a person can experiment with different thoughts, feelings, and sensations and get immediate feedback on their physical effects. For example, what thoughts result in increased heart rate? What thoughts result in decreased heart rate? With practice, and with the information provided by the sensitive biofeedback instrument, the trainee can learn to alter heart rate, or change the level of muscle tension, or learn to lower blood pressure, or even to increase skin temperature in parts of the body. This is biofeedback training.

(From Danskin and Crow, op. cit., p. 3)

a. What is this paragraph about? _____

_____

b. What is the difference between biofeedback and biofeedback training?

_____

_____

_____

c. What can a trainee learn to do? _____

_____

_____

9. All sounds are waves produced by the vibrations of material objects. In pianos and violins, the sound is produced by the vibrating strings; in a clarinet, by a vibrating reed. The human voice results from the vibration of the vocal cords. In each of these cases a vibrating source sends a disturbance through the surrounding medium in the form of longitudinal waves. The frequency of the sound wave is identical to the frequency of the vibrating source. The human ear can normally hear sounds made by vibrating bodies whose frequencies are between 16 and 20,000 hertz. Sound waves whose frequencies are below 16 hertz are called *infrasonic;* those with frequencies above 20,000 hertz are called *ultrasonic.* We cannot hear infrasonic or ultrasonic sound waves.

(From Conceptual Physics, 2d ed., by Paul G. Hewitt, Little, Brown and Co., 1971, p. 270)

a. What is the subject of this passage? _____

_____

_____

b. What causes sound? _____

_____

_____

c. Can you infer (guess through context) what a *hertz* is? _____

_____

_____

d. Could we hear something at the vibrating frequency of 22,000 hertz?

_____

10. In 1851, J. B. L. Foucault demonstrated the rotation of the earth by suspending a 200-foot pendulum in the Pantheon in Paris. It traced its path in sand on the floor. The pendulum continued to vibrate in a single plane as the earth rotated underneath it. This left a series of traces in the sand going in all directions. Thus, Foucault showed the earth does rotate.

a. Who is the paragraph about? _____
   _____

b. What is the paragraph about? _____
   _____

c. When did this happen? _____
   _____

d. How did the experiment prove the earth rotates? _____
   _____
   _____

e. Where else did you read about Foucault in this chapter?
   _____
   _____
   _____

COMPREHENDING SCIENCE TEXTBOOK PASSAGES: APPLYING STUDY-READING TECHNIQUES

Directions: The following passage is from an earth science textbook used in many colleges. It is not easy reading, but it is similar to the type of reading required of students in college. Apply the skills you have learned:

1. Prepare before you read by surveying the passage.
2. Read from section to section.
3. Use context clues to understand unfamiliar words.
4. Examine each section you read by marking, underlining, or taking notes.
5. Review the passage before answering the questions that follow it.

ORIGIN OF THE EARTH

ARTHUR BEISER AND KONRAD B. KRANSKOPF

Where does the planet earth fit into the evolution of the universe? Insignificant though it is in the grand scheme of the cosmos, it is nevertheless our home and therefore of considerable interest to us. Although nothing like a complete picture of the origin of the earth has been devised, some idea of the probable sequence of events in its formation is available.

The story begins with a local eddy [a current moving opposite from a main current] in the swirling gas and dust of the primordial [original] galaxy. This eddy in time condensed through the action of gravity into a cloud stable enough to resist disruption. The cloud, the so-called *protosun*, was as far across as the present solar system. Eventually it began to contract, taking perhaps 80 million years to make the transition from gas cloud to star, and, in the course of the contraction, some of the gas remained behind to form a diffuse spherical nebula [formless mass] about the nascent sun.

Protoplanets

In time the nebula cooled and flattened into a thin disk. In doing so it increased in density and ultimately reached the point at which mutual gravitational forces within the disk became as great as the tide-producing forces exerted by the sun. This created an unstable situation, which resolved itself when the flattened nebula broke up into separate smaller clouds. These were the *protoplanets* from which the planets of the present developed. Had the nebular density been less than it was, many tiny planets would have resulted; if it had been much greater one or more small stars would have been formed as companions to the sun.

While the protoplanets were coming into existence the sun was still dark, not yet having completed the shrinkage that, by increasing the pressure and temperature of its interior, would permit it to evolve energy and become luminous. The protoplanets were huge affairs, protoearth, for instance, being possibly 500 times more massive than and 2,000 times as far across as the current earth. With the sun in darkness the heavier constituents [parts] of the protoplanets migrated inward, collecting in the center of each protoplanet to form a heavy core surrounded by lighter gases. At this time the satellites got their start. In the case of protoearth, for some reason there was only a single large secondary body.

From Introduction to Earth Science, *by Arthur Beiser and Konrad B. Kranskopf, McGraw-Hill Book Co., copyright © 1975, pp. 331–333. Reprinted by permission.*

Effects of the Sun

Then the sun began to shine, and the peaceful evolution of the protoplanets reached a more dramatic phase. In addition to the light it emits, the sun puts out intense streams of fast, electrically charged particles. Today these particles lead to auroral [many-colored] displays and magnetic disturbances on the earth and the deflection of comet tails away from the sun, among other effects; during the early stages of planetary evolution they served to sweep the solar system free of the remnant nebular gas that pervaded interplanetary space. Meanwhile the cold protoplanets grew warm, and their own envelopes of gas and vapor began to boil away. The earth and the other planets nearest the sun suffered an immense diminution [growing smaller] in their sizes and weights, since the light hydrogen and helium of which they were largely composed could escape easily. Finally, after the greater part of a billion years, the relatively bare, shrunken planets of today emerged permanently from the mists that enshrouded them.

Meanwhile, the protoplanet cores were proceeding to consolidate themselves. In the case of the earth this led to pronounced heating, due partly to radioactivity. Ultimately the entire earth melted, and the iron and silicate components separated to form the core and mantle, respectively. Then, gravitational energy exhausted, the molten earth began to solidify, and, with the development of the crust and its continents, a recognizable ancestor of our present planet appeared. This occurred 4½ billion years ago, completing a process that had begun a billion or so years earlier.

Earth's Future

What of the future course of the earth? If the sun evolves as similar stars do, several billions of years from now it will begin to swell into a luminous giant, as large around as the orbit of Venus and emitting a hundred times more radiation than it does now. The earth will grow warmer, and ultimately the oceans will reach the boiling point. Steam will fill the atmosphere, and all life will perish except, conceivably, some exceedingly resistant spores. This situation will last perhaps a billion years, until the sun begins to decline in an evolutionary process that will end with it a feeble white dwarf. The steam will condense into new oceans as the earth cools, terminating in a globe completely covered with ice and snow. Doubtless a little volcanic and diastrophic [mountain-forming] activity will still persist, but the ultimate picture will be one of lifeless desolation as darkness draws near.

Other Solar Systems

The modern view of the origin of the solar system is that it is a natural aspect of the evolution of the sun. Since our sun is by no means an exceptional star in any respect, it is reasonable to suspect that other stars are also attended by planetary systems. If this suspicion is correct, and there is indirect evidence to support it, over a billion stars in our galaxy alone should have planetary systems of some kind, and many of them should resemble our own solar system. In fact, one other star has already been found to have planets circling it. Of the billions of planets in the galaxies of the universe, a certain proportion surely meet, in the words of Harlow Shapley, "the happy requirements of suitable distance from the star, near-circular orbit, proper mass, salubrious [favorable] atmosphere, and reasonable rotation period—all of which are necessary for life as we know it on earth." True, the combination of immense distances between stars and the impossibility of attaining speeds faster than that of light makes it unlikely that the hypothesis of life on other worlds will be directly verified in the near future, if indeed ever, but no serious arguments that dispute this hypothesis have been advanced. It seems probable that we are not alone in the universe.

Review your notes or markings before answering these questions.

RECALL

1. What is a *protosun?* _____

_____

2. What are *protoplanets?* _____

_____

3. What is meant by *protoearth?* _____

_____

4. How old is the earth? _____
5. How long did it take for the earth to get from its origin to its present stage?

_____

6. Was earth at one time smaller or larger than it is now?

_____

7. What are some future stages in the course of the earth?

_____

_____

_____

INTERPRETATION

8. According to the author, we earthlings may not be alone in the universe. What is your opinion of this? Why?

_____

_____

_____

_____

_____

9. Two reasons are provided in the last paragraph that explain why the author feels it is unlikely that we can prove other life exists in the universe. Do you feel those problems can be overcome? Explain.

_____

_____

_____

APPLICATION

10. Many people have religious beliefs in disagreement with the scientific views expressed here. Why would this theory disturb some people? _____

_____

_____

_____

_____

Name _____ Section _____ Date _____

UNIT 2   CHECK TEST (Chapters 4–6)

PART ONE: WORD KNOWLEDGE

A. Directions: Underline the root word in each of the following words.

1. unartistic
2. independent
3. accountable
4. uncreative
5. realistic
6. unsocial

B. Directions: Circle the prefixes in the following words, and define the meaning of each word in the blank following it. Try not to use the root word in your definition.

7. impersonal: _____

8. inactive: _____

9. disable: _____

10. preview: _____

11. redo: _____

12. uncommon: _____

13. irreplaceable: _____

14. disapprove: _____

C. Directions: Circle the suffixes in the following words, and define the meaning of the word in the blank following it.

15. painful: _____

16. careless: _____

17. securely: _____

18. foolish: _____

Unit 2 Check Test (Chapters 4–6) 225

19. responsible: _____

20. dependable: _____

D. Directions: In the following blanks, write words that go with the prefixes.

21. __anti_____   24. __mal_____

22. __post_____   25. __ante_____

23. __mis_____

PART TWO: WORD USAGE

Directions: Following are two columns. In the blank by the word in the first column, write in the letter of the definition from the second column.

1. _____ sham   a. a scientific study of the universe

2. _____ vast   b. sore; touchy

3. _____ sensitive   c. to take apart

4. _____ pervades   d. foul; nasty

5. _____ regimenting e. hidden

6. _____ vile   f. not true or real

7. _____ nebula   g. word for word

8. _____ astronomy   h. a mass of interstellar dust or gas

9. _____ dismantle   i. imitation; pretending

10. _____ obscure   j. over and over again

11. _____ anarchy   k. change; modify

12. _____ literal   l. disorder; confusion

13. _____ alter   m. spreads throughout

Copyright © 1988 Holt, Rinehart and Winston, Inc.

14. _____ simulation   n. large; great in size

15. _____ repetitive   o. organizing; systematizing

PART THREE: COMPREHENDING PARAGRAPHS

Directions: Read the following paragraphs and answer the questions that follow.

A. The Food and Drug Administration is constantly coming under attack from all sides. When a new drug that might cure some disease is first announced, the FDA usually withholds its approval until final test results are in. Yet the potential buyers cry that the FDA should do it sooner because the delay costs lives. Those performing the tests claim that hurrying to use the drug could cost lives. Sometimes the public doesn't want the FDA's advice.

   1. FDA stands for _____.

   2. What is the main idea of the paragraph? _____
   _____
   _____

B. The FDA, then, is caught in between. Its responsibilities are enormous. Its job is to ensure that "foods are safe and wholesome, drugs are safe and effective, household products are safe or carry adequate warning labels, and all of the above are honestly and informatively labeled and packaged for the consumer." This involves taking care of the contents, packaging, and labeling of almost all food items except eggs, poultry, and meat. The FDA is caught between giving the kind of protection consumers want and not placing a hardship on industry by making too many regulations. It's not easy with consumers becoming more critical and demanding. And with rising expenses, industry can't always afford to meet every standard demanded by consumers. The FDA can't please everybody, but it tries to continue to provide safe and nutritious food, keeping costs reasonable.

   1. Why is the FDA's job difficult? _____
   _____
   _____

Unit 2 Check Test (Chapters 4-6)

2. Is the author biased toward the FDA? _____ Explain.

_____

_____

_____

C. When the FDA started to consider banning the sweetener saccharin, its users became angry because they felt they should have been told sooner. At the same time, the diet-food industry accused the FDA of causing undue alarm based on incomplete evidence. But the FDA had no choice. Once tests prove a compound can cause cancer, it must be banned by law. With the banning of saccharin, the consumer would have no widely prevalent, non-caloric sweetener available. Consumers began demanding that the sweetener not be banned even if it did cause cancer. They wanted the right of choice to buy it or not.

1. What is the problem the FDA had to face?

_____

_____

_____

2. Based on the content of the paragraph, what do you think the FDA did? _____

_____

_____

_____

PART FOUR: ESSAY READING

Directions: Read the following essay, and answer the questions that follow.

BIG BUSINESS: SELLING CANCER
WALTER RALEIGH

1   Since the 1950s, more and more information has been publicized to show cigarette smoking is a health hazard. There is evidence that links smoking with cancer, heart problems, and lung disease (emphysema). Nevertheless, tobacco companies are making more profit than ever before. It seems the more dangerous smoking becomes, the more people smoke. Why? Cigarette advertising.

2   When cigarette companies realized they could not fight the truth about the danger of smoking, they created the so-called low tar and nicotine cigarettes. Advertising was so well done that smokers went for these "new" cigarettes. Cigarette makers were able to almost double the number of cigarettes they could produce from the same amount of tobacco. Tobacco profits are so high now that tobacco companies are forced to find ways to spend their money. Many tobacco companies are buying up farmlands, cosmetic companies, canned food businesses, soap companies, and other industries not related to smoking. Rather than losing money, the cigarette industry has become more solid than ever. All this because advertising has convinced 50,000,000 people they should smoke.

3   The smoker, the one who has made tobacco a big industry, is not doing as well. Many more smokers are developing cancer of the mouth, lungs, or throat. Others have fallen victim to lung disease where they often live like vegetables for years. Still others are dying from circulatory disease. A well-known physician has said, "Cancer is probably the most merciful of the diseases related to smoking. It kills—usually in six months or less.... Emphysema is different. Any smoker simply has to smoke a large enough quantity over a long enough time and he will develop emphysema. Emphysema patients sometimes struggle on pathetically for five to ten years as vegetables—needing constant care twenty-four hours a day." In 1972, 300,000 people died as a result of smoking. This is more than the American losses in both the Korean and Vietnam wars.

4   The U.S. Government's connection with the tobacco industry is interesting. They have been very careful to walk a middle line. They have forced the tobacco companies to put warning labels on their advertising and cigarette packs. But that's about it. They have to be cautious. Many Southern states' income depends on tobacco crops. Tax on tobacco at both the state and federal level is staggeringly high. And tobacco companies are big contributors to political campaigns. They spend millions on advertising, which helps the economy.

5   In 1970, the U.S. Congress spent $84 million to help the tobacco industry. The government guarantees a minimum price per acre for tobacco crops. It spent $2.7 million in research to find a new way to grow tobacco more cheaply. It also spent $250,000 in advertising overseas to get foreign nations to buy Amer-

Reprinted by permission of the author.

ican tobacco. In fact, the United States is the world's biggest tobacco exporter. And big business is more important than good health to some people.

6   Even though cigarettes cannot be advertised on television, cigarette sales are higher than ever. Magazines, newspapers, billboards—all carry ads making cigarette smoking seem a pleasure. Advertisers make smoking seem fun, exciting, adult, and glamorous. We're even told they taste good:

"Tastefully Cool"—(Kool)
"The Great *New* Taste"—(Kent)
"Tastes as Fresh as Springtime"—(Salem)
"Taste One! Taste Me!"—(Doral)
"The National Choice for a Lady with Taste"—(Eve)
"It's a Matter of Taste"—(Viceroy)

Research shows that very few people can tell the difference between brands.

7   Look carefully at any cigarette ad. Is it really selling cigarettes? More than likely it's selling an image, an idea that smoking is natural. The ads imply that smoking can win you a man or a woman. They imply you'll look like that rugged man or beautiful woman in the ad if you pop a cigarette in your mouth. They imply cigarettes are "fresh" and connected with green fields, running streams, or snow-covered mountains. The truth? Cigarettes kill.

8   Cigarette companies even use the evidence against them to sell us. When lists are published showing which cigarettes are high or low in tar and nicotine, some companies claim, "Look at us; we don't kill you as fast as Brand X." And the idea that filters cut down the amount of tar and nicotine is a fantasy. Advertising, however, has convinced us smoking is safer now.

9   One tobacco company recently claimed their cigarette was "a thinking man's cigarette." The truth is that if a man or woman were thinking for himself or herself, the tobacco industry would be out of business by now.

COMPREHENSION CHECK

RECALL

1. Which statement best reflects the main idea of the essay?
    a. Smoking is dangerous to one's health.
    b. Cigarette sales, thanks to advertising, are higher than they've ever been.
    c. Even though there is proof that smoking is harmful, cigarette companies are doing better than ever because of advertising.

d. The U.S. Government's connection with the tobacco industry is helping its sales.
2. Which of the following industries are some tobacco companies buying with their profits?
   a. farming
   b. cosmetics
   c. canned foods
   d. soap
   e. all of the above
3. Why does one doctor claim that cancer is more "merciful" as a disease than emphysema?

_____

_____

_____

4. Who is responsible for the tobacco industry's success?

_____

_____

INTERPRETATION

5. What seems strange about the connection between the tobacco industry and the U.S. Government?

_____

_____

_____

6. A bias, remember, is a preference for, or a leaning toward, something. Is the author of the essay biased for or against cigarette smoking?

_____

7. Give some examples of the author's bias.

_____

_____

_____

Unit 2 Check Test (Chapters 4–6)

8. We can infer or guess from the article that the author probably
   a. smokes
   b. does not smoke
9. We can infer from the article that the author does not care for the methods used in cigarette advertising.

   a. True, because _____

   _____

   b. False, because _____

   _____

APPLICATION

10. Why do you think more and more people are smoking even though evidence shows it's a health hazard? _____

_____

_____

_____

Name _____ **Section** _____ **Date** _____

UNIT 3

Chapter 7

Objectives

- **P: PREREADING DRILLS**
  Words to Know
  Warm-up Drills
- **R: READING DRILL**
  Reading and Thinking About What You Read
  "The Development of Writing" by Susan and Stephen Tchudi
  Comprehension Check
- **E: EXERCISES IN VOCABULARY**
  Drills
  - 1: Synonyms
  - 2: Antonyms
  - 3: Using the Correct Word
  - 4: Word Formation
  - 5: Definition Review

  Vocabulary Check
- **P: PERFECTING READING SKILLS**
  Comprehending Paragraphs
  Comprehending, Interpreting, and Evaluating: "How to Spell" by John Irving

Objectives

When you have finished with this chapter, you will

1. Recognize and be able to use at least 90 percent of the vocabulary words in the Words to Know section.
2. Know what synonyms are.
3. Know what antonyms are.
4. Know and be able to use at least fifty synonyms and antonyms discussed in this chapter.
5. Know how to change words to form different parts of speech, such as verbs to nouns, nouns to adjectives, and so on.
6. Have developed your reading comprehension skills in recognizing main ideas, cause-effect relationships, and an author's bias.

P: PREREADING DRILLS

WORDS TO KNOW

Directions: Read the following list of words aloud. Learn any you don't know. They all are defined as they appear in the essay you will read in this chapter.

1. *prior*—coming before.
Most of what we know about human life prior to writing—prior to "written history"—is based on guesswork.
2. *speculation*—guessing; reflection; using what is known to figure out what's unknown.
What we think life was like 20,000 years ago is based on speculation.
3. *natural phenomenon*—an unusual occurrence or happening in nature (the plural of phenomenon is phenomena).
For thousands of years, people have been observing and keeping records of natural phenomena, such as Halley's Comet.
4. *enhance*—make better.
Throughout the ages, people have used writing to enhance their existence with stories and plays and the like.
5. *flourish*—to succeed; to grow or do well.
Some of the great early civilizations flourished around the Mediterranean Sea.
6. *ingenious*—clever; resourceful.
Although it seems simple and obvious to us today, the development of the alphabet was an ingenious and remarkable achievement.
7. *hieroglyphics*—drawings used to represent things the way words do.
Egyptian hieroglyphics are an example of drawings gradually simplified and coming to stand for whole words in a language.
8. *stylus*—a sharp, pointed instrument used for writing.
Printing on a clay tablet with a stylus was a very slow and cumbersome procedure.
9. *papyrus*—a plant from which paper was made.
Egyptians pioneered in developing a better, lighter writing material, papyrus.
10. *inextricably*—unable to untie or get loose from.
People's needs to organize, control, and understand their worlds have been inextricably tied to writing.
11. *implement*—to carry out; to cause a plan to happen.
Preparation is necessary in order to implement the plan.
12. *Middle Ages*—the period in European history dating from A.D. 476 to A.D. 1453.
In the Middle Ages, books and manuscripts were rare and expensive, most of them owned by the Catholic Church.

WARM-UP DRILLS

DRILL 1

Directions: Move your eyes rapidly across each line, and mark the word by the number each time it appears on the same line. For example:

1. laugh   tough   ~~laugh~~   tough   ~~laugh~~   tough
2. right   night   night   ~~right~~   ~~right~~   night

Don't look back on any line. If you make a mistake, don't stop to change your answer. Try to finish in less than thirty seconds.
Begin timing.

1. accept   except accept except except except
2. except   accept accept accept except accept
3. advise   advice advise advise advice advise
4. affect   affect effect effect effect effect
5. alley   ally alley ally ally ally
6. alter   altar altar altar altar alter
7. angel   angle angle angel angle angle
8. berth   birth birth birth berth birth
9. brake   brake break break break break
10. bridal   bridle bridal bridle bridle bridle
11. capitol   capitol capital capital capital capital
12. coarse   course coarse course course course
13. counsel   council council council counsel council
14. quiet   quite quite quiet quite quite
15. forth   fourth fourth fourth forth fourth
16. fair   fare fair fare fare fare
17. dairy   dairy dairy diary dairy dairy
18. dessert   dessert desert desert desert desert
19. device   devise devise device devise devise
20. dual   duel dual duel duel duel

TIME: _____

P: Prereading Drills

Carefully check each line. Place the number correct in the blank that follows. Then go on to the next exercise.

TOTAL LINES CORRECT: _____

DRILL 2

Directions: The words in this list are the same words as in Exercise 1 but are printed in capitals. Follow the same directions as for the preceding exercise. Don't look back on any line.
Begin timing.

1.	ACCEPT	EXCEPT ACCEPT ACCEPT EXCEPT ACCEPT
2.	EXCEPT	ACCEPT ACCEPT EXCEPT ACCEPT ACCEPT
3.	ADVISE	ADVISE ADVICE ADVISE ADVICE ADVISE
4.	AFFECT	EFFECT AFFECT EFFECT EFFECT EFFECT
5.	ALLEY	ALLY ALLY ALLEY ALLY ALLY
6.	ALTER	ALTAR ALTAR ALTAR ALTER ALTAR
7.	ANGEL	ANGLE ANGEL ANGLE ANGLE ANGLE
8.	BERTH	BIRTH BIRTH BIRTH BIRTH BERTH
9.	BRAKE	BREAK BRAKE BREAK BREAK BREAK
10.	BRIDAL	BRIDAL BRIDLE BRIDLE BRIDLE BRIDLE
11.	CAPITOL	CAPITAL CAPITOL CAPITAL CAPITAL CAPITAL
12.	COARSE	COURSE COURSE COARSE COURSE COURSE
13.	COUNSEL	COUNCIL COUNCIL COUNCIL COUNSEL
14.	QUIET	QUITE QUITE QUITE QUIET QUITE
15.	FORTH	FOURTH FOURTH FOURTH FOURTH FORTH
16.	FAIR	FAIR FARE FARE FARE FARE
17.	DAIRY	DAIRY DAIRY DAIRY DIARY DAIRY
18.	DESSERT	DESERT DESSERT DESERT DESERT DESERT
19.	DEVICE	DEVISE DEVISE DEVISE DEVICE DEVISE
20.	DUAL	DUAL DUEL DUEL DUEL DUEL

TIME: _____

Carefully check each line. Place the number correct in the blank that follows.

NUMBER CORRECT: _____

DRILL 3

Directions: The following drills are the same as the previous drills except that now you will look for key phrases rather than single words. Keep your eyes focused near the center of the columns, and bring your eyes down the page. Every time the key phrase appears in the column, make a mark by it or underline it rapidly. You should finish in ten seconds or less. The key phrase for this exercise is **over the hill.**
Begin timing.

on the scale	on the middle
under the hill	take time out
the large park	on the middle
the small knot	over the hill
over the hill	price is right
near the hill	not so much
a round knot	the black hog
not the price	black and blue
sent a letter	send the letter
over the hill	over the hill
over the door	please move over
that he will	under the seat
hill and dale	over the hat
proud to be	near the hill
that we are	about ten o'clock
believe in them	front to back
name the horse	start the stripes
over the hill	if you fail
tame the horse	in the auditorium
over the hill	make it do now

TIME: _____

The key phrase appears six times. How did you do?

DRILL 4

Directions: Mark the key phrase **tame the horse** every time it appears in the following columns. You should finish in ten seconds or less.

make it do now	over the hill
in the auditorium	name the horse
tame the horse	believe in them
if you fail	that we are
front to back	proud to be
about ten o'clock	hill and dale

P: Prereading Drills 241

near the hill	that he will
over the hat	mane and horse
under the seat	over the hill
please move over	sent a letter
over the hill	not the price
send the letter	a round nail
black and blue	near the hill
the black hog	over the hill
not so much	the small know
price is right	the large park
over the hill	under the hill
name the horse	on the scale
take time out	stars and stripes
tame the horse	send the letter

TIME: _____

The key phrase appears only twice.

DRILL 5

Directions: Write the letter of the correct definition in the blank by the word. There are more definitions than words.

_____ 1. prior   a. nearly hopeless

_____ 2. speculation   b. to carry out; to do

_____ 3. phenomena   c. unable to get loose from

_____ 4. enhance   d. unusual occurrences

_____ 5. flourish   e. sharp, pointed instrument

_____ 6. ingenious   f. coming before

_____ 7. stylus   g. guessing

_____ 8. papyrus   h. to succeed; to do well

_____ 9. inextricably   i. make better

_____ 10. implement   j. clever; resourceful

                              k. type of paper

                              l. drawings used to represent words

Copyright © 1988 Holt, Rinehart and Winston, Inc.

R: READING DRILL

READING AND THINKING ABOUT WHAT YOU READ

Directions: Answer the following questions.

1. Based on the title of the following article, what do you think the selection will be about?

_____

2. Can you tell from the title if the author is biased regarding the subject?

_____

3. What do you know about the subject? _____

_____

4. What do you think you'll learn from reading this article?

_____

_____

5. Do you expect to be bored? _____ Explain. _____

_____

_____

Now read the selection.

THE DEVELOPMENT OF WRITING

SUSAN AND STEPHEN TCHUDI

Much of what we know about the history of humankind has come to us through writing. Indeed, most of what we know about human life prior to writing—prior to "written history"—is based on speculation and guesswork. For thousands of years, people have used writing to make records of their lives: They have written laws and treaties to maintain order and peace; they have made written agreements for trading goods and kept records of commerce; they have written down records of seasons, crops, plantings, and harvests; they have observed and written explanations of natural phenomena like day and night, winter and summer, water and earth, moons and stars, animals and plants; they have used writing to try to understand spiritual life and to create religions; they have written myths and legends to describe their views of the world; they have created educational books to teach their young; and they have written about their experiences and emotions in poetry, drama, song, and story. Throughout the ages people have used written language to enhance their existence, to explain themselves, and to understand themselves and their world.

Primitive people—those who lived about 20,000 years ago—used "writing" in the form of pictures. Evidence has been found that earliest humans made markings on cave walls, on stones, and on objects to denote ownership or to represent religious beliefs or experiences. However, these drawings were a far cry from writing as we know it.

The pictures and markings made about 5,000 years ago seemed to tell some sort of story or show connections among events in people's lives. The drawings became symbols, representing more than just a single object. These *pictograms* (or stories told through pictures) have been discovered throughout the world, carved or written on stone, shells, tree bark, and animal skins. Early stories told through pictograms, such as animals and hunters, seemingly in chase, reflected people's relationships with their environment. Still, these drawings were not true writing.

Somewhere around 3000–2000 B.C. the use of *ideograms* developed. People needed and wanted to express more in writing than they could with simple pictures. Ideograms are symbols in which a rough sketch, say, of the sun, could represent not just a single object—the sun itself—but several related ideas: day, good weather, the east (that place or direction where the sun rose). Soon ideograms could express ideas and emotions, not just actions, objects, or events. The ideogram of an eye with a tear, for example, was a symbol for sorrow in cultures as different as the Mayas and Aztecs in what is now Central America and the Chinese in the Orient.

The next stage in the development of writing seems to have taken place in western Asia and around the Mediterranean Sea, where some of the early great cultures flourished: Sumeria, Mesopotamia, Phoenicia, Egypt, Rome, and Greece. As these cultures came into contact with one another, they needed to find common systems of communication, including writing.

The *cuneiform* system—developed in Sumeria (now Iraq) around 3500 B.C.

Susan and Stephen Tchudi, "The Development of Writing," "The Uses of Writing Today," and "The Future of Writing" from The Young Writer's Handbook. *Copyright © 1984 Susan and Stephen Tchudi. Reprinted with the permission of Charles Scribner's Sons.*

and adopted by many ancient civilizations in that area—used marks made by pressing a wedge-shaped stylus or marking tool in wet clay. At first, the cuneiform markings represented objects, actions, and ideas as ideograms, but gradually the marks became "streamlined," looking less and less like "the real thing." At the same time those symbols stamped in wet clay came to represent or stand for specific words in the spoken language. Egyptian *hieroglyphics* are another example of drawings gradually simplified and coming to stand for whole words in the language. At this point in history, writing was rather close to what we conceive it to be, but one thing was missing: the alphabet.

This development took place in Phoenicia, a neighbor of both Greece and Rome, which was known for its manufacturing and trading throughout the Mediterranean and was a powerful influence in the development of Western culture. The Phoenicians adapted earlier writing systems, using marks to represent not whole words, but individual sounds in their language. This may seem rather simple or obvious to us, but it was an ingenious and remarkable achievement. Through letter-symbols, the Phoenicians could use just a few symbols, about two dozen, in place of thousands and thousands of cuneiform symbols or hieroglyphics. (You may know that written Chinese has never made this transition. Thus, learning to write Chinese is very difficult, and writers spend much of their lifetime learning to master tens of thousands of separate characters or word drawings.)

The modification of the alphabet to the point at which we can recognize the letters came through the Greeks and the Romans. The Greeks, who had contact with the Phoenicians through trade, borrowed their alphabet, adopting nineteen of their twenty-two symbols and adding some of their own to create a twenty-four-letter alphabet, beginning with the characters named *alpha* and *beta* that give us our word *alphabet*. The Romans—neighbors and successors of the Greeks as the major world power—took that basic system of alphabetic writing and carried it through their part of the world as the written form of their language, Latin. For centuries the Romans dominated a large part of the

Figure 7.1 The Evolution of the Letters *M* and *H* from Pictograms

world, and they left behind legacies of government, religion, language, and, of course, *writing*.

Along with the development of the alphabet, the "technology" of writing has steadily improved, making the use of writing and print more available to everyone. For the caveman who drew on walls, "writing" was slow and laborious and the writer had to depend upon someone walking by to examine his work. In the cuneiform system, printing on a clay tablet with a stylus, writing was faster and somewhat more portable, but still very slow and cumbersome. In Egypt, written language was at first used only by the priests, who had the materials and the slave labor to create writing, but later the Egyptians pioneered in developing better and lighter writing materials: papyrus, parchment, and vellum. On the other side of the globe, the Chinese developed paper about the first century A.D. When paper began to be used in Europe several centuries later, writing became much less expensive and more available to the people. Still, in the Middle Ages, books and manuscripts were rare and expensive, most of them having been created and owned by the Church, whose scribes spent lifetimes copying.

You probably know of Johann Gutenberg, who is generally credited with inventing "movable type" that made printing practicable. From Gutenberg's time on, there has been immense interest in our culture in letting every person learn to read and write. The United States has one of the highest literacy rates in the world. We value writing and reading so much that the acquisition of these skills is an absolutely central part of our educational system.

The story of the evolution of both the alphabet and writing materials shows how important writing is and has become to people. The entire course of civilization can be traced in and through writing. People's needs to organize, control, and understand their worlds have been inextricably tied to writing, providing ways to order and comprehend and define. That need has not diminished in our electronic age.

The Uses of Writing Today

Despite the development of sophisticated telecommunications systems and the widespread use of computers, much of the work (and fun) of the world is done through the written word. The laws of the land, their interpretation, and their enforcement are maintained through print. Agreements between nations on war and peace, commerce, and ecology are written and signed. Businesses and industries may need their phones and computers, but their work could not go on without the written word, and many business people worry about the "paper avalanche" that is created in their offices every day. Proposals for new products and services are developed, submitted, and approved in writing. Production, evaluation, and distribution depend on the writing and implementing of a plan. Scientists, doctors, and social scientists—people working on the problems in our lives—must have pen and paper handy to record their hypotheses and experiments and observations.

There are writers who interpret and explain the world for us: journalists, who report events of the world and new developments in education, science, medicine, art, politics, and religion; historians, philosophers, and social analysts, who give their opinions about the meaning of what's happening to us; authors of poems and plays and stories, who interpret experience in their own way through writing; reviewers, who give us their opinions of how successful things are in our world.

Many people write for small or private audiences. Even though the phone company advertises that telephones are personal and efficient, many of us prefer to keep in touch through letters. Many people keep journals and diaries that are meant for their eyes only. Most of us feel a need to keep a pen and a pad of paper handy for notes and scribbles, sometimes to ourselves, sometimes to others.

Is print dead? Not by a long shot.

The Future of Writing

We think it likely that in your lifetime you will see some remarkable changes in the way print is created, packaged, and distributed. For instance, your daily paper may soon not be printed on paper at all, but will arrive on your television screen. Instead of checking out a book at a library, you may someday borrow a computer or video disk that will display the text on a screen. Instead of writing with pen and ink on paper, you will certainly learn to use an electronic word processor, and you may even come to own a small portable word processor that you can carry around with you and type ideas into whenever you want. It is even conceivable that in your lifetime the alphabet itself may change as new letters and symbols, more suitable for use in computers and other electronic devices, come to stand alongside and then replace the letters developed so long ago by the Greeks and Romans.

However, the *word*—language—is here to stay. No matter what alphabet and what language develop, there will still be a need for *writers*—people who write in language—on the face of this planet.

COMPREHENSION CHECK

Directions: Answer the following questions without looking back unless you are told to do so.

RECALL

1. The thesis or main idea of the article is that
   a. no matter what, writing will always be important.
   b. forms of writing have changed over the centuries.

R: Reading Drill

    c. much of what we know about our history has come to us through writing.
    d. all of the above.
    e. none of the above.

2. People were writing as we know it as far back as 20,000 years ago.

    a. True

    b. False, because _____

_____

3. Define *pictograms*. _____

_____

4. Define *cuneiform*. _____

_____

5. Briefly discuss the history of our present alphabet. _____

_____

_____

_____

6. How may reading as we know it change in the future? _____

_____

_____

INTERPRETATION

7. Why do the authors feel that writing is so important? _____

_____

_____

8. Do you feel the authors are biased in their feelings about writing? _____

Explain. _____

_____

9. How might our lives be different if we did away with learning how to write? _____

_____

_____

APPLICATION

10. What did you learn from reading this selection? _____

_____

_____

_____

Name _____ **Section** _____ **Date** _____

E: EXERCISES IN VOCABULARY

DRILLS

DRILL 1: SYNONYMS

Directions: Synonyms are words that have the same or similar meanings. Read each line that follows from left to right. Underline the word that means the same or nearly the same as the word by the number. For example:

   1. large   round   small   <u>big</u>   short

Work as quickly as you can.

1. biggest   smallest shortest little largest
2. crew   group meaning students thank
3. situation   reach maid position valuable
4. blend   usual mix freedom method
5. craze   cigarette noise liberty fad
6. custom   promise pull habit correct
7. fashion   style wrong washer beside
8. aroma   several aid recall odor
9. persuade   shop convince union suppose
10. foul   catch fowl vile human
11. harmful   bad proper strong certain
12. curious   contend interested difficult crew
13. related   connected trouble actual ache
14. business   action address always work
15. expensive   around better costly article
16. beginning   apart start ancient among
17. colony   bridge apple cause group
18. amazed   surprised birth center bridge
19. stuffed   border amuse full candle
20. illegal   cheap unlawful chief engine
21. attempt   field excite force try
22. suppose   develop imagine fault dirty
23. occur   happen either contribute contain

250   E: Exercises in Vocabulary

24. sufficient   foolish   dirty   enough   declare
25. strike   famous   hit   furniture   courage

DRILL 2: ANTONYMS

Directions: Antonyms are words that are opposite in meaning. *Hot* and *cold*, *hard* and *soft*, *difficult* and *easy* are antonyms. Read each line that follows from left to right. Underline the word that means the opposite or nearly the opposite of the word by the number. Work as quickly as you can.

1. clean   clothes   dirty   dress   drummer
2. smooth   encounter   dinner   fortunate   rough
3. early   time   late   further   gasoline
4. lose   forest   loose   find   descendants
5. never   couple   deny   electric   always
6. distant   rear   fasten   near   crack
7. sell   college   grand   buy   happy
8. peace   journey   war   piece   nearly
9. fail   succeed   market   leaves   muscle
10. past   mention   present   feature   negative
11. dangerous   health   into   safe   library   lean
12. public   hospital   private   marriage   narrow
13. cheap   mouth   intend   judge   expensive
14. remember   hole   forget   handle   ground
15. enter   leave   iron   sheets   matter
16. beautiful   however   imagine   sense   ugly
17. alive   heavy   dead   booming   noses
18. awake   sleep   jewelry   priest   another
19. drop   opposite   round   lift   opinion
20. silent   relative   noisy   return   shame
21. village   pound   presence   shade   city
22. permit   radio   prevent   question   sometimes
23. amusing   wondrous   usually   sad   wind
24. ill   well   various   therefore   supply
25. sufficient   structure   though   lacking   through

Copyright © 1988 Holt, Rinehart and Winston, Inc.

E: Exercises in Vocabulary

DRILL 3: USING THE CORRECT WORD

Directions: Read the following sentences, and write in the correct word from the choices below each sentence.

1. Helen bought an _____ dress.
   expense   expensive

2. What _____ have you had in using the cash register?   instruction   instructed

3. Dress for the party is _____.
   informally   informal

4. It looks _____ made.
   cheap   cheaply

5. His list of _____ is three pages long.
   accomplish   accomplishments

    Notice that you had to select the correct response from two words with the same root. In #1, you needed an adjective to describe the dress: *expensive*, from the root *expense*, with the suffix *ive*. In #2, you needed a noun: *instruction*, from the root *instruct*, with the suffix *ion*. In #3, you needed an adjective to describe what kind of dress: *informal*. In #4, you needed an adverb to describe how it was made: *cheaply*, from the root *cheap*, with the suffix *ly*. In #5, you needed a noun, a thing, the object of the preposition *of*: *accomplishment*, from the root *accomplish*, with the suffix *ment*.
    While this is not a grammar book, it may help you to put together some of the information you've learned about roots and suffixes.
    Here are some terms you should learn:

1. *nouns*—people, places, things, ideas.
Some nouns: Jerry, Boston, accomplishments, abortion, democracy, instruction.
2. *verbs*—action words, or a state of being showing what the subject of the sentence does or is.
Some verbs: Jerry *thinks;* Boston *is;* birds *fly;* teachers *instruct.*
3. *adjectives*—describe or say something about nouns.
Some adjectives: *cheap* shirt; *expensive* car; *poor* instruction; *illegal* abortion; *controversial* subject.
4. *adverb*—describe or add to a verb or other adjectives, telling how, when, and where.

Some adverbs: made *cheaply;* decorated *expensively;* parked *illegally;* arrived *early.*

In English, many words can be changed from one part of speech to another by adding or changing some of the suffixes you've already learned. Study this list before doing the next drill.

Verb		*Suffix*	*Noun*
swim	+	er	*swimmer
instruct	+	or	instructor
guide	+	ance	**guidance
depend	+	ence	dependence
depend	+	ency	dependency
accomplish	+	ment	accomplishment
extend	+	sion	extension
act	+	ion	action

Noun		*Suffix*	*Adjective*
child	+	ish	*childish* person
operation	+	al	*operational* plan
pain	+	less	*painless* dentist
joy	+	ous	*joyous* reunion
revenge	+	ful	*revengeful* man
expense	+	ive	***expensive* coat

Adjective		*Suffix*	*Adverb*
cheap	+	ly	*cheaply* made
automatic	+	ally	*automatically* done

Verb		*Suffix*	*Adjective*
love	+	able	***lovable* baby
imagine	+	ed	*imagined* fears
fry		(change *y* to *i*)	*fried* chicken
run	+	y	*runny* nose
imitate	+	ive	***imitative* style
greet	+	ing	*greeting* card

* If a word has one syllable and one consonant at the end and one vowel before the consonant, the consonant is doubled when the suffix begins with a vowel.

** Notice that when a final *e* is silent, it is dropped.

E: *Exercises in Vocabulary*

DRILL 4: WORD FORMATION: PART A

Directions: Following are some words with the part of speech abbreviation. In the blanks at the right, write in the correct word needed to change the word by the number to other parts of speech. For example:

wide (adj.) ———— *width* ———— (n.)

Use a dictionary if you need to.

1. expense (n.) ———————————— (adj.)

2. fry (v.) ———————————— (adj.)

3. survival (n.) ———————————— (v.)

4. desire (v.) ———————————— (adj.)

5. flat (adj.) ———————————— (v.)

6. instruct (v.) ———————————— (n.)

7. informal (adj.) ———————————— (adv.)

8. greet (v.) ———————————— (n.)

9. sales (n.) ———————————— (v.)

10. detachment (n.) ———————————— (v.)

11. cheap (adj.) ———————————— (adv.)

12. inform (v.) ———————————— (n.)

13. resent (v.) ———————————— (n.)

14. accomplishments (n.) ———————————— (v.)

15. exaggerate (v.) ———————————— (n.)

17. monument (n.) ———————————— (adj.)

18. permit (v.) ———————————— (n.)

19. searcher (n.) _____ (v.)

20. swindler (n.) _____ (v.)

PART B

Directions: On a separate sheet of paper, write sentences for each word you changed in the preceding drill. Then, turn it in to your instructor.

DRILL 5: DEFINITION REVIEW

Directions: Write the letter of the correct definition in the blank in front of the word. There are more definitions than words.

_____ 1.	vast	a.	clever; resourceful
_____ 2.	simulation	b.	large; great in size
_____ 3.	repetitive	c.	unable to get loose or free
_____ 4.	trend	d.	causing public disagreement
_____ 5.	confrontation	e.	imitation; pretending
_____ 6.	enhance	f.	a movement in a certain way
_____ 7.	prior	g.	face-to-face disagreement
_____ 8.	ingenious	h.	nearly hopeless
_____ 9.	flourish	i.	coming before
_____ 10.	inextricably	j.	to make better
		k.	to succeed
		l.	over and over

VOCABULARY CHECK

PART A

Directions: In the blanks following each word, write a synonym or word that means the same.

E: Exercises in Vocabulary

For instance: correct: __right__

1. crew _____
2. blend _____
3. fad _____
4. custom _____
5. fashion _____

6. odor _____
7. persuade _____
8. costly _____
9. colony _____
10. amazed _____

PART B

Directions: In the blanks following each word, write an antonym or word that means the opposite.

1. smooth _____
2. peace _____
3. public _____
4. remember _____
5. ugly _____

6. permit _____
7. loose _____
8. lose _____
9. sufficient _____
10. amusing _____

PART C

Directions: Read each of the following sentences. In the blank write in the correct word by adding the proper suffix to the word in parentheses. For example:

The major ____*accomplishment*____ of the president will be forgotten by now. (accomplish)

1. Your _____ in the mountains will depend on your ability to deal with nature. (survive)

2. Please _____ that loose flap on the tent. (tight)

3. Mary seems _____ toward me because I dated her brother. (resent)

4. The _____ got away with $15,000. (swindle)

5. Doug's _____ takes time to make assignments clear. (instruct)

PART D

Directions: Use the list of suffixes to change the following verbs into nouns.

Verb	Noun	Suffix
1. govern	_____	or
		ence
2. guide	_____	ency
		ion
3. fulfill	_____	ance
		ment
4. sail	_____	sion
5. tend	_____	

PART E

Directions: Use the list of suffixes to change the following nouns into adjectives.

Noun	Adjective	Suffix
1. child	_____	al
		ish
2. convention	_____	less
		ous
3. humor	_____	ful
		ive
4. resource	_____	able
5. reason	_____	

Name _____ **Section** _____ **Date** _____

P: PERFECTING READING SKILLS

COMPREHENDING PARAGRAPHS

Directions: Carefully read the paragraphs, and answer the questions that follow. Look up any words you can't figure out in context.

1. (a) Rollo May, author of *Love and Will*, believes that authentic love is the result of love and will together. (b) Will is a decision to care for and be involved with another person. (c) It is a commitment to involve oneself with the other individual's feelings. (d) It is being vulnerable through the sharing of one's feelings and thoughts. (e) Love refers to the feelings that nourish that commitment. (f) May believes that will without love becomes manipulation and love without will becomes sentimental and may not last long.

    a. Which sentence is the topic sentence? _____

    b. Explain sentence f in your own words.

    _____

    _____

    c. What is this paragraph attempting to *define?*

    _____

    _____

2. (a) Most writers dealing with love claim there are four kinds. (b) The first, *agape*, refers to caring about others more than oneself. (c) The second, *philia*, refers to family ties, friendship, and companionship. (d) The third, *eros*, reflects excitement, spontaneity, and creativity. (e) The last, *libido*, is physical desire and expression. (f) Authentic love is a blending of these four kinds of love.

    a. Which sentence is the topic sentence? _____

    b. What is being defined? _____

    _____

    _____

257

c. Does this paragraph differ from paragraph 1 in its definition of authentic love? _____

_____

3. (a) For a person who feels strongly attracted to someone else, especially in the early stages, it is not easy to distinguish between infatuation and love. (b) These two emotional states are easily confused. (c) We can usually identify different levels of attraction we feel during a developing relationship. (d) But distinguishing between infatuation and love may not be so easy. (e) When infatuated with someone, faults are overlooked easily and conflicts avoided. (f) The relationship seems a dream; indeed, it is an unrealistic relationship with a dream person imagined in terms of one's own needs. (g) Logic and reason become alien as passion and excitement take over.

   a. Which sentence is the topic sentence? _____

   b. What is the effect of infatuation? _____

   _____

   _____

   c. Of the four loves described in paragraph 2, which one best fits infatuation? _____

   _____

4. (a) True love seems to have more substance. (b) There is a more thoughtful appreciation of one's partner. (c) There's a desire to be with the loved one long after the initial days of infatuation. (d) There's a tolerance for the other's shortcomings and a commitment to the partnership. (e) In effect, love is enduring, whereas infatuation is here and gone.

   a. Which sentence is the topic sentence? _____

   b. What effect does true love have on a relationship? _____

   _____

   _____

   _____

c. What does *enduring* mean as used in the paragraph?

5. Why do people fall in love? The answer is embedded in a myriad of psychosocial factors. Many of us have learned to expect to fall in love, and also to expect a variety of rewards from a loving relationship: emotional support, companionship, and sexual pleasure, for instance. Social pressure also plays a dominant role in many people's lives. Most of us receive many messages from friends, family, and society, all of which tell us that falling in love is the appropriate thing to do.

(From Our Sexuality *by Robert Crooks and Karla Bauer. Benjamin Cummings Publishing Co., 1980, p. 139)*

a. What is the main idea of this paragraph?

b. What causes people to fall in love?

c. What must *myriad* mean as used in the paragraph?

6. As with the question of why people fall in love, there are no simple answers to explain with whom people fall in love. There are a number of factors, however, that are often important. One of these is proximity. People often fall in love with individuals they see frequently—in school, at work, at church, or at parties. Another factor is similarity. It has been reported that people who fall in love often have highly similar social backgrounds, sharing like family histories, social class, religion, or other com-

mon traits. Commonality of interests also seems to be important to the long-term success of a relationship. People who have very similar attitudes and behavioral characteristics frequently become lovers. This does not mean, however, that people necessarily fall in love with individuals who are like them. Frequently, the needs of lovers complement each other. For example, a person who has a need to be assertive and feel in control may enter into a love relationship with someone who prefers a more passive role. *(From Crooks and Bauer, op. cit., p. 139.)*

a. What is the main idea of this paragraph?

_____

_____

_____

_____

b. What are some examples given to explain with whom people fall in love? _____

_____

_____

c. What must *proximity* mean as used in the preceding paragraph?

_____

7. Physical attractiveness also often plays a dominant role in drawing lovers together. In spite of the fact that many of us have been taught that "beauty is only skin deep," the physical appearance of another may greatly influence the degree of attraction we feel. It has been experimentally demonstrated that an individual's physical attractiveness frequently has a dramatic impact on his or her appeal to the opposite sex. Physical appearance seems to influence not only "sex appeal," but also many aspects of our initial attitudes toward other people. In one study, college students were shown photographs of males and females of differing degrees of physical attractiveness and asked to provide their impression of these people. The researchers reported that the most physically appealing individuals were

(From Crooks and Bauer, op. cit., p. 139.)

P: Perfecting Reading Skills 261

consistently rated as more interesting, sociable, kind, and sensitive than their less attractive counterparts.

a. What is the main idea?

_____

_____

_____

_____

b. What is the purpose of mentioning the college study?

_____

_____

_____

_____

c. Based on its use in this paragraph, what must *counterpart* mean?

_____

_____

_____

_____

COMPREHENDING, INTERPRETING, AND EVALUATING

Directions: Apply all the skills you have learned so far as you read the following selection by John Irving, author of *The World According to Garp* and *The Hotel New Hampshire*. See what he—once a hopelessly poor speller himself—has to say that might help you with your own spelling.

HOW TO SPELL

JOHN IRVING

Let's begin with the bad news.

If you're a bad speller, you probably think you always will be. There are exceptions to every spelling rule, and the rules themselves are easy to forget. George Bernard Shaw demonstrated how ridiculous some spelling rules are. By following the rules, he said, we could spell fish this way: ghoti. The "f" as it sounds in enough, the "i" as it sounds in women, and the "sh" as it sounds in fiction.

With such rules to follow, no one should feel stupid for being a bad speller. But there are ways to improve. Start by acknowledging the mess that English spelling is in—but have sympathy: English spelling changed with foreign influences. Chaucer wrote "gesse," but "guess," imported earlier by the Norman invaders, finally replaced it. Most early printers in England came from Holland; they brought "ghost" and "gherkin" with them.

If you'd like to intimidate yourself—and remain a bad speller forever—just try to remember the 13 different ways the sound "sh" can be written

shoe	suspicion
sugar	nauseous
ocean	conscious
issue	chaperone
nation	mansion
schist	fuchsia
pshaw	

Now the Good News

The good news is that 90 percent of all writing consists of 1,000 basic words. There is, also, a method to most English spelling and a great number of how-to-spell books. Remarkably, all these books propose learning the same rules! Not surprisingly, most of these books are humorless.

Just keep this in mind: If you're familiar with the words you use, you'll probably spell them correctly—and you shouldn't be writing words you're unfamiliar with anyway. USE a word—out loud, and more than once—before you try writing it, and make sure (with a new word) that you know what it means before you use it. This means you'll have to look it up in a dictionary, where you'll not only learn what it means, but you'll see how it's spelled. Choose a dictionary you enjoy browsing in, and guard it as you would a diary. You wouldn't lend a diary, would you?

Reprinted by permission of International Paper Company.

A Tip on Looking It Up

Beside every word I look up in my dictionary, I make a mark. Beside every word I look up more than once, I write a note to myself—about WHY I looked it up. I have looked up "strictly" 14 times since 1964. I prefer to spell it with a k—as in "stric<u>k</u>tly." I have looked up "ubiquitous" a dozen times. I can't remember what it means.

Another good way to use your dictionary: When you have to look up a word, for any reason, learn—and learn to *spell*—a *new* word at the same time. It can be any useful word on the same page as the word you looked up. Put the date beside this new word, and see how quickly, or in what way, you forget it. Eventually, you'll learn it.

Almost as important as knowing what a word means (in order to spell it) is knowing how it's pronounced. It's gover<u>n</u>ment, not goverment. It's Feb<u>r</u>uary, not Febuary. And if you know that <u>anti-</u> means against, you should know how to spell <u>anti</u>dote and <u>anti</u>biotic and <u>anti</u>freeze. If you know that <u>ante-</u> means before, you shouldn't have trouble spelling <u>ante</u>chamber or <u>ante</u>cedent.

Some Rules, Exceptions, and Two Tricks

I don't have room to touch on <u>all</u> the rules here. It would take a book to do that. But I can share a few that help me most:

Some spelling problems that seem hard are really easy. What about <u>-ary</u> or <u>ery</u>? Just remember that there are only six common words in English that end in <u>-ery</u>. Memorize them, and feel fairly secure that all the rest end in <u>-ary</u>.

cemetery   monastery
millinery   confectionery
distillery   stationery
                  (as in pap<u>e</u>r)

Here's another easy rule. Only four words end in <u>-efy</u>. Most people misspell them—with <u>-ify</u>, which is usually correct. Just memorize these, too, and use <u>-ify</u> for all the rest.

stupefy   putrefy
liquefy   rarefy

As a former bad speller, I have learned a few valuable tricks. Any good how-to-spell book will teach you more than these two, but these two are my favorites. Of the 800,000 words in the English language, the most frequently misspelled is <u>alright</u>; just remember that <u>alright</u> is <u>all</u> <u>wrong</u>. You wouldn't write <u>alwrong</u>, would you? That's how you know you should write <u>all</u> <u>right</u>.

The other trick is for the truly *worst* spellers. I mean those of you who spell so badly that you can't get close enough to the right way to spell a word in order to even FIND it in the dictionary. The word you're looking for is there, of course, but you won't find it the way you're trying to spell it. What to do is look up a synonym—another word that means the same thing. Chances are good that you'll find the word you're looking for under the definition of the synonym.

Demon Words and Bugbears

Everyone has a few demon words—they never look right, even when they're spelled correctly. Three of my demons are <u>medieval</u>, <u>ecstasy</u>, and <u>rhythm</u>. I have learned to hate these words, but I have not learned to spell them; I have to look them up every time.

And everyone has a spelling rule that's a bugbear—it's either too difficult to learn or it's impossible to remember. My personal bugbear among the rules is the one governing whether you add <u>-able</u> or <u>-ible</u>. I can teach it to you, but I can't remember it myself.

You add <u>-able</u> to a full word: adapt, adaptable; work, workable. You add <u>-able</u> to words that end in <u>e</u>—just remember to drop the final <u>e</u>: love, lovable. But if the word ends in two <u>e</u>'s, like agree, you keep them both: agreeable.

You add <u>-ible</u> if the base is not a full word that can stand on its own: credible, tangible, horrible, terrible. You add <u>-ible</u> if the root word ends in <u>-ns</u>: responsible. You add <u>-ible</u> if the root word ends in -miss: permissible. You add <u>-ible</u> if the root word ends in a soft <u>c</u> (but remember to drop the final <u>e</u>!): force, forcible.

Got that? I don't have it, and I was introduced to that rule in prep school; with that rule, I still learn one word at a time.

Poor President Jackson

You must remember that it is permissible for spelling to drive you crazy. Spelling had this effect on Andrew Jackson, who once blew his stack while trying to write a Presidential paper. "It's a damn poor mind that can think of only one way to spell a word!" the President cried.

When you have trouble, think of poor Andrew Jackson and know that you're not alone.

What's Really Important

And remember what's really important about good writing is not good spelling. If you spell badly but write well, you should hold your head up. As the poet T. S. Eliot recommended, "Write for as large and miscellaneous an audience as possible"—and don't be overly concerned if you can't spell "miscellaneous." Also remember that you can spell correctly and write well—and still be misunderstood. Hold your head up about that, too. As good old G. C. Lichtenberg said, "A book is a mirror: if an ass peers into it, you can't expect an apostle to look out"—whether you spell "apostle" correctly or not.

Now answer these questions.

RECALL

1. What is the main idea of the passage? _____

_____

_____

2. According to George Bernard Shaw, how else can we spell *fish* in English? _____

3. Ninety percent of all writing consists of _____ basic words.

4. There are only six common words in English that end in —*ry*. All the rest end in _____.

5. Approximately how many words are in the English language?

_____

6. If you can't find a word in the dictionary because you can't spell it, how might you find it in the dictionary?

_____

_____

INTERPRETATION

7. What is the author's attitude about poor spelling? _____

_____

_____

8. Why is knowing how to pronounce a word almost as important as knowing what it means? _____

_____

_____

9. Explain the quote by G. C. Lichtenberg in the last paragraph. _____

_____

_____

_____

APPLICATION

10. Even though Irving uses humor to show the difficulty in spelling many English words, state at least two ways he offers that you personally can use to help improve your spelling.

_____

_____

_____

_____

FURTHER APPLICATION

Directions: In the space that follows, write down at least five words you have difficulty spelling. Then apply what Irving tells you here to learn how to spell them correctly.

Problem Words	*Correct Spelling*	*Rule/Method*
1. _____	_____	_____
2. _____	_____	_____

Copyright © 1988 Holt, Rinehart and Winston, Inc.

3. _____   _____   _____

4. _____   _____   _____

5. _____   _____   _____

Chapter 8

Objectives

P: **PREREADING DRILLS**
Words to Know
Warm-up Drills

R: **READING DRILL**
Reading and Thinking About What You Read
"Newspaper Reading, How to" by Nancy Cage
Comprehension Check

E: **EXERCISES IN VOCABULARY**
Drills
    1: Greek Word Parts
    2: Latin Word Parts
    3: Root Words
    4: Definition Review
Vocabulary Check

P: **PERFECTING READING SKILLS**
Comprehending Newspaper Headlines
Comprehending Paragraphs: Main Ideas and Support
Comprehending Essays: Skimming and Scanning
"Making TV Commercials" by Roy Wilson
Comprehending Bias and Inference:
"News Is Meant to Inform, Not to Make an Impression" by Andy Rooney

Objectives

When you have finished this chapter, you will

1. Recognize and be able to use 90 percent of the vocabulary words in the Words to Know section.
2. Know what is meant by "word categories."
3. Learn the advantage of knowing word parts, such as roots, prefixes, and suffixes.
4. Know and be able to use at least eight Greek and Latin word parts.
5. Be able to name and know the meaning of at least ten words that contain Greek or Latin parts.
6. Be able to define skimming and scanning and to know when to use those skills.
7. Have developed your reading comprehension skills in locating the thesis or main idea of an essay, in locating information quickly through scanning, and, in general, in improving reading comprehension.

P: PREREADING DRILLS

WORDS TO KNOW

Directions: Read the following list of words aloud. Learn any you don't know well. They all are defined as they appear in the essay you will read later.

1. *condense*—shorten; make smaller.
We have magazines that condense the weekly news.
2. *narrate*—to tell a story or relate an event.
TV news is selected, edited, and then condensed into short, narrated "pictograms."
3. *essential*—extremely important; necessary.
Knowing the news is essential to your mental well-being.
4. *portion*—a section or part of something.
Don't just read that portion of the newspaper that interests you; read it all.
5. *influential*—having power to sway or affect someone.
Newspapers are often owned by large corporations or influential people who interpret the news as they see it.
6. *allege*—to claim something without proof.
The police alleged he was the burglar, but the jury found him innocent.
7. *columns*—articles or essays that appear regularly in the paper or magazines.
George Will, in addition to appearing as a commentator on the nightly TV news, writes regular columns for *Newsweek* and the newspapers.
8. *conservative*—cautious; preferring to keep things as they are; traditional.
George Will is considered to be a political conservative.
9. *liberal*—broad-minded; tolerant; open; believing in maximum freedom of the individual.
The regular reading of newspaper editorials will clue you in on whether or not a paper is liberal or conservative in its thinking.
10. *habitual*—usual; customary; acting out of habit.
Daily reading of the newspaper should become habitual.

WARM-UP DRILLS

DRILL 1

Directions: Move your eyes from left to right. Mark the word by the number every time it appears on the same line. Work rapidly. Don't look back on a line. Don't change any errors. Try to finish in thirty seconds or less. Begin timing.

P: Prereading Drills

1. heroes   heroine hero heroine heroes heroes
2. switch   switch swatch swarm switch swarm
3. initiate   imitating imitated imitate initiate imitate
4. worth   worthy worth would worthless worth
5. curtail   curtain curious cautious curtain curly
6. manifest   manner manifest mountain manipulate
7. women   woman woman women woman women
8. examine   exams examine examined exam examine
9. producer   produce produced produce producer product
10. promote   promise promote promise promote problem
11. studio   studio study started studs studio
12. feminist   female feminist female female feminist
13. function   luncheon functional function funky function
14. routine   route routine routine route routes
15. manager   marriages manager manages manager manages
16. impose   impossible impunge impose impress
17. monitor   manner monotone money monitor
18. valiant   valley valiant vanity valiant vary
19. lax   lox love lax lap land lax lox
20. colleague   college collegiate country colleague

TIME: _____

Check each line carefully. Make sure you marked the correct word each time it appears. Learn any words you don't know. Did you look back on item 5?

TOTAL LINES CORRECT: _____

DRILL 2

Directions: Move your eyes from left to right. Mark the word by the number every time it appears on the same line. Work rapidly. Don't look back on a line. Don't change any errors. Try to finish in thirty seconds or less. Begin timing.

1. location   motion lotion formation location
2. election   lotion election direction detective
3. direction   affection friction direction section
4. detective   active elective native detective

5. movement   monument movement document payment
6. friction   motion friction fraction section
7. sensitive   talkative objective sensitive native
8. objection   affection formation objection solution
9. objective   executive selective elective objective
10. intention   election question formation intention
11. dangerous   prosperous continuous studios dangerous
12. nervously   freely tenderly nervous frankly
13. assignment   agreement assignment payment amazement
14. fraction   solution fraction friction operation
15. continuous   dangerous continuous prosperous studious
16. poisonous   continuous dangerous poisonous prosperous
17. studious   studious dangerous poisonous prosperous
18. section   solution section location motion
19. talkative   active selective creative talkative
20. prosperous   dangerous prosperous continuous studious

TIME: _____

Check each line carefully. Make sure you marked the correct word each time it appears. Learn any words you don't know.

TOTAL LINES CORRECT: _____

DRILL 3

Directions: Follow the same directions as for the last drill. The only difference here is that you will be looking for a short phrase, not a single word. Try to finish in thirty seconds or less.
Begin timing.

1. a couple of   a lot of   a few of   a couple of   a couple is
2. make-believe heroes   make-believe hams   make-believe heroes make-believe show
3. larger-than-life   smaller-than-life larger-than-life larger-than-life
4. more recently   more receivers more recent more recently
5. not at all   not at me not at home not at all
6. private life   prior life private life private talks

P: Prereading Drills

7.	for that matter	for that mother for that matter for that middle
8.	a role model	a role model a role maker a role model
9.	on the ball	on the beach on the road on the ball
10.	a little wart	a little wad a little wart a little while
11.	playing up to	praying up to playing up to playing up to
12.	track down	track down trick down track down
13.	makes a pass	make a pan makes a puss makes a push
14.	create someone	create some create some create someone
15.	on the verge	on the vine on the verge on the hedge

TIME: _____

Check each line carefully. Make sure you marked the correct phrase. Sometimes it appears more than once on a line. Notice there is no phrase for item 13. Did you go back and look again? Remember, don't look back on a line. It slows you down.

TOTAL LINES CORRECT: _____

DRILL 4

Directions: Move your eyes straight down the following columns. Every time you see the key phrase *should initiate*, mark it quickly. Try to finish in fifteen seconds or less.
Begin timing.

has been curtailed	hopelessly dizzy
her new colleague	shared initials
should initiate	try to initial
should initial	try to initiate
vowed to ban	disappointed me
her valiant efforts	watch less TV
monitor the place	difficult decisions
should initiate	should initiate
far too lax	should be fine
should involve	had hysteria
should enter	fought valiantly
should engage	his pervasive ideas
try to initiate	should initiate
call him now	several colleagues
manifest destiny	curtail activities
should initiate	should initiate

manages to be	should enable
much better	should ideally

TIME: _____

The key phrase appears six times.

DRILL 5

Directions: Write the letter of the correct definition in the blank by the right word. There are more definitions than you need.

_____ 1. habitual   a. tolerant; open-minded

_____ 2. liberal   b. loose; not demanding

_____ 3. conservative   c. usual; done from habit

_____ 4. columns   d. shorten; make smaller

_____ 5. alleged   e. tell a story; read along

_____ 6. influential   f. necessary

_____ 7. portion   g. a section or part of

_____ 8. essential   h. having power to sway

_____ 9. narrate   i. to claim without proof

_____ 10. condense   j. articles appearing regularly in newspapers

                                                             k. cautious; slow to change

                                                             l. dried up

R: READING DRILL

READING AND THINKING ABOUT WHAT YOU READ

Directions: Answer the following questions. They are actually steps in surveying before reading carefully.

1. Read the title of the essay that follows. What can you guess will be the subject of the essay? _____

_____

_____

2. Read the opening paragraph. What now can you tell about the main idea of the essay? _____

_____

_____

3. Read the last paragraph. What does it tell you about the main idea of the essay? _____

_____

_____

4. Why is it sometimes a good idea to look at the title, opening, and closing paragraphs of an essay? _____

_____

_____

Now read the essay. Look for the main idea and how the author supports her thesis.

NEWSPAPER READING, HOW TO

NANCY CAGE

It seems as though we're all looking for shortcuts to everything these days. There are more things to do and more things to be done; there are more things to know and more things we need to know. As a result, we have magazines that condense the news of the week, books that are condensed or shortened, speed-reading books and courses, instant coffee, microwave meals, and vitamin pills for those too busy to eat right. Everything seems to be designed to cut down time or effort. It's no wonder some people think there must be a quick, easy solution to everything.

But as someone once said, you can't squeeze a Beethoven symphony into a capsule or expect to be informed about the day's news by swallowing a tiny pill at breakfast. Staying informed takes both time and effort. Unfortunately, most people today get their news information from watching TV news reports. But not only does that take more time to watch than reading the newspapers, it doesn't give you as much information. It's all selected, edited, and condensed into short, narrated "pictograms."

The best method for staying informed is to make newspaper reading a part of your daily routine. Theodore Bernstein says in his essay "How You Can Help Yourself" that reading a newspaper should become as habitual as brushing your teeth or eating your lunch: "Toothbrushing and lunching are essential to your physical well-being and growth; knowing the news is essential to your mental well-being and growth."

Reading the newspaper can take as much as an hour a day if you want to get the most from it. However, that hour does not have to be in one sitting. You can break that up into time slots that fit your schedule. Maybe you read a half hour in the morning and another half hour in the evening. Or you might break the hour into four fifteen-minute sessions. Whatever you do, the time will be well spent if you know how to go about reading the paper.

What can you do in a fifteen-minute session? Quite a bit if you go about it correctly. First, read every headline on the first page. Page one is called "the show window" of the newspaper. Most all of the major news stories are shown here. By reading every headline, you know what the major stories of the day are. This takes less than a minute.

Next, turn to the news summary or index if the newspaper has one. Most major newspapers do, usually on the second page. Here is where a brief statement about the major news stories is made, including some not appearing on the front page. Reading these summaries gives you a brief overview of the most important stories of the day. It also gives you more information than a TV news

Reprinted by permission of the author.

broadcast will. This might take five minutes. If there is no story summary page, go to the next step.

Spend the rest of the fifteen minutes moving through the paper page by page. Skim by looking at the headlines and the pictures. You'll see many advertisements throughout, which you can ignore, not like the ads on TV. By going through the newspaper this way, you won't *know* the news, but you will know something about the news. You won't be well-informed, but you'll know what items in the news you want to spend more time on later.

When you have some more time to spend, you begin reading news items more carefully. You should read all of the stories. Skipping items that appear uninteresting is up to you, but it is not advisable. What you skip from lack of interest might be the most important part of the paper to someone else. But you'll learn that the more you read of the paper, the wider your interests become. People, places, events in the news—these may be foreign to you when you first start reading on a daily basis. But as you continue to read daily, these names and events will seem familiar and more interesting.

Tips on Reading the Paper

Here are some tips on reading the newspaper. *Don't just read the headlines.* The paper is limited in space. Often, there is not enough room on the front page to place all the major stories. That means other important events appear elsewhere.

A small story today may be a big story tomorrow. *Read as many news stories as possible.* If you skip reading a small story and it develops into a big news event, you will have missed out on the beginning events that led up to the big one.

Don't Be a One-Subject Reader

Some people read only one part of the paper, such as the sports section, the business portion, or the local happenings. Widen your field of information. The better informed you are, the better citizen you will be.

Look for Facts Before Forming Opinions

Facts appear in the news stories that are written to give information on Who, What, Why, When, and Where. Usually, the "5 W's" appear within the first sentence or two of a news story. *News stories* are about events or issues of importance from around the world. *Feature stories* are of high interest but usually about things that are not as important as news stories. Animals, people, strange happenings, local history, and the like are subjects of feature stories. They may contain the 5 W's too, but they are not written in a news story style. They may be sad, amusing, clever, suspenseful, descriptive, or written in any number of ways that will grab a reader's interest. Like editorials, they may reflect the author's bias.

Don't Readily Accept What the Editors of the Paper Say in Their Editorials

You must guard against accepting as truth whatever is said. Newspapers are often owned by corporations or influential people who interpret the news as they see it. Their positions on politics, ecology, current events, and the like are *their* positions. You have yours, and if you are informed, you'll know whether or not to agree or disagree with their viewpoints.

Don't Jump to Conclusions When You Read

Watch out for words such as "alleged" when you read about someone being arrested and charged with a crime. The story of the arrest might appear on the front page at the time, and some readers immediately think the person is guilty. Often weeks or months later the person is found not guilty, but the news story, being less sensational, is only a small notice somewhere in the back of the paper.

Other Newspaper Features

Newspapers also contain many other features that you should read. There are the comics, the crossword puzzles, letters to the editors, and regular columns. If you must skip part of the paper, skip all of these except the letters to the editor and the regular featured columns. The letters to the editor allow people to give their opinions and reactions to news events and editorial statements. They give you an opportunity to see how other people feel and why. The featured columns range from writers such as Ann Landers to George Will. Many columnists are syndicated, meaning they appear in newspapers sold all across the United States. Get in the habit of reading both conservative and liberal columnists, not just the ones with whom you agree.

The Danger in Being Uninformed

A democracy works only when the citizens are informed of the facts and make up their own minds. Unfortunately, most people tend to accept the opinions of others and don't even realize or care that they are. Because we are all busy with our day-to-day lives, we often avoid taking the time to become informed so that we can make the right decisions during voting time. We parrot what we hear on TV or the radio or someone we respect without really investigating for ourselves. But if we citizens are to perform our duty, we must think for ourselves. And we cannot do that unless we take the time to become informed and act on our information. Otherwise, we will wake up one day and wonder how we allowed "those others" to get us so far away from a true democratic society.

R: Reading Drill

COMPREHENSION CHECK

Directions: Answer the following questions without looking back.

RECALL

1. What is the thesis of the essay? _____

   _____

   _____

2. How much time should be spent daily reading the newspaper? _____

   _____

3. If you are unable to read the entire paper all at once, what might you do? _____

   _____

4. What is the difference between a news story and a feature story? _____

   _____

5. The author suggests that you skip parts of the paper that don't interest you.

   a. True.

   b. False, because _____

   _____

   _____

6. List the three steps the author suggests as a way to approach reading the newspaper during the first fifteen minutes.

   Step One: _____

   Step Two: _____

   Step Three: _____

Copyright © 1988 Holt, Rinehart and Winston, Inc.

INTERPRETATION

7. Why do you have to be careful not to accept as truth what is said in editorials? _____

   _____

   _____

8. What do you think is the author's opinion regarding TV news? _____

   _____

   _____

   Why? _____

   _____

   _____

   Do you agree or disagree with the author's opinion? _____
   Why? _____

   _____

   _____

APPLICATION

9. Compare watching the news on television with reading the newspaper Watch fifteen minutes of a major network's evening news (ABC, CBS, or NBC), and take notes on what is reported. Then spend fifteen minutes reading the newspaper, using the technique described in the essay you just read. Is it true that you get more and better information from reading the paper than from watching the news? _____ Explain. _____

   _____

   _____

R: Reading Drill

_____

_____

_____

10. Look through today's newspaper for fifteen minutes, using the technique the author describes. Make a list of four major news items that you do not really know too much about but feel you should. For the next week, make a point to read about those items on a daily basis. Remember also to look for editorials, columnists' essays, and letters to the editor that may deal with one of your news items. Start a file for each news item by cutting out the newspaper selections you find. Present them to your instructor when the week is over.

News item #1: _____

News item #2: _____

News item #3: _____

News item #4: _____

Name _____ Section _____ Date _____

E: EXERCISES IN VOCABULARY

DRILLS

DRILL 1: GREEK WORD PARTS (PART A)

Directions: Many English words come from Greek prefixes and roots. Study the following Greek word parts. Then answer the questions that follow. The first one has been done for you.

anti = against
graph, gram = writing, record
micro = small
phone = sound
scope = sight
tele = far

1. Explain why a *telephone* is called what it is. *If "tele" means far and "phone" means sound, a telephone receives and sends sound from far distances.*

2. Why is a *microscope* called what it is? _____

3. How does a *microscope* differ from a *telescope*? _____

4. How does a *telephone* differ from a *telegram*? _____

5. If a person is against having or using telephones, what one word could you make up that would mean this? _____

6. Explain why a *telescope* is called what it is. _____

E: Exercises in Vocabulary

DRILL 1: GREEK WORD PARTS (PART B)

Directions: Study the following Greek word parts. Then answer the questions that follow. You may need to refer to Part A for some answers. Also, when two word parts are joined and the first part ends with a vowel and the second part begins with a vowel, the vowel in the second part is dropped *(geoølogy, bioølogy)*.

auto = self   *hydro* = water
bio = life   *meter* = measure
geo = earth   *ology* = study of

1. If *auto* means self and *graph* means writing, what is an *autograph*?

2. If *bio* means life and *ology* means study of, what is *biology*?

3. If *hydro* means water and *meter* means measure, what is a *hydrometer*?

4. What word means the study of the earth?

5. What word means the study of water?

6. What word means a life story or record of someone?

7. What word means a life story written by the person it's about?

8. What word means an instrument that measures small things?

9. What word means an instrument that picks up sounds in the water?

10. Why is a phonograph called what it is?

DRILL 2: LATIN WORD PARTS

Directions: Many English words are also made up of Latin word parts. Study the following Latin word parts.

inter = between, among
mis = wrong, incorrect
non = not
post = after
trans = across

aqua = water
port = carry
spec(t) = look
via, vis = see
voc = call

Using the preceding word parts and the key words in the definitions that follow, make English words that fit the following definitions. The first one has been done for you. Notice how a preceding Latin word part was added to the key word *mingle* in this definition.

1. to mingle among people   *intermingle*
2. to carry across   _____
3. able to be seen   _____
4. not a resident   _____
5. after the conference   _____
6. taking place in water   _____
7. spelled wrong   _____
8. talks a lot   _____
9. to look into something   _____
10. something you can carry   _____
11. someone who looks on   _____
12. across the Atlantic   _____

DRILL 3: ROOT WORDS

Directions: Following are some phrase groups. In each group, three of the four phrases have words that are from the same root or root word. Check the

E: Exercises in Vocabulary 285

blank in front of the phrase that does *not* have a word from the same root or root word. Write the root or root word in the blank space. For example:

a. _____ a changeable person

b. _____ the changing weather

c. ___√___ the chained bear

d. _____ the unchanged man

Root word: *change*

Notice that the root word is *change* in all but the third phrase. Now you try it.

1. a. _____ the invisible man
   b. _____ visibility is high
   c. _____ poor vision
   d. _____ division of work
   Root word: _____

2. a. _____ a portable TV
   b. _____ portray a villain
   c. _____ good transportation
   d. _____ import tax
   Root word: _____

3. a. _____ a creative mind
   b. _____ create your own
   c. _____ a lovely creation
   d. _____ crated vegetables
   Root word: _____

4. a. _____ it's unreal
   b. _____ realize now
   c. _____ face reality
   d. _____ fishing reel
   Root word: _____

5. a. _____ the new inspector
   b. _____ to speculate
   c. _____ new spectacles
   d. _____ specific instance
   Root word: _____

6. a. _____ no plans now
   b. _____ a late plane
   c. _____ the planning stages
   d. _____ planned to go
   Root word: _____

Copyright © 1988 Holt, Rinehart and Winston, Inc.

7. a. _____ equal opportunity
    b. _____ equipped wrong
    c. _____ unequal pay
    d. _____ equally measured

    Root word: _____

8. a. _____ probably true
    b. _____ improbable mess
    c. _____ preferable to this
    d. _____ not probable

    Root word: _____

DRILL 4: DEFINITION REVIEW

Directions: Write the letter of the correct definition in the blank by the word. There are more definitions than words.

_____ 1. concepts   a. a fellow member
_____ 2. preference   b. possible
_____ 3. potential   c. capacity to remember or hold
_____ 4. humiliation   d. take apart
_____ 5. retention   e. rosy; chubby; innocent
_____ 6. alien   f. ideas; beliefs; feelings
_____ 7. obscure   g. claimed without proof
_____ 8. dismantle   h. hidden; out of sight
_____ 9. cherubic   i. foreign; not familiar
_____ 10. alleged   j. shame; embarrassment
                           k. devoted to
                           l. what you want over something else

VOCABULARY CHECK

PART A

Directions: Define the following word parts.

E: Exercises in Vocabulary

1. tele: _____
2. micro: _____
3. phone: _____
4. graph: _____
5. ology: _____
6. auto: _____
7. geo: _____
8. meter: _____
9. bio: _____
10. scope: _____

PART B

Directions: Using the word parts from Part A, write five words and define each one.

1. word: _____

definition: _____

2. word: _____

definition: _____

3. word: _____

definition: _____

4. word: _____

definition: _____

5. word: _____

definition: _____

PART C

Directions: Define the following words.

1. transport: _____
2. intermingle: _____
3. vocal: _____
4. inspect: _____
5. spectator: _____
6. nonresident: _____
7. invisible: _____
8. postwar: _____
9. portable: _____
10. aquarium: _____
11. hydrometer: _____
12. biography: _____
13. biology: _____
14. geology: _____
15. autograph: _____
16. curtail: _____
17. impose: _____
18. colleague: _____
19. monitor: _____
20. vowed: _____

P: PERFECTING READING SKILLS

COMPREHENDING NEWSPAPER HEADLINES

Directions: Sometimes newspapers goof, and a headline does not say what it is supposed to say. Following are some headlines that appeared in newspapers around the country. Read each one and decide what you think was meant and what is really being said.

1. "Teacher Strikes Idle Kids" (Las Vegas *Sun*)

Intended meaning: _____

_____

2. "Air Force Considers Dropping Some New Weapons" (New Orleans *Times Press*)

Intended Meaning: _____

_____

3. "Doctor Testifies in Horse Suit" (Waterbury *Republican*)

Intended meaning: _____

_____

4. "Utah Girl Does Well in Dog Show" (Salt Lake *Tribune*)

Intended meaning: _____

_____

5. "Husband Beats Republican Wife" (Indianapolis *News*)

Intended meaning: _____

_____

6. "Red Tape Holds Up New Bridge" (Milford *Citizen*)

Intended meaning: _____

_____

_____

COMPREHENDING PARAGRAPHS: MAIN IDEAS AND SUPPORT

Directions: Read the following paragraphs and answer the questions. Try not to look back to find an answer, but do so if necessary.

1. The TV quiz show is really a form of advertising. The amount of advertising on TV is limited to the times available. As a means of getting around this, the TV quiz show was created. The quiz show allows dozens of products to be seen on TV outside the paid commercial time. Manufacturers give free products and sometimes pay a fee to have their name mentioned when someone wins their product. A study of TV quiz shows revealed that as much as 40 percent of a thirty-minute show was given over to some form of advertising.

    a. What is the paragraph about? _____

    _____

    _____

    b. Why was the TV quiz show created? _____

    _____

    _____

    c. What percentage of a thirty-minute quiz show is given to some form of advertising? _____

    d. Do manufacturers pay a fee to have their name mentioned on quiz shows? _____

2. Automobile makers give free cars to TV series if their brand is made to look good. The "good guys" on the show will use the free cars provided. The "bad guys" will use a different brand. Mannix always drove a Chevrolet Camaro. Mod Squad members drove a Chrysler. Starsky and Hutch drove a Ford Torino. A Firebird was used on "The Rockford Files." A Challenger is used on "The Dukes of Hazard," and a Ferrari on "Magnum, P.I." Notice how "good" shots or scenes using the free car show up in programs of this type. A Chrysler official says that the cars they "donate" to the program must be used right. If they aren't, this is pointed out to the TV show's producer. The number of cars given is reduced if their product isn't given enough show time.

Copyright © 1988 Holt, Rinehart and Winston, Inc.

a. What is the paragraph about? _____

_____

_____

b. What examples are mentioned? _____

_____

c. What happens if a "donated" brand car does not get the coverage on

TV that the manufacturers want? _____

_____

_____

d. Why do automakers give free cars to some TV series? _____

_____

3. The average American spends more time watching TV than any other activity but sleep. For millions, the time they go to bed depends on when the late news is over or whether or not Johnny Carson will be on the "Tonight Show." Even bathroom habits are controlled by TV. The water department in one city proved this. When the movie *Airport* was shown on TV, there was a record drop on the water department gauges at 9:00 P.M. Why? It seems that at 8:30 P.M., a bomb exploded on the airplane in the movie. Little water was used during this time. But when the pilot landed the plane safely and the movie ended, 26,000 people flushed their toilets, causing 80,000 gallons of water to be used at the same time. The power of television seems to be controlling even our toilet habits.

a. What is the main idea of the paragraph? _____

_____

_____

b. What example is used to back up the main idea of the paragraph?

_____

_____

c. When did the water gauges drop? _____

_____

d. How many people flushed their toilets at the same time? _____

_____

4. Children aged five and under watch an average of 23.5 hours of TV a week. (Adults watch 44 hours per week.) This means that by the time the child graduates from high school, he or she will have watched about 15,000 hours of TV. He or she will have seen 350,000 commercials and watched 18,000 murders. Next to peers, TV has become the most powerful influence on the beliefs, attitudes, and values of young people. Television is affecting the way humans learn to become human beings. Based on what is on TV, the human race is in trouble.

a. What is the main idea of the paragraph? _____

_____

_____

b. Does the author approve of young people watching so much TV?

_____

c. How many hours of TV per week does the average adult watch?

_____

d. How many commercials has the average high school graduate watched? _____

5. One way to measure how television influences the way we live would be to find a community (perhaps a town of at least 1,000) where people are not exposed to television. We could watch these people very closely to see how their lives are different because of their lack of television. But finding such a community is nearly impossible, for there is hardly a place in the United States without television. Even in the most remote and mountainous areas, at least 90 percent of the households have television. Since there is no city that would suit our experiment in tubelessness, perhaps we could look for 1,000 average people who don't watch television. But since these people are such a minority, they can hardly be considered average. To measure the effect of television is indeed difficult precisely because television has become so much a part of ordinary life in America.

(From Understanding Mass Media by Jeffrey Schrank, National Textbook Co., 1981.)

P: Perfecting Reading Skills

a. What is the main idea of the paragraph? _____

_____

_____

b. How could we measure how television influences the way we live?

_____

_____

_____

c. Why is it impossible to do that in the United States? _____

_____

6. One experiment on the absence of television was conducted in Germany, where 184 volunteer television viewers were paid to give up TV for one year. At first the volunteers reported that they spent more time with their children, went to movies more frequently, read and played more games, and visited friends and relatives more than they did before they gave up television. But within a few weeks things began to change. Even though the people were paid not to watch, one man dropped out after only three weeks. No one lasted more than five months. Why? Tension, fighting, and quarreling increased among families without television. When the experiment was over and the sets were back on, these effects disappeared.

(From Jeffrey Schrank, op. cit., p. 21.)

a. How would your family react to such an experiment?

_____

_____

_____

b. Would you be willing to give up television for one year? _____

Why? _____

_____

_____

c. Why do you think tension, fighting, and arguing rose when TV was removed? _____

_____

_____

7. One of the psychologists who conducted the experiment believes that watching TV tends to cover up conflicts and disagreements between habitual viewers. That is, instead of working out problems, people avoid them by watching TV. TV works as sort of a buffer between people, helping them to be together without having to work out their conflicts. Take away the TV set and the rough edges begin to show.

   a. How does this answer compare with yours in question 6c above?

   _____

   _____

   _____

   b. Is the psychologist's answer fact or opinion? _____

   Explain. _____

   _____

COMPREHENDING ESSAYS: SKIMMING AND SCANNING

Directions: *Skimming* is quickly looking over something to get a general idea what it is about. Skimming is used when you don't need to read every word but only want to get a general idea of what you are reading. You look for main ideas and ignore the details. *Scanning*, on the other hand, is used when you know what you are looking for, such as a name, a date, a page number, a word in a dictionary, or a telephone number.

The following essay should be used to practice both skimming and scanning. First you will be asked to skim the essay, not read it. Try to take less than two minutes to read the title, the opening paragraph, the first sentence of each paragraph, and then the last paragraph. After you answer some skimming questions, you will then be given some questions to answer by scanning for them. Time yourself or have someone time you.

MAKING TV COMMERCIALS
ROY WILSON

1   According to the magazine *Advertising Age,* last year over $30 billion was spent on advertising. Television advertising alone cost over $5 billion. For most of us, billions of dollars are too much to really comprehend. Let's put it this way. If you want to sell something on one of the major television networks, it will cost you anywhere from $160,000 to $380,000 for just thirty seconds of prime time on a top-rated show. In 1986, because of the popularity of the Bill Cosby Show, advertisers were willing to spend $380,000 for only a thirty-second spot to reach that audience.

2   Now those large dollar amounts represent only the cost of *time.* The cost of writing, designing, and filming an ad for TV can be more than $200,000 for one thirty-second commercial. Then there is the cost of paying well-known people to be in the ads. Polaroid Camera is reported to have paid Laurence Olivier $250,000 to do one ad for them. The late John Wayne received over $1,000,000 to do a series of thirty-second commercials that were not even broadcast nationally.

3   Making an advertisement for television often costs more to make than a movie for television. Take a two-hour movie that costs $6 million to make. Costs average out to about $50,000 a minute, or $833 a second. A TV commercial by comparison can cost more than $6,000 a second. And that does not include the cost of paying for air time.

4   A major television network pays an average of about $300,000 for one episode of an hour TV series. That's about $5,000 a minute, or $85 a second. Compare $85 a second with $6,000 a second for a TV commercial. Which one is obviously more valuable, the program or the commercial? In terms of money—and making money is what television is all about—the commercial is by far more important.

5   Because of the importance of a TV ad, advertising agencies do much preparation before shooting a commercial. Research, market testing, talent, time, and money—all come together to make us want to buy a product. No matter how bad we think a commercial is, it works. Jeff Greenfield wrote in his article "Down to the Last Detail," that "... Charmin bathroom tissue commercials (they can't bear to call it toilet paper) will be a contributing factor to the fall of

Reprinted by permission of the author.

American civilization, should that happen. But those commercials carved out a substantial share of the market for a product that had nothing unusual to offer except a public impression formed from advertising."

6   In other words, we may think it's silly to hear the store owner say, "Please don't squeeze the Charmin." But silly or not, the commercial works. The sales of Charmin went up once the ads began. TV commercials actually buy their way into our heads. We, in turn, buy the product.

7   And the ads work because so much time and attention are given them. For example, making a beer ad is not easy. An advertising man tells of the effort that went into making one 30-second commercial. "The 'pour' shot is the key to a beer ad. How the beer looks going down the glass; whether the glass is completely clean and suggests ice-cold beer; how the bubbles look, whether the head on the beer is big enough, but not too big. Our standard order for a 'pour' shot was ten cases of beer—240 cans. And it wasn't overdoing it. I remember one pour shot which took 124 takes before the beer looked exactly right."

8   Such attention and time go into making all ads. Here are some rules of commercial ad making. If you want to get the blue-collar, lower-middle-class buyer, make sure the announcer has a tough, manly voice. Put some people in the ad who look as if they work with their hands. If you want to sell to an upper-class audience, make sure that the house, the furniture, the books on the shelves, the clothes, the hairstyle, and so forth are the type that group identifies with. If you want to make the buyer feel superior to the character selling the product, then make that person so stupid or silly everyone will feel great about himself or herself.

9   We laugh at commercials. We think we're above them. We think they don't affect us. We don't think we pay that much attention to them. But evidence shows we are kidding ourselves. The making of a TV commercial that costs more than $6,000 a second, plus the cost of buying TV time, is not kid stuff. It's big, big business. And it's telling us what to think, what we need, and what to buy. To put it simply, the TV commercial is a legal form of brainwashing.

SKIMMING QUESTIONS

See if you can answer these questions without looking back at the article.

1. What is the title of the essay? _____

_____

2. What is the main point of the essay? _____

_____

_____

P: Perfecting Reading Skills

3. Which often costs more, making a television commercial or a two-hour movie? _____

4. List at least four things you remember from skimming the essay.

_____

_____

_____

_____

SCANNING QUESTIONS

Scan back through the essay to answer these questions.

5. How much money was spent on TV advertising last year? _____

_____

6. What does it cost per second to make a two-hour movie? _____

_____

7. What does it cost per second to make a 30-second commercial? _____

_____

8. How many cans of beer are usually ordered to make a "pour" ad?

_____

9. What is the point of paragraph 4? _____

_____

_____

10. What is the point of paragraph 9? _____

_____

_____

COMPREHENDING BIAS AND INFERENCE

Directions: The following reading selection was written by a famous syndicated newspaper columnist, Andy Rooney. He frequently appears on the television news magazine "60 Minutes." This selection serves as an example of the type of writing you will find on the editorial pages of newspapers.

Read the following essay looking for bias and inference. *Bias,* you'll remember, is having a leaning or prejudice for or against something. An *inference* is an educated guess or conclusion made on information available. An author may imply something by not stating thoughts or feelings directly. You then make an inference based on the information given. As you read Andy Rooney's essay, see if you can identify what he is biased against (it's what caused him to write this essay). Also look for points he may imply but not state directly.

NEWS IS MEANT TO INFORM, NOT TO MAKE AN IMPRESSION

ANDY ROONEY

1   Last week I spoke to a group of people in San Diego and, by any standard, you'd have to say they were above average. They were asking me questions about things I didn't know a whole lot about, but they didn't seem to mind and we were all having fun until one fellow got up and asked me the question that people in the news business are asked most often:

2   "How come you never report any of the good things that happen in this country?"

3   I say it's a question, but it's usually asked in such a manner as to suggest you are the agent of a foreign government trying to bring down the United States of America.

4   There's something that people who ask that question don't understand, and I don't suppose anything I say here is going to help but I'm going to say it anyway.

5   In the first place, news by its very nature is often negative. News is change, a deviation from what's normal or the way things have been. Mount St. Helens at rest is normal, and when it doesn't erupt you won't find pictures of it on Page 1. When it erupts it is a news story because it's an abrupt change that has a negative effect on the lives of a lot of people. You could say the same of a ship-

Reprinted with permission of the author, Andrew A. Rooney. From And More *by Andy Rooney,* Atheneum, 1982.

P: Perfecting Reading Skills 299

wreck or Congress. Congressmen are honest for the most part, and it is only news when one of them steals and is caught.

6   My questioner in this case went so far as to suggest that newspapers and television journalism ought to seek out stories that show America in a good light. In other words, he thinks we should put news to work creating an effect. We should choose our stories, not for their news value, but for the impression they will have on readers.

7   I'm sure this man is good to his wife and children and works hard at his job, but he doesn't know a damned thing about what makes this country great and free.

8   Who would he suggest choose these "good" stories about America? Could anything so important be left to editors? Wouldn't it be better to have a government agency oversee the choice? There's plenty of precedent for this around the world. Our government agency could take a trip to the Soviet Union to see how they do it there. It isn't as oppressive as we think. They just don't let the journalists create a lot of negative ideas in people's heads by letting them report "bad" stories.

9   For instance, Russian readers never have to read about an airplane crash.

10 Aeroflot, the Soviet airline, is run by the government, and why undermine confidence in the government, right, Ivan?

11 Russians didn't have to worry about wheat production falling 20 percent below predictions in the Soviet Union this year, either, because that bad news wasn't reported in the papers. They'll find out about it soon enough when there's not enough bread to go around this winter.

12 It's difficult for anyone in the news business to understand how anyone can think news ought to be used for any purpose but to inform. As soon as it is used to promote one good cause, such as patriotism, by having positive allusions to that cause inserted in its news columns, that's the end of a free press . . .

13 There's no doubt about it, news is tough to take here sometimes. In a single day's paper you can read of one politician calling another a liar, you can read of murder, drug busts, bribery of elected officials, dishonest police and 12 percent inflation, but if some Americans find it more difficult to believe this is a great country because of the negative stories they read about it, that's their problem. It's right for us all to love America because you have to love your own in the world. But we ought to love it enough and believe in it enough to know that it will stand up in open competition with any country in the world, even when all the unpleasant facts about it are known.

Now answer these questions.

RECALL

1. Which of the following best states the thesis of the essay?
    a. Some people don't understand the purpose of reporting the news.
    b. The news is meant to inform, not to make an impression.

c. The news reporting in the United States is better and more informative than the news reporting the Russians get.
   d. Continually hearing bad news is tough to take, and news reporters should look for good news to give us.
2. The author believes that news people should select stories to report that show America in a good light.

   a. True

   b. False, because _____

   _____

   _____

3. How does Rooney define news? _____

   _____

   _____

INTERPRETATION

4. We can infer from paragraph 4 that the author doesn't think what he has to say will change the questioner's mind.

   a. True

   b. False, because _____

   _____

5. What bias toward the questioner does Rooney show in paragraph 7?

   _____

   _____

   _____

6. Can we infer that Rooney means what he says in paragraph 8 regarding a government agency selecting what news to give the people? _____

   _____

P: Perfecting Reading Skills 301

7. What is the purpose of paragraph 11; that is, what is the point Rooney is making? _____

_____

_____

_____

8. What does Rooney think is the purpose of news reporting?

_____

_____

_____

Why do you agree or disagree? _____

_____

_____

_____

APPLICATION

9. Skim through today's newspaper to see how many reported events could be called "good news" as compared with what might be termed "bad news." What news items do you think are used to make an impression, and which ones are used to inform? Bring them in to share with the class.
10. Look carefully at the stories that appear on the first page of today's newspaper. Do you think they all deserve to be major, front-page news items, or are some of them used to grab your attention so you will buy the paper? Discuss them in class.

Name _____ **Section** _____ **Date** _____

Chapter 9

Objectives

- **P:** **PREREADING DRILLS**
  Words to Know
  Warm-up Drills
- **R:** **READING DRILL**
  Reading and Thinking About What You Read
  "Increasing Aesthetic Comprehension" by W. Royce Adams
  Comprehension Check
- **E:** **EXERCISES IN VOCABULARY**
  Drills
  - 1: Word Categories
  - 2: Greek Word Parts
  - 3: Latin Word Parts
  - 4: Root Words
  - 5: Words in Context

  Vocabulary Check
- **P:** **PERFECTING READING SKILLS**
  Comprehending Reference Materials
  Comprehending Maps, Tables, and Graphs
  Comprehending What You Read
  "The Idea Killers" by Kurt Vonnegut, Jr.
- **UNIT 3 CHECK TEST (CHAPTERS 7–9)**
  - 1: Word Knowledge
  - 2: Word Usage
  - 3: Comprehending Paragraphs
  - 4: Essay Reading

  "The Right Answer" by Roger von Oech

Objectives

When you have finished this chapter, you will

1. Recognize and be able to use at least 90 percent of the vocabulary words from the Words to Know section.
2. Have developed your ability to organize information by dealing with word categories.
3. Have developed your ability to make and understand outlines.
4. Know and be able to use at least fifteen more Greek and Latin word parts.
5. Be able to name and use at least twenty more words containing Greek and Latin word parts.
6. Have developed further your ability to deal with words in context.
7. Have developed your ability to use skimming and scanning skills with reference materials such as a table of contents, an index, a glossary, maps, tables, and graphs.
8. Have developed your reading skills in all areas of comprehension.

P: PREREADING DRILLS

WORDS TO KNOW

Directions: Read the following words aloud. Learn the definitions of any words you don't know.

1. *aesthetic*—pertaining to artistic beauty.
People who don't read much literature never get a chance to develop their aesthetic level of comprehension.
2. *sensory impressions*—feeling, smelling, seeing, hearing, or tasting.
Some readers are able to get strong sensory impressions from good, descriptive writing.
3. *hypocrisy*—pretending to believe or feel something you don't.
In his novel *Huckleberry Finn,* Mark Twain makes a strong attack on hypocrisy and the inhumanity of human beings to each other.
4. *retain*—to hold on to or keep.
William Golding's *Lord of the Flies* shows the useless attempts the boys make to retain their British upbringing.
5. *conveyed*—communicated; carried; passed on.
The theme and ideas conveyed in the story are very real.
6. *itinerant*—traveling from place to place.
John Steinbeck's *Grapes of Wrath* reflects many facts about the itinerant farmer during the depression period.
7. *expository prose*—information presented in a clear, precise way, such as an essay; nonfiction.
Sometimes good fiction can be more powerful and memorable than expository prose.
8. *superficial*—what's apparent rather than under the surface.
Most study guides for novels are rather superficial and do not deal with the aesthetic levels of the book.
9. *sarcasm*—poking fun at someone or something, often by stating the opposite of what is meant by using bitter, harsh language.
Figures of speech can often reflect sarcasm, such as saying "Nice work!" when someone drops a dish.
10. *participant*—someone who takes part in an event.
In first-person novels, the narrator is usually a participant in what goes on in the story.

P: Prereading Drills

WARM-UP DRILLS

DRILL 1

Directions: Read from left to right. Mark the word by the number each time it appears on the same line. Don't look back on any line. Don't change any errors you notice. Just keep moving. Try to finish in twenty-five seconds or less. Begin timing.

1.	sense	sensory sensible sense senseless since
2.	rapid	rabid rabbit rapid rabid ranch ripe
3.	escape	enjoy essence escape essential enjoy
4.	aesthetic	aerial aesthetic aeroplane astronauts
5.	author	authority authors author authority audit
6.	mature	nature maturate mother mature nature
7.	evaluate	elevate elevator evaluate evaluation
8.	morals	morale more morbid moral morals moral
9.	hypocrisy	hypocrite hypodermic hyperactive hypocrite
10.	gradual	graduate gradually gradual gradual grade
11.	conveyed	convoy conveyed convey conveyed confess
12.	depicts	deride depicts depicted depiction deep
13.	itinerant	itinerant itinerary itinerant itchy indent
14.	symbolic	symbol symbolic symbolically symbol sump
15.	primitive	primary prim properly primitive primeval
16.	retain	remain retaliate refrain report retrain
17.	expository	expose explain expository repository
18.	superficial	supergirl super supper superficial super
19.	universal	universe unicycle universal universe unit
20.	figurative	figure figures finger fugitive figurative

TIME: _____

Check each line carefully. Make sure you have marked each word correctly. The words by the numbers all appear in the essay you will soon read. Make sure you know their meanings.

TOTAL LINES CORRECT: _____

Copyright © 1988 Holt, Rinehart and Winston, Inc.

DRILL 2

Directions: Read from left to right. Mark the word by the number each time it appears on the same line. Don't look back on the same line. Don't change any errors you may make. Work rapidly. Try to finish in twenty-five seconds or less. Begin timing.

1. weather   whether   weather   whether   weather   whether
2. further   further   farther   farther   farther   further
3. former   farmer   former   former   farmer   farmer
4. tended   tender   tender   tended   tender   tender
5. sightings   sighings   sightings   sighings   signings   sightings
6. ridge   ridge   bridge   ridge   bridge   ridge
7. radar   radio   radar   redder   radar   radio
8. gulley   galley   galley   gulley   galley   gulley
9. orbit   order   orbit   order   orbit   order
10. booster   brother   bother   booster   brother   booster
11. tumble   tumbling   thumb   thimble   tumbled   thumb
12. debris   debris   debts   debris   debts   depth
13. advance   advice   advances   advancement   advance   advance
14. mirage   mirror   mirage   mirage   mirror   minor
15. hoaxes   horses   horses   hoaxes   horses   hoaxes
16. peer   pear   pair   peer   perm   peer
17. mirage   mirror   manor   miner   mirage   miracle
18. extensive   extension   extensive   extension   extensive
19. debris   denude   debris   decant   debris   detonate
20. galaxy   galley   galaxy   gulley   gulf   galaxy

TIME: _____

Check each line to see if you marked the correct word. Learn the meanings of any words you don't know. Notice there is no word to mark for item 11. Did you look back on that line?

TOTAL LINES CORRECT: _____

DRILL 3

Directions: Follow the same directions as for the previous drill. Try to finish in twenty-five seconds or less.
Begin timing.

P: Prereading Drills

1. peer   pear   peer   pear   peer   pear   pear
2. outright   outside   outright   outdoors   outright   outside
3. discredit   disobey   disorder   discredit   disobey   disorder
4. launch   lunch   lurch   launch   lunch   lurch
5. charred   charred   chained   charred   chained   char
6. cirrus   circus   cirrus   circus   circle   cirrus
7. disc   desk   disc   disco   discs   disco
8. credibility   credit   credibility   credentials   credited
9. galactic   galaxy   gala   galactic   galaxy   galactic
10. claim   chain   chair   chain   claim   clams
11. survey   serve   survey   service   serve   survey
12. disturbed   disturb   disturbed   distress   disturb   disturbed
13. visible   visual   vision   visible   vision   visual
14. craft   crop   crafty   crusty   craft   craft
15. meteors   meters   meteors   meters   meaty   meteors
16. hoax   howl   hoax   howdy   here   hex
17. justified   justice   just   juice   justified
18. luminous   lusty   luminous   luminous   luxury
19. biology   biography   biography   biology   biography
20. parallel   parallax   parallel   parachute   perfect

TIME: _____

Check each line carefully. Make sure you have marked the correct word every time it appears. Learn any words you may not know.

TOTAL LINES CORRECT: _____

DRILL 4: DEFINITION REVIEW

Directions: Write the letter of the correct definition in the blank by the word.

_____   1. aesthetic   a. moving about

_____   2. sensory   b. lacking depth

_____   3. hypocrisy   c. to keep

_____   4. retain   d. pertaining to beauty

_____ 5. convey   e. single-minded

_____ 6. itinerant   f. one who takes part

_____ 7. expository   g. providing information

_____ 8. superficial   h. to tell or pass along

_____ 9. sarcasm   i. dealing with the senses

_____ 10. participant   j. phoniness; saying one thing but doing another

k. nasty humor

l. a belt

R: READING DRILL

READING AND THINKING ABOUT WHAT YOU READ

Directions: Before reading the following selection, answer these questions.

1. Look at the title of the following essay. What do you think it will say about aesthetic comprehension? _____

_____

_____

2. What do you think aesthetic comprehension is? _____

_____

3. Look at each of the headings. Write down what you think each section will cover.

_____

_____

_____

_____

_____

4. What do you think you might learn from this selection that could help you develop your reading skills? _____

_____

_____

Now read the article.

INCREASING AESTHETIC COMPREHENSION
W. ROYCE ADAMS

What Is Aesthetic Comprehension?

There are at least three levels of comprehension: literal, critical, and aesthetic. Literal comprehension is the level you use to understand and recall main ideas, to follow directions, and to summarize what you have read. It's the most basic level. Critical comprehension is what you need to understand the difference between fact and opinion, to recognize bias and inference. It's the level of understanding that allows you to make valid judgments. Aesthetic comprehension is the awareness of the art and beauty of writing. Appreciating an author's humor, irony, satire, use of language, and quality in writing requires the development of aesthetic comprehension.

The three levels of comprehension really are needed for total understanding of what we read. Even though we talk about them as separate parts, all three levels should work together at the same time. We have difficulty reading when all three levels are *not* working together. It is then that we have to pay attention to one or more parts of total comprehension before we understand what we are reading. For instance, we may have to learn the literal meaning of a word before we can understand a sentence. Once we understand the literal meaning, we have to respond critically by making sure whether we are reading fact, opinion, bias, or inference so that we can accept or reject the ideas in the sentence. Then we can react to the quality of the way the language is used in the sentence. Good readers usually have all three levels of comprehension working at the same time.

Unfortunately, the aesthetic level of comprehension doesn't usually get the teaching attention the other levels get. But it should. It is that level of understanding that helps us appreciate sensory impressions: to feel, hear, see, taste, and smell the descriptive images created by words. It enables us to understand characters, plot, conflict, and emotions in fictional writings. But most important, it helps us see the deeper meanings and social commentaries of the authors we read. Above all, it is that level of comprehension that deals with making reading enjoyable.

There are, of course, many levels of enjoyment. Some readers enjoy factual prose rather than fiction. Some readers prefer science fiction to Westerns. Others prefer short stories to novels. But it doesn't matter what form of literature mature readers prefer; they read for the aesthetic experience. And the fact that they read much means that their enjoyment and taste grow with each reading of something new.

Reprinted with the author's permission.

Fiction Versus Fact

Some readers feel that fiction is not "real," that reading fiction is just a way to escape from the world's realities for a while. But good fiction is a mixture of fiction and reality. Mark Twain's *The Adventures of Huckleberry Finn* may be classified as fiction because the characters, events, and dialogue are all "made up." Yet the book gives us a very real account of the life along the Mississippi River in the 1830s. The values of the people, their morals, their dress, their eating habits, their speech are all "real." That book provides us with a better and more interesting view of that period than any American history book can. But readers who read only for a story never utilize their aesthetic level of comprehension. They can never really feel sympathy for Huck with his moral struggle regarding his relationship with a black slave, his friend Jim. They can never see that Twain was writing a bitter attack on hypocrisy, stupidity, and the inhumanity of people to each other. For the purely literal reader, the book is just a story, make-believe. And for still other poor readers, the story is taken so literally that it offends them, and they ask for the book to be banned from schools and libraries.

Another book, *Lord of the Flies* by William Golding, is a fictional account of a group of young English boys planewrecked on an island during an atomic war. Golding shows in the story the useless attempts of the boys to retain their British upbringing and shows their gradual destruction of one another. Though a sad story in many ways, it is a powerfully symbolic account of Golding's belief that the problems we have in society are caused by the defects or flaws of human nature. So, though the story is fiction, the theme and ideas of the story are very real and provide the good reader with food for thought. However, those readers who have not yet developed their three levels of comprehension find certain ideas offensive, so they want books such as this banned.

Writers of good fiction attempt to communicate real experience. They know that telling an experience or relating ideas factually in expository prose is often less effective than sharing through fiction. We usually feel an experience we are shown rather than just told. In fiction, we feel the characters' happiness and sorrow. Some of the most interesting characters we ever meet are in literature. Characters such as Holden Caulfield in *Catcher in the Rye*, Captain Ahab in *Moby-Dick*, Willy Loman in *Death of a Salesman*, Boo Radley in *To Kill a Mockingbird*, to name a few, have become as real to readers as any person who ever lived.

Depending on the book you pick, you can read fiction and still be dealing with fact. John Steinbeck's *The Grapes of Wrath*, for example, portrays many facts about the itinerant farmer during the depression of the late 1920s and early 1930s. Read James T. Farrell's *Young Lonigan* to learn about the influence environment plays on a teenager growing up. Read Joseph Conrad's *Heart of Darkness* to learn what happens to a man who "goes native" and how close we all are to our primitive desires in spite of our civilized codes. Read Robert Ruark's *Something of Value* for facts about racial issues in Africa. Read Irving

Stone's *Lust for Life* for facts regarding the artist Vincent van Gogh. Read Ray Bradbury's *Fahrenheit 451* for a fictional view of what could be a factual future if humans lose their desire to read and be challenged by ideas. The list could go on and on. The point is that good fiction is generally based on facts of life, facts that are far more powerfully stated than can usually be done in expository prose.

Some works deserve more than one reading. You may read *Huckleberry Finn* as a child and delight in the adventures of Huck and Jim as they float on a raft down the river. If you read the novel in college, you may become aware of the social commentaries you weren't prepared for as a child. If you read the novel again after you've become a parent, it may bring back memories of your own youth. Such novels are considered "classics" because they offer something new with every reading. Their characters, their themes, their conflicts are universal and apply to our human characteristics no matter when the novels were written.

Aesthetic Comprehension and Figurative Language

Developing aesthetic comprehension requires not only having good literal and critical reading skills but also an appreciation of how language is used. Skillful writers often use figurative language. Figurative language is language used in an imaginative way. Here we will discuss four figures of speech: *simile* (sim'i lē), *metaphor* (met'a for), *hyperbole* (hī per'bō lē), and *litotes* (lī'tō tēs).

The two familiar figures of speech are *similes* and *metaphors*. A simile (from the word *similar*) likens one thing with another by using the words *like* or *as*. Here's a simile using *as:* "She has a heart as big as a whale." Here's a simile using *like:* "My love is like a red, red rose."

Not all uses of the word *like* create similes. When you hear, "Your mother is just like mine," that's not a simile because the comparison is not being made of two different things, such as a heart that is the size of a whale or love that is like a rose. Similes, then, liken two unlike objects as being similar.

A metaphor does the same thing as a simile but does *not* use the words *like* or *as*. A metaphor suggests or implies there is a likeness between two things. Here are a couple of metaphors: (1) "All the world's a stage." (2) "I cried so hard the cards in my hands ran in a river of mascara." Notice (1) likens the world to a stage. Metaphor (2) compares tears with a "river of mascara."

Another effective figure of speech is a *hyperbole*. A hyperbole is an extreme exaggeration and is used in an attempt to emphasize a point. When someone says, "Man, the winds last night must have blown a hundred miles an hour," the attempt is to emphasize the fact that the winds blew hard, not necessarily an actual 100 mph. Here are some other hyperboles: (1) "It'll take me a thousand years to finish this assignment!" (2) "Her head is in the clouds." (3) "If mom finds out, I'm dead!"

A *litotes* is a figure of speech that is almost the opposite of hyperbole. Whereas hyperboles exaggerate, litotes understate. They usually have a touch of irony or sarcasm behind their meaning and state the opposite of what is meant. A woman, shopping for a dress, is shown a dress that costs $600. "Only $600, you say," she tells the sales clerk, meaning actually, "You've got to be crazy." A husband is looking at his body in a mirror and says to his wife, "Not bad for a man of forty, huh?" She replies, "Sure, you'll live to be a hundred and twenty." Her real intent is a put-down. A father looks at his daughter's report card: all *D*'s. He tells her, "You're a regular genius." A student tells his literature instructor that William Faulkner was a great writer. The instructor answers, "Not bad, not bad." In all cases, the figures of speech used mean the opposite and imply sarcasm or irony.

Knowing how to respond to figures of speech is part of knowing how to read well. The more you read, the more you encounter figures of speech; the more you feel comfortable with them, the more you will comprehend. The more you can comprehend, the more rewarding reading can be, and the more you will be tuned in to the artful side of writing.

Why read literature? We need to read literature because it reflects the ideas, the beliefs, the feelings, the intellect of humankind. It exposes us to the thoughts, actions, and conclusions of others. It exposes us to comedy and tragedy, to ugliness and beauty, to romanticism and realism, to emotion and rationality. It reflects the success and failure of others and helps us shape a code of values by which to live. Though fiction may be based on a made-up world, it enriches our lives by showing us what is real or what could be real, in an artistic and emotional manner.

A good reader finds literature the best doorway to understanding others and, above all, to understanding himself or herself.

COMPREHENSION CHECK

Directions: Answer the following questions. Don't look back unless you are asked to do so.

RECALL

1. What is aesthetic comprehension? _____

    _____

2. What is figurative language? _____

    _____

3. What is the difference between similes and metaphors? _____

    _____

    _____

4. What is the difference between hyperbole and litotes? _____

_____

_____

_____

5. What are some of the reasons given for reading fictional literature? _____

_____

_____

_____

INTERPRETATION

6. We can infer that the author likes reading fiction.

    a. True

    b. False, because _____

    _____

7. We can infer that the author believes most people read superficially.

    a. True

    b. False, because _____

    _____

8. How does the author define "classical" fiction?

_____

_____

_____

R: Reading Drill

APPLICATION

9. Make up an example of a simile and a metaphor.

   _____

   _____

   _____

   _____

10. Go to the library and read the first few pages of one of the books mentioned in the essay. Decide on one of them and check it out to read. Let your instructor know which one you selected and why.

Name _____ Section _____ Date _____

E: EXERCISES IN VOCABULARY

DRILLS

DRILL 1: WORD CATEGORIES (PART A)

Directions: Following are two lists of words. Write the letter of the word from the right-hand column in the blank in front of the word by the number that means the same thing or almost the same thing. Use your dictionary when needed.

_____ 1. hallucination   a. trick

_____ 2. protagonist   b. expose

_____ 3. haughty   c. delusion

_____ 4. mentor   d. stuck-up

_____ 5. tote   e. bright

_____ 6. botch   f. hero

_____ 7. discredit   g. supervision; observation

_____ 8. hoax   h. wreck

_____ 9. luminous   i. carry

_____ 10. surveillance   j. teacher

PART B

Directions: Following are a list of words and an unfinished outline. Complete the outline by writing the words from the list in the correct category. The first word has been done for you.

weapons	comedy	guard	armor
luminous	fort	sparkling	wittiness
astronauts	satellites	orbit	brilliant
joking	intelligent	levity	clown

E: Exercises in Vocabulary

I. defense

   A. _weapons_

   B. _____

   C. _____

   D. _____

II. humor

   A. _____

   B. _____

   C. _____

   D. _____

   E. _____

III. bright

   A. _____

   B. _____

   C. _____

   D. _____

IV. space

   A. _____

   B. _____

   C. _____

DRILL 2: GREEK WORD PARTS

Directions: In the last chapter you learned some Greek word parts. Study the Greek word parts that follow. Review the ones in the last chapter if you need to. Then answer the questions that follow.

anthrop = man
derm = skin
path = feeling, disease
phil = love
phob = fear
psych = mind
zo = animal

aster (astro) = star
bibl = book
dem = people
crat, cracy = power, rule
gam = marriage
miso = hatred
pseudo = false

1. If biology is the study of life, what is *anthropology*? _____

2. If *a* means without, what does *apathy* mean? _____

3. What is *astrology*? _____

4. What is a *philanthropist*? _____

5. What word means the study of the mind? _____

6. If *phobia* means fear of, what does *anthropophobia* mean? _____

7. What does *democracy* mean? _____

8. What word means the study of animals? _____

9. What would *galactic zoology* refer to? _____

E: Exercises in Vocabulary

10. If *graph* means writing or record, what is *bibliography?* _____

_____

11. What is a *misogamist?* _____

_____

12. If *nym* means name, what is a *pseudonym?* _____

_____

13. What is a *pseudopsychologist?* _____

_____

14. What is a *bibliophile?* _____

_____

15. If *poly* means many, what is *polygamy?* _____

_____

16. What word means the opposite of *philanthropist?* _____

_____

17. What word means the study of skin disorders? _____

_____

18. What is the opposite of a *philogamist?* _____

_____

19. What is *pseudoscience?* _____

_____

20. What is the opposite of a *misanthrope?* _____

_____

DRILL 3: LATIN WORD PARTS

Directions: Here are some more Latin word parts. Study them, and then answer the questions that follow.

aud, audit = hear, listen to
dic(t) = tell, speak
mit, miss = send, sent
ped, pod = foot
fac = make, do
man, manu = hand

cred = believe
fort = strong
gen = race, birth, kind
contra = against
cap = take, hold
de = down from, reverse

1. If you have an *auditory* problem, what kind of problem is it? _____

2. If you *contradict* someone's story, what are you doing? _____

3. If you did not know what *manufacture* means, how could you figure it out? _____

4. What does it mean to *transmit* something? _____

5. If *credible* means believable, what does *incredible* mean?

6. If you say someone has *fortitude* when it comes to not eating too much, what does it mean?

7. Why do you think the first book in the Bible is called *Genesis*?

8. If an actress *captivates* an audience, what does it mean?

E: Exercises in Vocabulary

9. If someone gives you an *audition,* what are they giving you? _____
   _____

10. If *tri* means three, what is a *tripod?* _____
    _____

11. To do something *manually* is to do it by _____

12. *Genes* have to do with _____

13. *Pedal, pedestrian, peds*—all have the root _____ , which means
    _____

14. When you *deplane,* you are _____
    _____

15. When you give *credence* to someone's story, you _____
    _____

16. Circle the Latin roots in the following words:

    a. auditorium   b. factory   c. dictation   d. captive

DRILL 4: ROOT WORDS

Directions: Some phrases in groups follow. In each group, three of the four phrases have words that are from the same root word. Fill in the root word, and check the blank in front of the phrase that does *not* have a word from the same root.
For example:

   a. _____ a portable TV

   b. __✓__ portray a villain

   c. _____ good transportation

   d. _____ import tax

   Root: ___*port*___

1. a. _____ had countless bills
    b. _____ needs to recount
    c. _____ hilly country
    d. _____ he miscounted

    Root: _____

2. a. _____ the missing factor
    b. _____ not on factory time
    c. _____ a facial massage
    d. _____ manufactures toys

    Root: _____

3. a. _____ a new automobile
    b. _____ what the mob wants
    c. _____ it's very mobile
    d. _____ let's mobilize now

    Root: _____

4. a. _____ throw the dice
    b. _____ a little dictator
    c. _____ take dictation
    d. _____ has good diction

    Root: _____

5. a. _____ she captivated him
    b. _____ they captured four
    c. _____ take no captives
    d. _____ six or seven caps

    Root: _____

6. a. _____ telephone
    b. _____ he's a phony
    c. _____ phonograph record
    d. _____ study of phonics

    Root: _____

DRILL 5: WORDS IN CONTEXT

Directions: In the following passage, every fifth word is left out. See if you can figure out what words fit in the blanks. The first ones have been done for you.

When most people think ___*of*___ flying saucers or, as ___*UFOs*___ are mostly austerely called, "___*unidentified*___ flying objects" (UFOs), they think _____ them as spaceships coming

E: Exercises in Vocabulary   **323**

_____ outside Earth and manned

_____ intelligent beings. Is there

_____ chance of this? Do _____

"little green men" really _____? There are arguments

pro _____ con.

　　There is, according _____ the best astronomical

thinking _____, a strong chance that

_____ is very common in _____

universe. Our own galaxy, _____ over a hundred billion

_____, is only one of _____ a

hundred billion galaxies.

　　Current _____ about how stars are

_____ make it seem likely _____

planets are formed also _____ that every star may

_____ planets about it. Surely _____

of those planets would _____ like our Earth in

_____ and temperature.

　　Current theories _____ how life got its

_____ make it seem that _____

planet with something like _____ chemistry and

temperature would _____ sure to develop life.

_____ reasonable estimate advanced by

_____ astronomer was that there

Copyright © 1988 Holt, Rinehart and Winston, Inc.

_____ be as many as 640,000,000

_____ in our galaxy alone _____

are Earthlike and that _____ life.

But on how _____ of these planets is

_____ intelligent life? We can't

_____, but suppose that only _____

out of a million _____ planets develops intelligent life

_____ and that only one _____ of

ten of these _____ a technological civilization more

_____ than our own. There _____

still be as many _____ 1,000 different advanced

civilizations _____ our galaxy, and perhaps

_____ hundred more in every

_____ galaxy. Why shouldn't some

_____ them have reached us?

VOCABULARY CHECK

PART ONE

Directions: Define the following words.

1. phobia: _____

2. astrology: _____

3. democracy: _____

4. anthropology: _____

Copyright © 1988 Holt, Rinehart and Winston, Inc.

E: Exercises in Vocabulary

5. zoology: _____

6. credible: _____

7. contradict: _____

8. captivate: _____

9. deplane: _____

10. credence: _____

PART TWO

Directions: Supply the word that fits the following definitions.

1. to do by hand   _____

2. a person walking   _____

3. to send a message   _____

4. a place to hear speakers and concerts   _____

5. believable   _____

6. a book lover   _____

7. a phony lover   _____

8. many marriages   _____

9. someone who hates humans   _____

10. a list of books   _____

Name _____ **Section** _____ **Date** _____

P: PERFECTING READING SKILLS

COMPREHENDING REFERENCE MATERIALS

DRILL 1: THE TABLE OF CONTENTS

Directions: A table of contents appears in the front of nearly every book. It is a table or list of the book's contents. By skimming a book's table of contents, you get a good idea of what the book will cover. A table of contents appears on page 327. First, *skim* over the table of contents. Then answer each of the following questions by *scanning* the table of contents for the answer.

1. Can you tell from skimming and scanning if the book takes UFOs seriously? _____ Why? _____
   _____

2. If you did not know what is meant by "Close Encounters of the Third Kind," where could you find the answer? _____
3. If you were going to write a paper on the history of UFOs, would this book contain any information to help you? _____
   Where? _____

4. What type of photographs are in the book? _____
   _____

5. If you wanted to read more about UFOs, is there anything in the book to help you? _____ What? _____
6. On what page would you find out about scientists' attitudes about UFOs?
   _____

7. On what page would you find out about the Air Force's Blue Book?
   _____

8. If you started reading on page 141, what would you learn about?
   _____

326

Copyright © 1988 Holt, Rinehart and Winston, Inc.

Contents

Preface v

Part 1: The Reality of UFOs

Chapter 1: Science Laughs at UFOs 3
Chapter 2: History of UFO Reports 17
Chapter 3: UFO Reports: Update 29
Chapter 4: UFOs Are Real 42

Part 2: The Information and the Problem

Chapter 5: UFO Night Sightings 52
Chapter 6: UFO Daylight Sightings 76
Chapter 7: Close Encounters of the First Kind 84
Chapter 8: Close Encounters of the Second Kind ... 102
Chapter 9: Close Encounters of the Third Kind 126

Part 3: The Future

Chapter 10: The Center for UFO Studies 141
Chapter 11: The Air Force's Blue Book 162
Chapter 12: What's Next? 186

Appendix 1: Photos of Hoaxes 197
Appendix 2: Photos of Sightings Thought to Be Real .. 201
Bibliography of Readings On UFOs 226
Index 233

9. By just reading the titles to the three parts of the book, what can you guess

the book will cover? _____
10. If you were doing a report on UFOs, would this book be helpful?

_____Why? _____

_____

DRILL 2: THE INDEX

Directions: An index appears at the end of a book. An index lists in alphabetical order the subjects, names, and terms used in the book. Page numbers are given so you can easily find something or see if the book covers what you are looking for. Part of an index is shown on page 329. Scan the index to answer the following questions.

1. On what pages would you find information about "Close Encounters of the

Second Kind"? _____

2. On what page would you find information about a "Close Encounter of the

Second Kind" in Canada? _____
3. Does the book have any information on UFO sightings by astronauts?

_____

4. Is there some coverage in the book on Air Force Blue Book cases?

_____

5. Was there a report of a "Close Encounter of the Third Kind" in New

Guinea? _____

6. What does ATIC stand for? _____

_____

7. If you wanted to know what the Condon Committee was, where would you

look? _____
8. Pretend you had to read the first eighty-three pages of this book. Tomorrow you are going to have a test on those pages. Scan the index for all the listings from page 1 to page 83. What subjects, names, or terms would you need to

Copyright © 1988 Holt, Rinehart and Winston, Inc.

P: Perfecting Reading Skills

review before the test? _____

_____

_____

Index

A

ATIC (Air Technical Intelligence Center), 5, 102
American Institute of Aeronautics and
    Astronautics, 78, 84, 110
Astronaut UFO sightings, 167–169
Astronomer, 19, 31–33

B

Blue Book unidentified cases, 164, 167, 170, 177–179
British Air Ministry, 89

C

Close Encounters of the First Kind, 84–101; Beverly, Ma., 53, 85–86; Missouri Case, 92–93; reporters' coverage, 98
Close Encounters of the Second Kind, 102–125; car stoppings, 103–105; Cochrane, Wis., 107–109; Levelland, Tex., 111–113; Quebec, Canada, 115; Van Horne, Iowa, case, 121–124; Vins-sur-Calamy, France, 119–120.
Close Encounters of the Third Kind, 84, 102, 105, 126–140; Dexter, Mich., 137; North Dakota case, 128–130; Papua, New Guinea, 131–133; Socorro, New Mex., 137–139; Walton Travis case, 139–140.
Condon, E. U., 18, 20–27; Condon Committee, 21–25

D

Data, hard core, 31–38
Daylight sightings, 76–83

9. How can what you did with question 8 help you in preparing for exams in other classes? _____

_____

_____

DRILL 3: GLOSSARIES

Directions: A glossary is a short dictionary of words and terms used in the book you are reading. Not all books have glossaries. Usually, such books as history texts, psychology texts, chemistry texts, and so on, or books dealing with special subjects have glossaries. You can save a trip to the dictionary when a book has a glossary. Many words are usually defined as they are used in the context of the book. Scan the partial glossary on page 331 to answer the following questions.

1. What subject does the book from which this glossary is taken deal with?

_____

How do you know? _____
2. What is the difference between the earth's equator and a celestial equator?

_____

_____

_____

3. What is a constellation? _____

_____

_____

4. How does a constellation differ from a galaxy? _____

_____

_____

_____

P: Perfecting Reading Skills 331

5. How far does light travel in a year? _____

_____

6. What is an astronomical unit? _____

_____

7. What's the average distance of the earth from the sun? _____

_____

_____

Glossary of Terms

apastron The point of greatest distance of separation of two stars circling each other.
astronomical unit The average distance of earth from the sun; about 150,000,000 kilometers.
atom A particle of matter made up of a central nucleus surrounded by electrons.
atomic nucleus A small structure at the center of an atom, containing nearly all the mass of the atom.
axis of rotation The imaginary straight line about which an object spins.
binary stars Two stars that are close together in space and that revolve about each other.
celestial equator An imaginary circle about the sky, lying exactly above every point on earth's equator.
celestial poles Imaginary points in the sky that are directly above earth's North and South Poles.
constellation A grouping of stars in the sky, often pictured in some familiar shape (the Big and Little Dippers.)
double stars Two stars that appear to be close together in the sky.
galaxy A huge collection of millions and trillions of stars (our sun is a part of a galaxy).
light-year The distance light travels in a year, about 9,500,000,000,000 kilometers.

Copyright © 1988 Holt, Rinehart and Winston, Inc.

8. How can a glossary be helpful to you? _____

_____

_____

_____

DRILL 4: BIBLIOGRAPHIES

Directions: A bibliography, as you learned in the vocabulary section, is a list of books that can be used to find more information about a subject. Often, bibliographies appear at the end of chapters or at the end of a book. A bibliography appears on page 333. Scan it to find the answers to the following questions.

1. What subject does this bibliography cover? _____

_____

2. Is this bibliography a fairly recent list of books on the subject?

   _____ How do you know? _____

   _____

3. If you wanted to read more about galaxies, what are the names of the books that probably would be most helpful? _____

   _____

   _____

4. Which of the following is the correct way the bibliography is written? Circle one.
   a. Publisher, title, author, date.
   b. Title, author, publisher, date.
   c. Author, title, publisher, date.
   d. None of the above.
5. Why do you suppose there is no author's name for the second book listing? _____

   _____

P: *Perfecting Reading Skills*   333

6. What publisher has more than one book on the list? _____

   _____

7. Why are Isaac Asimov's books listed first? _____

   _____

8. Which of the books on the list would probably be best for someone who did not know much about astronomy? _____

   _____

   _____

Bibliography

Asimov, Isaac. *Alpha Centauri.* Lothrop, Lee & Shepard Company, 1976.

———. *To the Ends of the Universe.* Revised Edition. Walker and Company, 1976.

Bok, B. J., and P. F. Bok. *The Milky Way,* 4th edition. Harvard University Press, 1974.

Cleminshaw, C. H. *The Beginner's Guide to the Stars.* Thomas Y. Crowell Company, 1977.

Field, George B., et al. *The Redshift Controversy.* W. A. Benjamin Co., 1973.

Hoyle, Fred. *Astronomy and Cosmology.* W. H. Freeman & Co., 1973.

Hynek, J. Allen. *The UFO Experience.* Henry Regnery Co., 1972.

Mitton, Simon. *Exploring the Galaxies.* Charles Scribner's Sons, 1976.

Shapley, Harlow. *Galaxies,* 3d edition. Harvard University Press, 1972.

Whitney, Charles A. *The Discovery of Our Galaxy.* Angus and Robertson, 1972.

COMPREHENDING MAPS, TABLES, AND GRAPHS

DRILL 1: READING MAPS

Problem: At 5:45 P.M. on April 24, 1964, a "Close Encounter of the Third Kind" occurred in Socorro, New Mexico, which lasted between five and ten minutes. A Socorro police officer, Lonnie Zamora, was chasing a speeding car south of town. The speeding car escaped when Officer Zamora saw a descending object that was spouting flames and making explosive noises. The craft landed, and he saw two white-cloaked figures. Shortly after, the craft took off and disappeared. It left burn marks on the ground where it landed.

Use the map on page 335 to answer the following questions.

1. If Zamora did see an alien spaceship, what is near Socorro that would be of interest to creatures from outer space? _____

2. Is Albuquerque north or south of Socorro? _____
3. If you were in Las Vegas and wanted to drive to the spot where the spacecraft is supposed to have landed, what would be the fastest route to get there?

4. About how far is Socorro from Lincoln National Forest? _____

5. Which is closer to Socorro, Albuquerque or Las Cruces? _____

6. Which city is farthest east of Socorro?
   a. Tucumcari   b. Roswell   c. Artesia

7. What highway goes from Alamogordo to Tucumcari? _____

8. What highway runs through the Apache Indian Reservation? _____

P: Perfecting Reading Skills

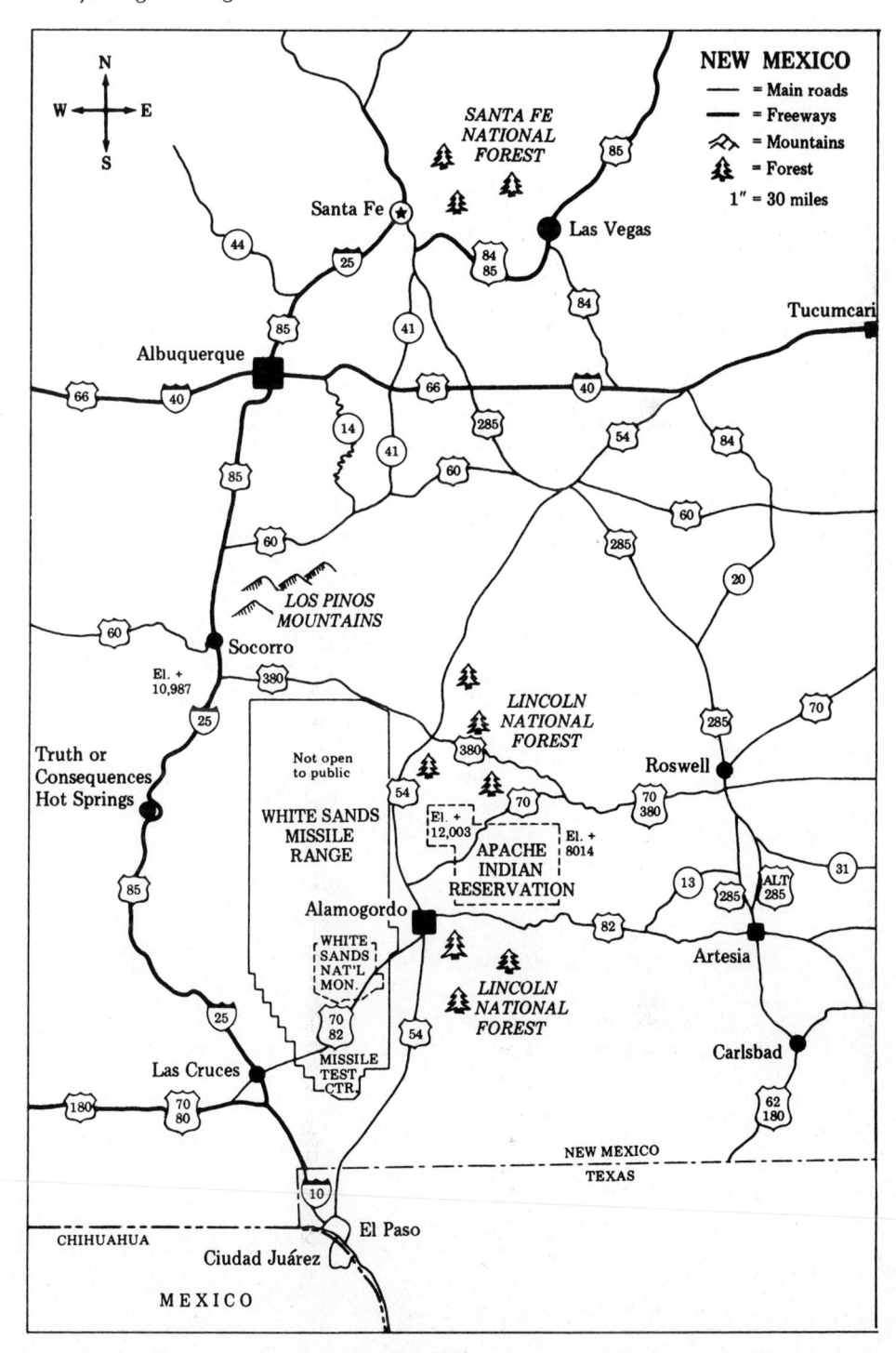

336 P: Perfecting Reading Skills

9. On what highways was the speeding car that Officer Zamora was chasing probably traveling? _____

10. What is the first highway the driver of the speeding car could turn off?

_____

DRILL 2: READING TABLES

Directions: Tables, charts, and graphs are used to show information that is easier to find visually than in paragraph form. A table or chart is arranged to make it possible to find specific facts quickly, to compare information, and to show relationships. For instance, look at the table on page 337. Notice that it gives information on "Major UFO Encounters of the First Kind." The table is divided into five columns. Use the table to scan for the answers to the following questions.

1. How many years does the table cover? _____

2. What is the longest length of sighting listed in the table? _____

3. What is the shortest length of sighting listed? _____

4. Where did a UFO sighting occur that the largest number of people saw?

_____

5. Did more sightings occur during A.M. or P.M.? _____

6. What year has the most sightings listed? ____ _____
7. What state has had more than one "Close Encounter of the First Kind"?

_____

8. Are the sightings listed in Table 1 the only ones that occurred between 1954 and 1967? _____

How do you know? _____

9. What is meant by 2 + 1 + 1 observers? _____

_____

Copyright © 1988 Holt, Rinehart and Winston, Inc.

P: Perfecting Reading Skills

Table 1

Major UFO Encounters of the First Kind Recorded by the Air Force (1954–1967)

Date	Time	Place	No. of Observers	Length of Sighting
8-20-55	10:45 P.M.	Kenora, Ont.	2	4 mins
6-26-63	1:00 A.M.	Weymouth, Mass.	2	1 min
4-3-64	9:00 P.M.	Monticello, Wis.	3	5-10 mins
3-8-65	7:40 P.M.	Mt. Airy, Md.	3	3 mins
6-19-65	4:00 A.M.	Rocky, Okla.	2	2-3 mins
1-11-66	7:40 P.M.	Meyerstown, Pa.	4	10 mins
2-6-66	6:05 A.M.	Nederland, Tex.	3	5 mins
4-17-66	5:05 A.M.	Portage County, Ohio	*2+1+1	1 hr 35 mins
4-22-66	9:00 P.M.	Beverly, Mass.	10	30 mins
7-22-66	11:30 P.M.	Freemont, Ind.	2	5-8 mins
10-10-66	5:20 P.M.	Newton, Ill.	6	3-4 mins
4-17-67	9:00 P.M.	Jefferson City, Mo.	*1+1+2	10-15 mins
10-14-67	2:30 A.M.	Mendota, Ca.	3	3 mins
10-27-67	3:05 A.M.	Parshall, N.D.	*1+1	5 mins

(There are many other sightings not listed here)

*Refers to separate groups or individual observers.
**The Air Force stopped recording UFO sightings after 1969.

10. Why are there no listings after 1969? _____

_____

DRILL 3: READING GRAPHS

Directions: Graphs can be drawn in several ways: bar graphs, line graphs, and circle graphs. Which type is used depends on which form can best explain the information being presented. Use the graphs on pages 338 and 339 to answer the following questions.

1. Which is the largest planet in diameter?

_____

2. Which is the smallest?

_____

3. Which planet is the closest to the sun?

_____

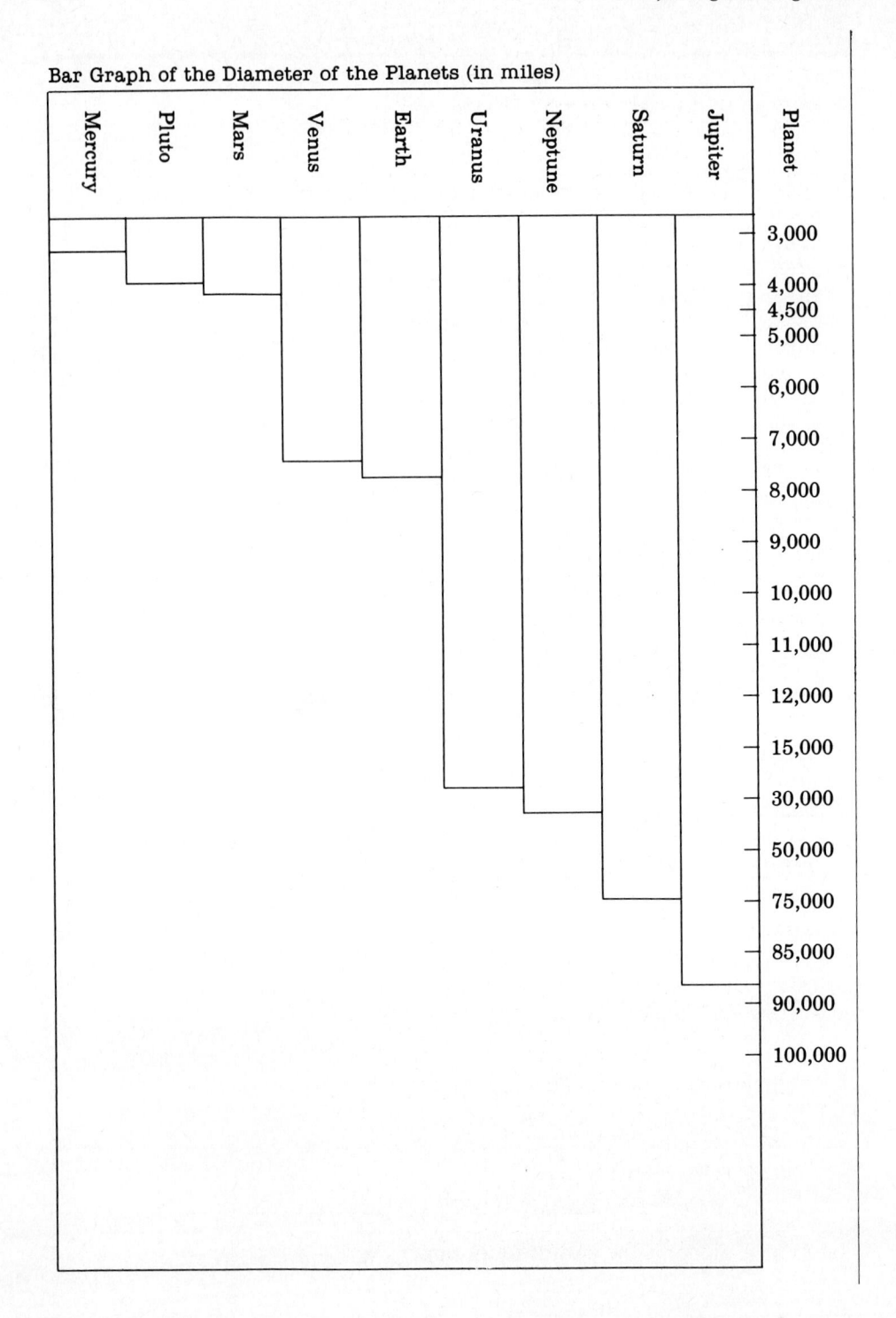

Bar Graph of the Diameter of the Planets (in miles)

Planet	Diameter
Mercury	3,000
Pluto	4,000
Mars	4,500
Venus	8,000
Earth	8,000
Uranus	30,000
Neptune	30,000
Saturn	75,000
Jupiter	85,000

P: Perfecting Reading Skills

4. Which planet is the farthest from the sun?

5. Which is closer to the sun, Uranus or Earth?

Line Graph of Distance of Planets from the Sun (in miles)

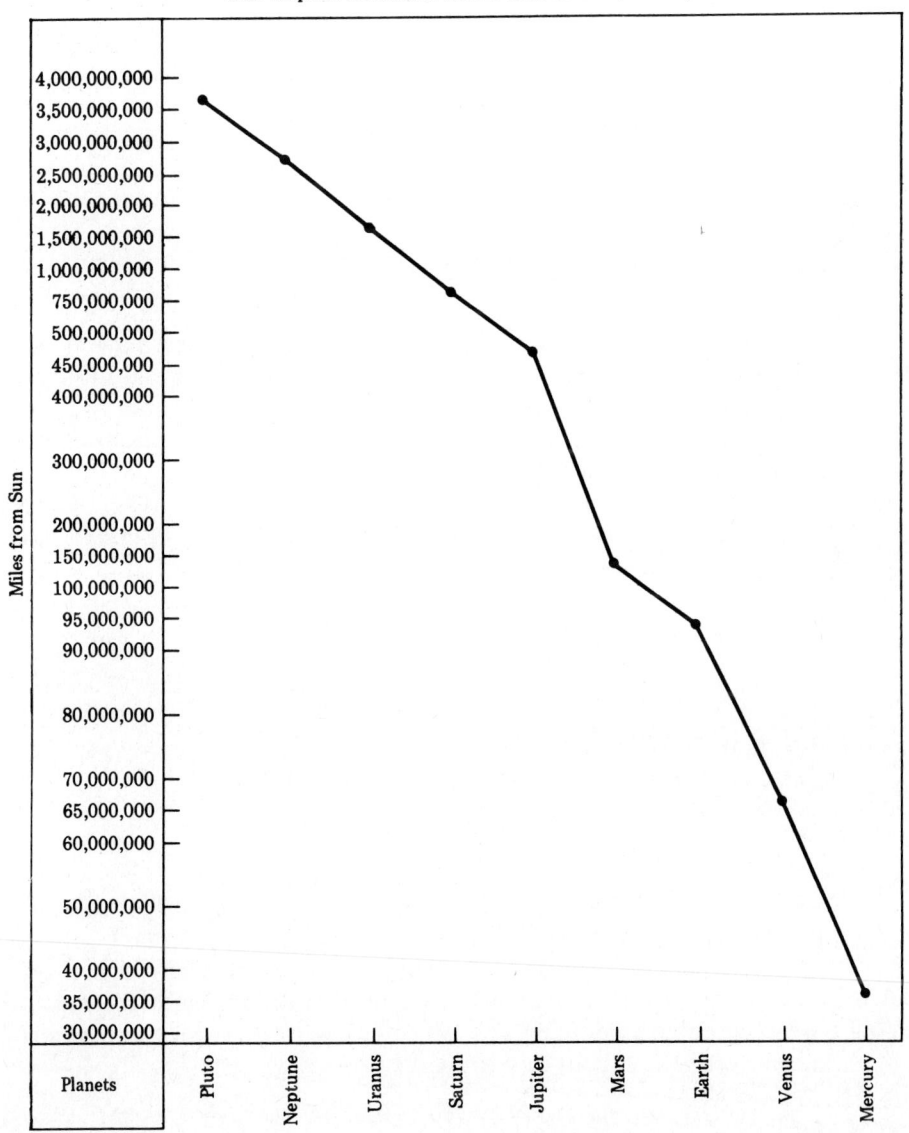

6. How many planets are closer to the sun than Earth?

7. How many planets are smaller than Earth?

8. About how many miles in diameter is Earth?

9. How far away from the sun is Earth?

10. Which planet is the coldest and why?

COMPREHENDING WHAT YOU READ

Directions: Read the following essay using all the skills you have learned. Read for the main idea, noting what information the author uses to support his thesis. Look for author bias and inference, while being careful not to let your own biases interfere with your comprehension. Use context clues to help you with words you may not know.

The author, Kurt Vonnegut, Jr., has written many novels, among them *The Sirens of Titan, Piano Player, Slaughterhouse Five, Breakfast of Champions,* and *Galapagos.*

THE IDEA KILLERS

KURT VONNEGUT, JR.

1   The American Civil Liberties Union, of which I am an ardent supporter, has suggested that I may be the most censored writer in America. I only wish that my parents had lived to hear that said of me. My father's dying words were, "You will never amount to a hill of beans." He didn't really say that. I am making what we call a joke. Jokes are protected by the First Amendment to our Constitution. Even jokes about God Almighty.

Originally appeared in Playboy *Magazine: Copyright © 1983 by* Playboy.

P: Perfecting Reading Skills

2   Teachers and librarians have been unbelievably brave and honorable and patriotic, and also intelligent, during all the recent attacks on the First Amendment, which says, among other things, that all Americans are free to read or publish whatever they please. Slander and libel, of course, are excepted from the law's protection.

3   If I have been censored a lot, then teachers and librarians have had to defend my books a lot. I do not imagine for a microsecond that they have done that because what I write is so true and beautiful. Many of them may hate what I write, even though I am, at my worst, no more dangerous than a banana split. They defend my books, and anybody else's, because they are law-abiding and because they understand, as did our founding fathers, that it is vital in a democracy that voters have access to every sort of opinion and information.

4   Thanks to our founding fathers, it is the law in this country that, once any idea is expressed here, no matter how repugnant it may be to some persons or, simply, to everybody, it must never be erased by the Government. Even if the overwhelming majority of our people voted to have this or that idea killed, the killing would be illegal because of the First Amendment, which says:

> Article I—Congress shall make no law respecting an establishment of religion or prohibiting the free exercise thereof; or abridging the freedom of speech or of the press; or the right of the people peaceably to assemble and to petition the Government for a redress of grievances.

5   I am mainly concerned with freedom of speech here, but that right is surely intertwined, as it is in the First Amendment, with the separation of church and state and the right to have our complaints heard by our Government.

6   Is there now a war about the First Amendment going on in this usually serene democracy of ours? Well—an earlier draft of this essay was full of warlike images. I am, after all, a war hero. I allowed myself to be captured by the Germans during World War Two in order to save lives.

7   In the warlike version—which, if read aloud, would sound a lot like the *1812 Overture*—I had the teachers and the librarians draped over barbed wire, drowning in water-filled shell holes, and so on.

8   Concerned citizens such as you and I were in an officers' club in a bomb shelter 200 miles behind the lines. Up at the front, the censors and the book burners were wearing spiked helmets and using dumdums and mustard gas. They were yelling at the teachers and the librarians to surrender the First Amendment. The teachers and the librarians were yelling what General Anthony C. McAuliffe said to the Germans when they told him his situation was hopeless during the Battle of the Bulge. They were yelling, "Nuts! Nuts! Nuts!"

9   But the book burners and the censors are not, in fact, subhuman, maniacal enemies. They are ordinary, usually likable, usually honorable neighbors of yours and mine. There is trouble between them and people like us, which often reaches courtrooms, because they believe, honestly, that they fully understand

two sorts of laws that are superior to the Constitution: the laws of nature—and, above those, the laws of God.

10   To them, the hierarchy of laws is like a deck of playing cards. Laws made by God are aces. Laws made by nature are kings. Laws made by men are queens. The law against double parking would be the deuce of clubs, I suppose.

11   So when a censor sees or hears an idea that is being freely circulated in this democracy, an idea that tremendously offends him and probably a lot of other people, too, he tries to get rid of whatever is carrying that idea—a book, a magazine, a movie or whatever—by means of vigilante action or with the help of the Government.

12   When somebody opposes him, saying that he is behaving in an unconstitutional manner, he replies that constitutional law is only a queen. He reaches into his pocket and pulls out four kings, natural laws that say that no real man will allow unpopular ideas to be expressed while he's around, and so on.

13   He lets that sink in, and then he pulls out four aces, which are God's laws. God Almighty Himself hates the idea that he wants squashed.

14   Does he win his case? Not in America. Maybe in Iran he could, but he had better know his Koran.

15   In this country, we do not play with a full deck of cards, which is what the censors find so hard to accept. We have agreed with one another, through the instrument of our Constitution, that we will not, when engaged in public business, behave as though the laws of God and nature were fully understood.

16   This agreement is not some newfangled contraption that came in with rock 'n' roll and frontal nudity. Censors commonly talk about getting back to good old American fundamentals. How can they disagree with us that, when we and they respect the First Amendment, no matter how troubling that amendment can be from time to time, we are being as fundamentally American as we can get?

17   Perhaps the censors will agree with us, too, that the most disgraceful episodes in our treatment of human beings within our borders have taken place when some people's ideas of God's law or natural law have been allowed to supersede our Constitution. I refer to human slavery, which so many Americans believed to be natural and even ordained by God only the day before yesterday, in my great-grandfather's time. It was finally the enforcement of mere man's law that made slavery illegal.

18   During the first half of my own lifetime, lynchings were shockingly common and always had been. Not many people said that lynchings were in accordance with God's law, but it seems likely that a majority felt them to be in harmony with natural law. What could be more natural, after all, than that a community came to hate somebody so much that its members strung him up or burned him alive? (Castrating the offenders, incidentally, was a natural preliminary to those natural rites. What better way to protect the family?)

19   Fifty years ago, then, we might have been protesting the lynchings of human beings. How much less we have to complain of today—the lynchings of mere ideas, which cannot scream in pain.

P: Perfecting Reading Skills 343

20 Still, the issue remains the same: Can the Constitution of the United States be made a scrap of paper by appeals to what sincere persons believe the laws of God and nature to be? If we let that happen, I see no reason why we can't get back to the good old American practices of lynchings and even slavery again. What better way to fight crime?

21 If we did get back to slavery, then ideas might become truly dangerous, which they are not now. Just imagine what slaves might do if they got hold of a copy of the Constitution, for instance, and learned that all people, regardless of their opinions or their color or whatever, should be allowed to say whatever they like and to be otherwise free and equal.

22 I have alluded to the pain, the screams emitted by a lynched person. I will mention pain yet again. It is very often real pain that censors feel when they see this idea or that one, this image or that one, freely circulated for all to contemplate. I myself often feel that pain. New York's 42nd Street makes me want to die. There can't be many thoughtful Americans who were not sickened by the beliefs that the American Nazi party proposed to celebrate in Skokie, Illinois, a few years ago. We endured that Skokie pain in order that we ourselves might have the right to speak our minds, no matter how unpopular some of our views might be.

23 Our founding fathers never promised us that this would be a painless form of Government, that adhering to the Bill of Rights would invariably be delightful. Nor are Americans proud of avoiding pain at all costs. On patriotic holidays, in fact, we boast of how much pain Americans have stood in order to protect their freedoms—draped over barbed wire, drowning in water-filled shell holes, and so on.

24 So it is not too much to ask of Americans that they not be censors, that they run the risk of being deeply wounded by ideas so that we may all be free. If we are wounded by an ugly idea, we must count it as part of the cost of freedom and, like American heroes in days gone by, bravely carry on.

Now answer these questions.

RECALL

1. What is Vonnegut's thesis? _____

   _____

   _____

2. Vonnegut believes that those who have defined his works have done so because they feel his writing is "true and beautiful."

   a. True

Copyright © 1988 Holt, Rinehart and Winston, Inc.

b. False, because _____

_____

3. What does Vonnegut claim we must do when we are "wounded by an ugly idea"? _____

_____

_____

INTERPRETATION

4. Why do you think the essay is called "The Idea Killers"?

_____

_____

5. Why do you think Vonnegut's first draft of his essay was full of warlike images? _____

_____

6. The author uses an analogy. He says that for censors the hierarchy of laws is like a deck of playing cards. Explain what he means. _____

_____

_____

_____

7. For what reason does Vonnegut discuss slavery? _____

_____

_____

_____

P: Perfecting Reading Skills 345

8. In paragraph 7, Vonnegut makes reference to the *1812 Overture*. Even though we may not be familiar with it, what can we infer about it? _____

_____

_____

9. Vonnegut uses sarcasm in his essay.

   a. True

   b. False, because _____

   _____

   _____

APPLICATION

10. Do you believe certain books should be banned? _____

    Explain your position. _____

    _____

    _____

    _____

    _____

    _____

Name _____ Section _____ Date _____

UNIT 3

CHECK TEST (CHAPTERS 7–9)

PART ONE: WORD KNOWLEDGE

A. Directions: Following are two columns. Write the letter of the synonym in column B in the blank by the number.

A   *B*

1. _____ fad   a. odor

2. _____ aroma   b. unlawful

3. _____ expensive   c. craze

4. _____ illegal   d. enough

5. _____ sufficient   e. costly

B. Directions: Following are two columns. Write the letter of the antonym in column B in the blank by the number.

A   *B*

1. _____ safe   a. enter

2. _____ expensive   b. lacking

3. _____ leave   c. dangerous

4. _____ permit   d. prevent

5. _____ sufficient   e. cheap

C. Directions: Define the following word parts.

1. tele: _____

2. micro: _____

Unit 3   347

3. graph: _____

4. ology: _____

5. auto: _____

6. geo: _____

7. bio: _____

8. scope: _____

9. aud: _____

10. cred: _____

11. gen: _____

12. ped, pod: _____

13. manu: _____

14. meter: _____

15. contra: _____

PART TWO: WORD USAGE

Directions: Following are two columns. In the blank by the word in the first column, write the letter of the definition from the second column that best fits. There are more definitions than words.

1. _____ prior   a. to carry out; to put in use

2. _____ speculation   b. unable to get loose

3. _____ enhance   c. to succeed

4. _____ ingenious   d. make better

5. _____ flourish (v.)   e. action based on guessing

6. _____ implement (v.)   f. coming before

Copyright © 1988 Holt, Rinehart and Winston, Inc.

348   Unit 3

7. _____ inextricable   g. clever

8. _____ condense   h. shorten

9. _____ essential   i. to claim without proof

10. _____ allege   j. having power over

11. _____ liberal   k. necessary; extremely important

12. _____ portion   l. a section or part of

13. _____ influential   m. tolerant; broad-minded

14. _____ aesthetic   n. pretending to believe or feel things one doesn't

15. _____ hypocrisy   o. pass on; communicate

16. _____ retain   p. apparent; lacks depth

17. _____ convey   q. someone who takes part

18. _____ itinerant   r. pertaining to beauty

19. _____ participant   s. to hold on; keep back

20. _____ superficial   t. feelings

u. traveling from place to place

v. nasty humor

PART THREE: COMPREHENDING PARAGRAPHS

Directions: Read the following paragraphs and answer the questions.

A. Research has discovered that a physical attractiveness stereotype exists. When most people form first impressions of others, they tend to base their judgments on the unspoken notion that "what is beautiful is good." Physically attractive individuals are judged to be sensitive, kind, strong, interesting, modest, poised, sociable, outgoing, and sexually warm and responsive. This is true

Name _____ Section _____ Date _____

regardless of whether males or females are being judged, or whether males or females are doing the judging.

(From V. Derlega and L. Janda, Personal Adjustment, Scott, Foresman, 1981.)

1. What is the "physical stereotype" that exists? _____

_____

_____

2. Females react differently from males when judging physically attractive people.
   a. True
   b. False

B. The physical attractiveness stereotype begins very early in life. As young as the age of six, attractive boys and girls tend to be more popular than their less attractive classmates. Children believe that their unattractive classmates fight a lot, hit and yell at the teacher, and say more angry things than attractive children. Perhaps even more unfortunate for unattractive children, adults hold similar views. Given information about misbehavior supposedly acted out by an unattractive child, adults thought the misbehavior resulted from an "antisocial nature." If the child was attractive, adults thought the misbehavior occurred because the child "just had a bad day." Such beliefs about a child's attractiveness can have profound effects.

(Derlega and Janda, op. cit.)

1. When does the physical attractiveness stereotype begin?

_____

2. What advantage do physically attractive children have over less attractive children? _____

_____

_____

3. How do adults excuse an attractive child's misbehavior?

_____

_____

C. In essence the world is as we perceive it, and our perceptions are based in part on the input of our senses as well as what we personally do with that input:

accept it, reject it, interpret it, change it, color it—essentially, put our own meaning on it. The study of how people experience their world is called **phenomenology**. It is important to realize that most people react to their perceptions of the world rather than to what the world may be in scientific reality. A simple example may clarify this point. Let's say we place a straight metal rod halfway into a pool of clear water. The rod will appear bent or broken because of the refraction of the light waves by the water. Yet because we have measured and examined the rod scientifically, we know it is straight. But how would people react if they knew nothing about light refraction and had never before seen a partially submerged object? To them the rod is bent, and they would act on that perception. On the other hand, most of us have learned that light waves will be refracted by the water and appear bent, so we will assume that the rod is straight even though our eyes tell us it looks bent. In other words, because of our training, we have learned that our perceptions do not always reflect the objective world—we have learned that appearances can be deceptive.

1. State the main idea of the paragraph. _____

_____

_____

_____

2. Define phenomenology. _____

_____

_____

3. Do you perceive this paragraph as difficult? Why? _____

_____

_____

_____

PART FOUR: ESSAY READING

Directions: Read the following selection and answer the questions that follow.

Name _____ **Section** _____ **Date** _____

Unit 3   **351**

THE RIGHT ANSWER

ROGER VON OECH

Five figures are shown as follows. Select the one that is different from all the others.

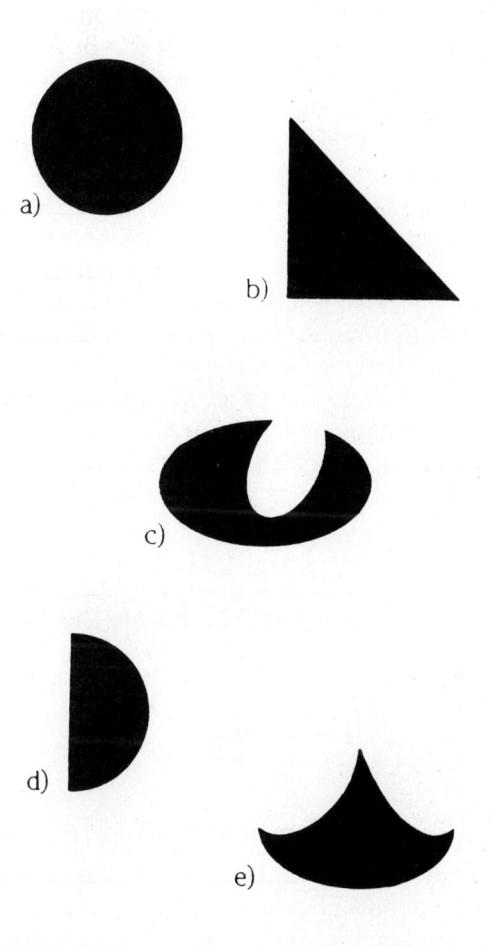

a) ●

b) ▲

c) ◐

d) ◑

e) ⌣

Learning How to Think

Where do you learn how to think? One important source is your formal schooling. From your education you learn what is appropriate and what is not. You learn many of the questions you use to probe your surroundings. You learn

From Roger von Oech, A Whack on the Side of the Head *(New York: Warner Books, 1983). Copyright © 1983 by Roger von Oech. Reprinted with permission.*

where to search for information, which kinds of ideas to pay attention to, and how to think about these ideas. In short, your educational training gives you many of the concepts you use to order and understand the world.

Speaking of education, how did you do on the five-figure exercise on the previous page? If you chose figure B, congratulations! You've picked the right answer. Figure B is the only one that has all straight lines. Give yourself a pat on the back!

Some of you, however, may have chosen figure C, thinking that C is unique because it is the only one which is asymmetrical. And you are also right! C is the right answer. A case can also be made for figure A: it is the only one with no points of discontinuity. Therefore, A is the right answer. What about D? It is the only one that has both a straight line and a curved line. So, D is the right answer too. And E? Among other things, E is the only one which looks like a projection of a non-Euclidean triangle into Euclidean space. It is also the right answer. In other words, they are all right depending on your point of view.

Much of our educational system, however, is geared toward teaching people the *one right answer.* By the time the average person finishes college, he or she will have taken over 2,600 tests, quizzes, and exams—many similar to the one you just took. Thus, the "right answer" approach becomes deeply ingrained in our thinking. This may be fine for some mathematical problems where there is in fact only one right answer. The difficulty is that most of life doesn't present itself in this way. Life is ambiguous; there are many right answers—all depending on what you are looking for. But if you think there is only one right answer, then you will stop looking as soon as you find one.

The Chalk Dot

When I was a sophomore in high school, my English teacher put a small chalk dot like the one below on the blackboard.

He asked the class what it was. A few seconds passed and then someone said, "A chalk dot on the blackboard." The rest of the class seemed relieved that the obvious had been stated, and no one else had anything more to say. "I'm surprised at you," the teacher told the class. "I did the same exercise yesterday with a group of kindergartners and they thought of fifty different things the chalk mark could be: an owl's eye, a cigar butt, the top of a telephone pole, a star, a pebble, a squashed bug, a rotten egg, and so on. They really had their imaginations in high gear."

In the ten-year period between kindergarten and high school, not only had we learned how to find the right answer, we had also lost the ability to look for more than one right answer. We had learned how to be specific, but we had lost much of our imaginative power. As noted educator Neil Postman has remarked, "Children enter school as question marks and leave as periods."

The Sufi Judge

These "right answer" examples bring to mind the following Sufi story.

Two men had an argument. To settle the matter, they went to a Sufi judge for arbitration. The plaintiff made his case. He was very eloquent and persuasive in his reasoning. When he finished, the judge nodded in approval and said, "That's right, that's right."

On hearing this, the defendant jumped up and said, "Wait a second, judge, you haven't even heard my side of the case yet." So the judge told the defendant to state his case. And he, too, was very persuasive and eloquent. When he finished, the judge said, "That's right, that's right."

When the clerk of court heard this, he jumped up and said, "Judge, they both can't be right." The judge looked at the clerk of court and said, "That's right, that's right."

Moral: Truth is all around you; what matters is where you put your focus.

Consequences

The practice of looking for the "one right answer" can have serious consequences on the way we think and confront problems. Most people don't like problems, and when they encounter them, they usually react by taking the first way out they can find. I can't overstate the danger in this. If you have only one idea, you have only one course of action open to you, and this is quite risky in a world where flexibility is a requirement for survival.

An idea is like a musical note. In the same way that a musical note can only be understood in relation to other notes (either as a part of a melody line or a chord), an idea is best understood in the context of other ideas. Thus, if you have only one idea you can't compare it to anything. You don't know its strengths and weaknesses. I believe that the French philosopher Emilè Chartier hit the nail squarely on the head when he said,

> Nothing is more dangerous than an
> idea when it is the only one you have.

For more effective thinking, we need different points of view.

The Second Right Answer

Not long ago I did a series of creative thinking workshops for the executive staff of a large high-technology company. The president had called me in because he was concerned about the thinking environment at the top. It seemed that whenever his subordinates would make a proposal, that's all they'd make—just one; they wouldn't offer any alternative ideas. Since they had been trained to look for the right answer, they usually didn't go beyond the first one they found. The president knew that it was easier to make good decisions if he had a variety of ideas from which to choose. He was also concerned with how conservative this "one-idea" tendency had made his people's thinking. If a person were presenting only one idea, he would generally propose the "sure thing" rather than take a chance on a less likely offbeat idea. This state of affairs created a less than ideal climate for generating innovative ideas.

I told these people that one way to be more creative is to "look for the second right answer." Often, it is the second right answer which, although offbeat or unusual, is exactly what you need to solve a problem in an innovative way.

One technique for finding the second right answer is to change the questions you use to probe a problem. For example, how many times have you heard someone say, "What is the answer?" or "What is the meaning of this?" or "What is the result?" These people are looking for *the* answer, and *the* meaning, and *the* result. If you train yourself to ask, "What are the answers?" and "What are the meanings?" and "What are the results?" you will find that people will think a little more deeply and offer more than one idea.

Another technique to find more answers is to change the wording in your questions. Here's an example of how such a strategy can work. Several centuries ago, a curious but deadly plague appeared in a small village in Lithuania. What was curious about this disease was its grip on its victim; as soon as a person contracted it, he would go into a very deep almost deathlike coma. Most individuals would die within twenty-four hours, but occasionally a hardy soul would make it back to the full bloom of health. The problem was that since early eighteenth-century medical technology was not very advanced, the unafflicted had quite a difficult time telling whether a victim was dead or alive. This didn't matter too much, though, because most of the people were, in fact, dead.

Then one day it was discovered that someone had been buried alive. This alarmed the townspeople, so they called a town meeting to decide what should be done to prevent such a situation from happening again. After much discussion, most people agreed on the following solution. They decided to put food and water in every casket next to the body. They would even put an air hole up from the casket to the earth's surface. These procedures would be expensive, but they would be more than worthwhile if they would save some people's lives.

Another group came up with a second, less expensive, right answer. They proposed implanting a twelve inch long stake in every coffin lid directly over where the victim's heart would be. Then whatever doubts there were about whether the person was dead or alive would be eliminated as soon as the coffin lid was closed.

What differentiated the two solutions were the questions used to find them. Whereas the first group asked, "What should we do in the event we bury somebody *alive*," the second group wondered, "How can we make sure everyone we bury is *dead?*"

Unit 3

There are many other ways to look for the second right answer—asking what if, playing the fool, reversing the problem, breaking assumed rules, etc.... The important thing, however, is to look for the second right answer, because unless you do, you won't find it.

Summary

Much of our educational system has taught us to look for *the one right answer*. This approach is fine for some situations, but many of us have a tendency to stop looking for alternative right answers after the first one has been found. This is unfortunate because often it's the second, or third, or tenth right answer which is what we need to solve a problem in an innovative way.

☐ *TIP #1:* A good way to be more creative is to look for the second right answer. There are many ways to pursue these answers, but the important thing is to do it. Often the really creative idea is just around the corner.

☐ *TIP #2:* The answers you get depend on the questions you ask. Play with your wording to get different answers. One technique is to solicit plural answers. Another is ask questions that whack people's thinking. One woman told me she had a manager who would keep her mind on its toes by asking questions such as, "What are three things you feel totally neutral about?"

Now answer these questions.

1. What is the main idea of the essay?
   a. Most of our formal schooling does not teach us to think, and we must learn to think better.
   b. You should stop looking once you find the right answer.
   c. Sometimes there's no such thing as the right answer.
   d. To solve problems in an innovative way, we should not be satisfied with one answer but look for several.
2. Which of the following are ways to go about looking for a second right answer? Circle all that apply.
   a. asking, "What if?"
   b. playing the fool
   c. reversing the problem
   d. asking for the plural answers
   e. none of the above
3. We can infer that the author does not think schools do an adequate job of teaching thinking.

   a. True

Copyright © 1988 Holt, Rinehart and Winston, Inc.

    b. False, because _____

    _____

 4. Which of the figures in the exercise at the beginning of the reading selection is the right answer?
    a. Figure a
    b. Figure b
    c. Figure c
    d. Figure d
    e. Figure e
 5. When the author says, "Life is ambiguous," what does he mean? _____

    _____

 6. Why is the quotation of Neil Postman, "Children enter school as question marks and leave as periods," a good one to use in this essay? _____

    _____

    _____

 7. The author says that an idea is like a musical note. What does he mean by this? _____

    _____

    _____

 8. What is meant by the statement, "Nothing is more dangerous than an idea when it is the only one you have"? _____

    _____

    _____

 9. We can infer that the author is in the business of helping companies train their employees to think more creatively.

a. True

b. False, because _____

_____

_____

10. Explain why the author believes that most of us look only for the "right answer." _____

_____

_____

_____

Appendix I

Roots and Affixes Reference Lists

Here are three reference lists of word parts you may want to study to help you comprehend college textbooks more easily. List A contains the Greek root word parts that appear in Chapters 8 and 9, plus a few extra. Most of the words listed appear frequently in social studies textbooks.

List B contains a more comprehensive and sophisticated list of Greek roots and affixes. Many of the example words appear frequently in science textbooks.

List C contains a comprehensive list of Latin word roots and affixes. The example words appear frequently in general college textbooks.

The vocabulary in all three also appears on many standardized reading tests.

LIST A

GREEK WORD ROOTS AND AFFIXES

Root or Affix	Meaning	Word Using Root or Affix
a	without	amoral
anti	against	antislavery
bi	two	bipartisan
cent	one hundred	centennial
chron	time	chronological
circum	around	circumstance
com	put together	community
dec	ten	decade
dis	away from	disembark
ex	out from	expel
im	not	improper
in	not or into	independent
inter	among or between	interstate
intra	within	intramural
ism	act or condition of being; manner	capitalism
less	without	defenseless
ment	act or state of being	armament
mis	wrong	misinterpret
mono	one	monarchy
multi	many	multinational
pre	before	prehistoric
re	do again	reconstruct
sub	below	submarine
tele	at a distance	telephone
tion	act or state of	abolition
trans	across or beyond	transcontinental
un	not	undemocratic

LIST B

GREEK WORD ROOTS AND AFFIXES

Root or Affix	Meaning	Word Using Root or Affix
acou, acu	to hear	acoustics
auto	self	automatic
amphi	on both sides	amphitheater
anti	against, opposite	antibiotic
arthr	joint	arthritis
anthro, anthrop	man, mankind	philanthropy
biblio	book	bibliography
bio	life	biology
cardi	heart	cardiac
cephal	head	cephalopod
chlor	green	chlorophyll
chron	time	chronological
cyt	cell	cytology
dia	across, through	diameter
eu	good	euphony
epi	upon	epidemic
gen	kinds, race, origin	genealogy
geo	earth	geology
graph	write, record	biography
hedron	solid figure with many faces	octahedron
helio	sun	heliotherapy
hemo	blood	hemophile
hetero	mixed	heterogeneous
homo	same, alike	homogeneous
hydro	water	hydrolysis
itis	inflammation of	tonsillitis
log	word; reason	logo; logic
log(y)	study of	astrology
macro	large	macroscopic
mania	craze for	maniac
meter	measure	chronometer
micro	small	microscope
mono	one	monopoly
neuro	nerve	neurotic
octo	eight	octopus
ost; osteo	bone	osteopath
para	beside, aside from	parameter
path	feeling	sympathy
patho	disease of	pathology
peri	around	periscope

List B

Root or Affix	Meaning	Word Using Root or Affix
phil	love	bibliophile
phobos	fear	phobia
phon	sound	phonograph
poly	many	polygamy
psyche	mind, soul	psychology
scope	examine	stethoscope
som, somat	body	chromosome
syn	together	synchronize
tach, tachy	swift, speed	tachometer
tele	far, distance	telephone
thera	to nurse	therapy
theo	god	theology
zoo	animals	zoo

LIST C

LATIN WORD ROOTS AND AFFIXES

Root or Affix	Meaning	Word Using Root or Affix
ante	before	antecedent
aqua	water	aqualung
audio	hear	audiometer
aur	ear	aural
bene	well	benefit
cap, cip, cept	take	capacious, capacity, accept
carn	flesh	carnivorous
circum	around	circumference
cord	heart	cordial
corpus	body	corpse
credo	belief	incredulous
digit	finger; toe	digital
dis	not; apart	disappear
dominus	lord	dominate
dorm	sleep	dormant
duc, duct	lead	conductor
ego	I, self	egotist
ex	out	exit
frater	brother	fraternize
in	not	incredible
inter	between	interact
locus	place	locality
mitto, mit	send	transmit
mortis, mort	death	mortality
ocul	eye	oculist
pater	father	paternal
ped	foot	octopod
port	carry	porter, transport
post	after	postgraduate
pre	before	premedical
pro	before	project, procambium
sanguin, sangui	blood	consanguinity
scribe	write	transcribe
solus	alone	solo
somn	sleep	insomnia
son	sound	ultrasonic
subter	under; secret	subterranean
trans	across	transport
ultilis	useful	utility
video	see	videotape

Appendix II

Student Record Charts

Comprehension Record Chart

Directions: Write in the number of comprehension questions you got correct for each of three comprehension sections: Recall, Interpretation, and Application.

Comprehension Scores

Chapter	Essay Title	Recall	Interpretation	Application
1	Succeeding on Campus	___ of 3	___ of 4	___ of 3
	How to Use a Library	___ of 5	___ of 2	___ of 3
2	We Are What We Think...	___ of 4	___ of 3	___ of 2
	Search for Self-actualization	___ of 3	___ of 4	___ of 3
3	How to Study-Read	___ of 2	___ of 5	___ of 3
	Mnemonics—Memory Magic	___ of 3	___ of 2	___ of 2
4	Reading the Social Sciences	___ of 4	___ of 3	___ of 3
	The Kennedy Administration	___ of 4	___ of 1	___ of 2
5	Computers and Work	___ of 5	___ of 3	___ of 2
	Vitamin E	___ of 5	___ of 1	___ of 2
6	On Teaching the First Grade	___ of 4	___ of 3	___ of 3
	Origin of the Earth	___ of 7	___ of 2	___ of 1
7	Development of Writing	___ of 6	___ of 3	___ of 1
	How to Spell	___ of 6	___ of 3	___ of 1
8	Newspaper Reading	___ of 6	___ of 2	___ of 2
	News Is Meant to Inform	___ of 3	___ of 5	___ of 2
9	Increasing Aesthetic Comprehension	___ of 5	___ of 3	___ of 2
	The Idea Killers	___ of 3	___ of 6	___ of 1

Unit Review Test Scores Chart

Directions: Record the results of each unit test in the correct blanks.

Unit 1
Part 1: Work Knowledge   _____ correct of 25 items
Part 2: Word Usage   _____ correct of 20 items
Part 3: Comprehending Paragraphs   _____ correct of 8 items
Part 4: Essay Reading   _____ correct of 10 items
Self-evaluation: In the space that follows write a brief self-evaluation on how well you think you are doing, what you need to review, and what you could do to improve your scores.

Unit 2
Part 1: Word Knowledge   _____ correct of 25 items
Part 2: Word Usage   _____ correct of 15 items
Part 3: Comprehending Paragraphs   _____ correct of 6 items
Part 4: Essay Reading   _____ correct of 10 items
Self-evaluation: In the space that follows write a brief self-evaluation on how well you think you are doing, what you need to review, and what you could do to improve your scores.

Unit 3
Part 1: Word Knowledge   _____ correct of 25 items
Part 2: Word Usage   _____ correct of 20 items
Part 3: Comprehending Paragraphs   _____ correct of 8 items
Part 4: Essay Reading   _____ correct of 10 items
Self-evaluation: In the space that follows write a brief self-evaluation on how well you think you are doing, what you need to review, and what you could do to improve your scores.

Name _____ Section _____ Date _____

INDEX

antonyms, 250

"Big Business: Selling Cancer" by Walter Raleigh, 228

compound words, 174, 207
comprehending
  bias and inference, 298
  maps, tables, and graphs, 334
  paragraphs, 29–34, 65–67, 98–99, 144–148, 183–186, 257–261, 290–294
  reference materials, 326–333
  sentences, 26–29, 63–65, 99–103, 143–144, 181–183, 213–214
"Computers and Work" by Arthur Luehrmann and Herbert Peckham, 165
consonant blends, 18
context clues, 136
  words in, 176, 208, 322

"Development of Writing" by Susan and Stephen Tchudi, 242
dictionary
  abbreviations, 88
  definitions, 136
  entry words, 87
  pronunciation key, 89
"Do Large Doses of Vitamin E Retard the Aging Process?" by Eva May Hamilton and Eleanor Noss Whitney, 186

Greek word parts, 282–283, 317
Greek word roots and affixes, list of, 359–361

homonyms, 21, 57, 175
"How to Spell" by John Irving, 262
"How to Study-Read" by Michele Learned, 80
"How to Use a Dictionary" by James A. Michener, 35

"Idea Killers, The" by Kurt Vonnegut, Jr., 340

idiomatic phrases, 62
"Increasing Aesthetic Comprehension" by W. Royce Adams, 310

Latin word parts, 284–320
Latin word roots and affixes, list of, 362

"Making TV Commercials" by Roy Wilson, 295
marking and underlining, 148
"Mnemonics—Memory Magic" by Dennis Coon, 104

"News Is Meant to Inform" by Andy Rooney, 298
"Newspaper Reading, How To" by Nancy Cage, 276

"On Teaching the First Grade" by Carl Sagan, 199
"Origin of the Earth" by Arthur Beiser and Konrad B. Kranskopf, 220

prefixes, 133, 171, 205, 206

"Reading the Social Sciences" by Scott Forbes, 126
"Right Answer, The" by Roger von Oech, 351
root words, 133, 284, 321

schwa, 56
"Search for Self-actualization, The" by Dennis Coon, 68
skimming and scanning, 294
"Succeeding on Campus" by Adam Ribb, 11
suffixes, 134, 172, 206–207
synonyms, 249

"Uses of Error, The" by Isaac Asimov, 115

vowel sounds, 18, 20

"We Are What We Think We Are" by John Hubris, 47